Contemporary Developments in Games Teaching

The teaching of games is a central component of any physical education or youth sport programme. *Contemporary Developments in Games Teaching* brings together leading international researchers and practitioners in physical education and sports coaching to examine new approaches in games teaching and team sport coaching that are player/student centred and inquiry based.

The book aims to bridge the gap between research and practice by exploring contemporary games teaching from pedagogical, policy and research perspectives. It offers interesting new commentary and research data on well-established models such as teaching games for understanding (TFfU), Game Sense, Play Practice and the games concept approach (GCA), as well as introducing innovative and exciting approaches emerging in East Asia, including Singapore and Japan.

Representing the most up-to-date survey of new work in contemporary games teaching around the world, this book is invaluable reading for any student, researcher, in-service teacher or sports coach with an interest in games teaching or physical education.

Richard Light is Professorial Research Fellow in Human Movement in the School of Health Sciences at the University of Ballarat, Australia.

John Quay is Senior Lecturer in Curriculum and Pedagogy with a focus on Health and Physical Education at the Melbourne Graduate School of Education, Australia.

Stephen Harvey is an Associate Professor in Instructional Methods and member of the Physical Education Teacher Education faculty in the College of Physical Activity and Sport Sciences at West Virginia University, USA.

Amanda Mooney Senior Lecturer in Health and Physical Education and Course Director for the Bachelor of Health and Physical Education at Deakin University, Australia.

Routledge Studies in Physical Education and Youth Sport

Series Editor: David Kirk, University of Bedfordshire, UK

The Routledge Studies in Physical Education and Youth Sport Series is a forum for the discussion of the latest and most important ideas and issues in physical education, sport and active leisure for young people across school, club and recreational settings. The series presents the work of the best well-established and emerging scholars from around the world, offering a truly international perspective on policy and practice. It aims to enhance our understanding of key challenges, to inform academic debate, and to have a high impact on both policy and practice, and is thus an essential resource for all serious students of physical education and youth sport.

Also available in this series:

Children, Obesity and Exercise
A practical approach to prevention, treatment and management of childhood and adolescent obesity
Edited by Andrew P. Hills, Neil A. King and Nuala M. Byrne

Disability and Youth Sport
Edited by Hayley Fitzgerald

Rethinking Gender and Youth Sport
Edited by Ian Wellard

Pedagogy and Human Movement
Richard Tinning

Positive Youth Development Through Sport
Edited by Nicholas Holt

Young People's Voices in PE and Youth Sport
Edited by Mary O'Sullivan and Ann Macphail

Physical Literacy
Throughout the lifecourse
Edited by Margaret Whitehead

Physical Education Futures
David Kirk

Young People, Physical Activity and the Everyday
Living physical activity
Edited by Jan Wright and Doune Macdonald

Muslim Women and Sport
Edited by Tansin Benn, Gertrud Pfister and Haifaa Jawad

Inclusion and Exclusion Through Youth Sport
Edited by Symeon Dagkas and Kathleen Armour

Sport Education
International perspectives
Edited by Peter Hastie

Cooperative Learning in Physical Education
An international perspective
Edited by Ben Dyson and Ashley Casey

Equity and Difference in Physical Education, Youth Sport and Health
A narrative approach
Edited by Fiona Dowling, Hayley Fitzgerald and Anne Flintoff

Game Sense
Pedagogy for performance, participation and enjoyment
Richard Light

Ethics in Youth Sport
Policy and pedagogical applications
Stephen Harvey and Richard Light

Assessment in Physical Education
A sociocultural perspective
Peter Hay and Dawn Penney

Complexity Thinking in Physical Education
Reframing curriculum, pedagogy and research
Edited by Alan Ovens, Tim Hopper and Joy Butler

Pedagogies, Physical Culture, and Visual Methods
Edited by Laura Azzarito and David Kirk

Contemporary Developments in Games Teaching
Edited by Richard Light, John Quay, Stephen Harvey and Amanda Mooney

Contemporary Developments in Games Teaching

Edited by
Richard Light, John Quay,
Stephen Harvey and
Amanda Mooney

Routledge
Taylor & Francis Group

LONDON AND NEW YORK

First published 2014
by Routledge
2 Park Square, Milton Park, Abingdon, Oxfordshire OX14 4RN

Simultaneously published in the USA and Canada
by Routledge
711 Third Avenue, New York, NY 10017

First issued in paperback 2014

Routledge is an imprint of the Taylor and Francis Group, an informa business

British Library Cataloguing in Publication Data
A catalogue record for this book is available from the British Library

Library of Congress Cataloging in Publication Data
Contemporary developments in games teaching / edited by Richard Light, John Quay, Stephen Harvey, and Amanda Mooney
pages cm. -- (Routledge studies in physical education and youth sport)
1. Team sports--Study and teaching. 2. Group games--Study and teaching. 3. Physical education and training. I. Light, Richard, 1951- editor of compilation.
GV361.C653 2014
796.07--dc23
2013008419

ISBN 978-0-415-82119-3 (hbk)
ISBN 978-1-138-90819-2 (pbk)
ISBN 978-0-203-79773-0 (ebk)

Typeset in Times
by Taylor & Francis Books

Contents

Contributors

Meghan Casey is a research fellow in the School of Health Sciences at the University of Ballarat. Her research focuses on the design, implementation and evaluation of school–community linked sport and physical activity programmes for adolescents and health promotion strategies applied in the sport and recreation sector.

Edward Cope is a PhD student in the Institute of Sport and Physical Activity Research at the University of Bedfordshire. His research interests include coaches' use of pedagogy, coach learning and young people's experiences of sport.

Christina Curry is a lecturer in Health and Physical Education (HPE) in the School of Education at the University of Western Sydney, Australia. She was previously head of a HPE department in a Sydney secondary school and has taught in both primary and secondary schools in Australia for 14 years. Christina has presented in Australia, Singapore and the UK and was an invited presenter on Game Sense at the 2008 ISCPES (International Society for Comparative Physical Education and Sport) World Congress in Macau. She researches on physical education pedagogy with a focus on game-based approaches to teaching games.

John Robert Evans is a senior lecturer in Indigenous Health Studies in the Faculty of Education and Social Work at The University of Sydney. He has an extensive background in rugby as a player and coach, is the first Indigenous Australian to gain a PhD in the Faculty of Education and Social Work and was a recipient of the prestigious Endeavour Indigenous Scholarship in 2007. John's research focuses on rugby coaching with a particular interest in the use of Game Sense in rugby coaching.

Greg Forrest lectures in games and sports and pedagogy courses at the University of Wollongong after a teaching career of 21 years in NSW high schools. He is completing his doctoral study on enhancing understanding of game-centred approaches for both physical education teachers and sports coaches.

Joan Marian Fry is an Australian working in Singapore at the National Institute of Education and has taught in higher education settings in Asia, Australia and North America. Her research interests are curriculum development and students' perceptions of physical education.

Stephen Harvey is an associate professor in Instructional Methods and member of the Physical Education Teacher Education faculty in the College of Physical Activity and Sport Sciences at West Virginia University, USA. Prior to this, Stephen was a senior lecturer at the University of Bedfordshire, UK. He has also worked as a physical education teacher and a further education lecturer, gaining extensive experience of pedagogical models via his work as a teacher, sports coach and academic researcher.

Rémy Hassanin is a French national who grew up and learnt to play rugby in South Africa and is undertaking a PhD at the University of Ballarat (Australia). His study inquires into the ways in which socio-cultural context shapes what and how high-performance rugby coaches learn to coach through experience in Australia, South Africa and France.

Kendall Jarrett is a senior lecturer in physical education at Canterbury Christ Church University in the UK and has held educational appointments in Australia, Japan, the United Kingdom and Ireland. He has a background as a primary and secondary school physical education teacher and is undertaking a PhD through the University of Ballarat that inquires into the interpretation and use of game-based approaches by teachers to teaching games in the UK and Asia.

Ruan Jones is a doctoral student within the Institute of Sport and Physical Activity Research at the University of Bedfordshire, UK. Prior to this he worked as a senior lecturer in physical education at Canterbury Christ Church University and the University of Worcester. Ruan has 11 years of physical education teaching experience.

Richard L. Light is Professorial Research Fellow in Human Movement at the University of Ballarat prior to which he held the 75th Carnegie Anniversary Chair in Sport Pedagogy at Leeds Metropolitan University. He was a founding member of the International TGfU Task Force from 2002 to 2009, convened the 2003 International TGfU Conference in Melbourne, the 2006 Asia Pacific Conference on Teaching Sport and Physical Education for Understanding in Sydney and the symposia on TGfU at the AIESEP World Congress in Finland (2006) and Japan (2008). He is author of *Game Sense: Pedagogy for Performance, Participation and Enjoyment* published in 2013 by Routledge.

Michael Charles McNeill is an associate professor at the National Institute of Education, Nanyang Technological University, Singapore. Heavily involved in the research and promotion of the games concept approach (GCA) since 1999, he has 12 refereed publications on the teaching of games, as well as a significant number of theoretical and practical international conference presentations.

Amanda Mooney is a senior lecturer in health and physical education and the course director for the Bachelor of Health and Physical Education at Deakin University, Australia. Her research interests focus on cultural and societal factors that influence pedagogical practice and gendered identity formation in physical education and sport with an interest in exploring more productive and inclusive practices.

Alain Mouchet is 'Maître de Conférences', University Paris East, Department of Sciences and Techniques in Physical Activities and Sports, Créteil, France. He coordinates a Masters Degree Diploma 'Coaching of elite athletes' and teaches in PE, sport coaching, rugby pedagogy and research methods. His research activities focus on the analysis of subjective experience of people (i.e. implicit and explicit knowledge of players, coaches and others) in their usual context. This work focuses on: (1) decision making of elite rugby players in match; (2) in-match coaching behaviour; (3) comparative studies between national teams during movement game in rugby.

Wendy Piltz is a senior lecturer at the University of South Australia working in pre-service teacher education in health and physical education. She has worked as an advisor to the American Sport Education Program in games-based coaching, conducts professional development for teachers through ACHPER (Australian Council for Health, Physical Education and Recreation) and has consulted with national and state sporting bodies in Australia. She is well known for her research and writing on Play Practice with Alan Launder.

John Quay is programme director and lecturer in Pedagogy, Health and Physical Education at the Melbourne Graduate School of Education. His research interests focus on physical and outdoor education, human movement and sports science, and the deeper philosophical understandings of teaching and learning. He is co-author with Jacqui Peters of the recently published book, *Creative Physical Education*.

Steven Stolz is a lecturer in the Faculty of Education at La Trobe University, Australia. His present research interests include continental philosophy, applied ethics, sport ethics, and the philosophy of education, particularly the philosophical justifications surrounding the place of sport and physical education in educational institutions.

Naoki Suzuki is an associate professor at Tokyo Gakugei University, a leading teacher education programme in Japan. Dr Suzuki's research focus is on games teaching, on which he has published widely in Japanese, and he edits a regular series of books with recent chapters on Game Sense. He also presents and publishes in English in the US, the UK, Australia and other English-speaking countries.

Adrian P. Turner is an associate professor in physical education teacher education at Bowling Green State University in Ohio, US. His scholarship focuses on teaching games for understanding and he has published and presented both nationally and internationally on games instruction over the past two decades. Adrian conducts in-service workshops on tactical games teaching for physical educators and coaches. He teaches a school-based pedagogical methods course for pre-service teachers and collaborates with coaches in the Bowling Green Youth Soccer Club to maintain close links with local schools and organisations at the grass roots level.

Introduction

Richard L. Light and Amanda Mooney

For individuals interested in contemporary physical education and sports coaching practices, the well-known saying, 'may you live in interesting times' (sometimes referred to as the Chinese curse) will hold some resonance. As debate occurs about the very nature of what constitutes physical education and sports coaching, and 'which' knowledge should be privileged through pedagogical encounters, we do live in interesting times characterised by profound social and cultural changes (Wright, Macdonald and Burrows 2004). For some, these changes have produced professional working lives that are extremely fast-paced and time-poor. With many commercial enterprises claiming to offer 'innovative' and 'cutting-edge' practical solutions and 'quick fixes' for highly complex problems, as professionals we are now required to become critical consumers of what others have termed the global information explosion (Wright *et al.* 2004). In relation to physical education and coaching we believe that in order to be effective critical consumers, 'context' matters and as such, we need local, nuanced examples of how various teaching and coaching approaches are applied to consider their relevance for the issues we face in our own practice.

Contemporary Developments in Games Teaching draws on research into, and thinking about, learner-centred, inquiry-based approaches to teaching and coaching games and team sports from Europe, the UK, the US, Australia and Asia. It presents recent developments in games teaching from pedagogical, policy and research perspectives. It is built around a critical mass of established researchers/authors, supported by emerging authors and a few 'new faces'. Common to each contribution is a belief in the efficacy of student/player-centred, inquiry-based approaches to teaching games in physical education and coaching team sports and the ways in which recent developments and research can offer various perspectives to inform its implementation and ongoing improvement.

Despite the emergence of arguments for a wide array of 'movement' experiences to address issues of youth physical inactivity, games and team sports still appear to hold significance for many young people and continue to dominate global school-based physical activity experiences (Williams and Kentel in press). Although we have witnessed a growing movement committed to the continual improvement of games teaching and coaching through what others have termed 'game-centred approaches' (Oslin and Mitchell 2006), critics argue that more sophisticated ways of thinking about games teaching and coaching are required if their potential for student-centred and 'contextually' relevant learning experiences are to be achieved (Wright and Forrest 2007). In particular these authors argue much of the game-centred approaches research to date fails to:

> go beyond an unquestioning acceptance of the intrinsic value of games, and of the community of practice that games and sports constitute. Nor does it question how what actually happens in TGfU [teaching games for understanding] lessons realises TGfU outcomes, or outcomes that are associated with empowering young people to take a more active part in their own learning about games and the place of games in society.
>
> (Wright and Forrest 2007: 280)

Put simply, Wright and Forrest (2007) argue that there is relatively little evidence in either the theoretical or the empirical literature of what a game-centred approach 'looks like in real lessons' (p. 274). Recent work has sought to address this gap (see Light 2013) and the contributions in this collection in particular provide a range of examples of what we collectively term game-based approaches (GBA) in various teaching and coaching contexts that can be used to inform individual practitioner reflections and practice. We prefer to use GBA rather than 'game-centred approach' to avoid confusion with the Singaporean games concept approach (GCA). Common to each of these pedagogical approaches is a focus on the game instead of decontextualised techniques or skills to locate learning within modified games or game-like activities (Light 2013) and that emphasise questioning to stimulate thinking and interaction (see, for example, Wright and Forrest 2007).

While TGfU remains a dominant approach in the literature the proliferation of variations on it and the emergence of similar approaches such as Play Practice (Launder 2001) and the tactical-decision learning model (see Gréhaigne, Richard and Griffin 2005), which have much in common but have originated independently from TGfU, creates a need for an umbrella term.

The origins of the ideas underpinning GBA can be located in the 1960s and earlier in the work of people such as Wade (1967) in the UK and Mahlo (1974) in France, and others, but in terms of direct influence the publication of Bunker and Thorpe's (1982) ideas on teaching games have had the biggest influence. For this reason we provide a brief historical summary of the development of GBA, beginning with TGfU, to situate the contemporary developments presented in this volume. This collection focuses on some of the most recent developments in games teaching over the last few years. It does not attempt to cover all recent developments but does present innovative ideas on teaching and learning and on conducting current, cutting-edge empirical research. It also presents contemporary developments in pedagogy and policy in Asia as largely underrepresented in the games teaching literature. In addition to contributions from well-established scholars in the field this book showcases the work of some emerging scholars and early career researchers in physical education and sport pedagogy. Further, the book features chapters in English from authors who are well published in their first language but have published little in English. It comprises contributions from Australia, the UK, France, Japan, Singapore and the US.

Detail on the content of the collection is preceded by a brief historical outline for the development of GBA.

The development of GBA

TGfU was first proposed by David Bunker and Rod Thorpe in 1982 but since then has been further developed through research and practitioner interest in it. Their ideas on teaching games inspired a brief period of interest at the time but it was not sustained (Holt, Strean and Bengoechea 2002). The TGfU approach to teaching games by teaching *in* and *through* games did not really begin to take off until a decade later, evident in interest from North American scholars. These scholars recognised the importance of tactics and decision making in games and the limitations of an exclusive focus on the decontextualised drilling of technique in promoting better games players and making learning enjoyable (see, for example, Mitchell, Oslin and Griffin 1995). The growth of interest in games-based teaching over the early 1990s is reflected in a special issue of the *Journal of Teaching in Physical Education* in 1996 edited by Judith Rink and entitled, 'Tactical and skill approaches to teaching sport and games'.

This development led to the conceptualisation of a North American approach called the tactical games approach (Griffin, Mitchell and Oslin 1997). Tactical games followed a pattern of using modified games for learners to understand the meaning and place of skills in games, followed by focusing on developing the skill(s), then returning to the game or a more complex and demanding form of it, building up the games as skill and understanding developed. This period of development also led to the design and implementation of authentic assessment approaches that suited the very different teaching approach taken. The two main assessment instruments were the Game Performance Assessment Instrument (GPAI) developed in North America (see Oslin, Mitchell and Griffin 1998) and the Team Sport Assessment Procedure (TSAP) developed by French and French-Canadian researchers (see, for example, Richard and Godbout 2000). The general debate over this period tended to be around the comparative importance of technique and tactics (see, for example, Mitchell *et al.* 1995; Turner and Martinek 1992).

Over this period Rod Thorpe made regular visits to Australia to work with local coaches and the Australian Sports Commission (ASC) to develop a version of TGfU focused on sport coaching called 'Game Sense' (Light 2004, 2013). He built upon coaches' existing use of practice games but introduced a more systematic approach and an emphasis on questioning to promote thinking and dialogue. The ASC produced a Game Sense package comprising a handbook (den Duyn 1997), a video and a useful set of modified practice games divided into the four game categories of invasion, striking, net/wall and target games. Geared more toward sport coaching than physical education classes (and receiving far less attention from researchers) the Game Sense approach has remained close to the original ideas of Bunker and Thorpe while TGfU has become more defined and specific in its implementation and developed in parallel with tactical games (Light 2013).

Toward the end of the 1990s interest developed in constructivist theories of learning and other theories that sit upon the same epistemological assumptions about what knowledge is and how it is acquired (see, for example, Light 2008). This provided new ways of understanding how learning occurred in TGfU and similar approaches (Gréhaigne and Godbout 1998; Kirk and Macdonald 1998) that were further developed by prominent figures in physical education research such as Rovegno (see, for example, Rovegno and Dolly 2006), Gréhaigne (see, for example, Gréhaigne *et al.* 2005) and Wallian (see, for example, Wallian and Chang 2007; Light and Wallian 2008). The concept of situated learning (Lave and Wenger 1991), first proposed in a physical education context by Kirk and Macdonald (1998), has also influenced thinking about learning and pedagogy. Such work now underpins other theoretical perspectives that promote enhanced understanding and learning in and through games such as self-determination theory (see Deci and Ryan 2000) and the constraints-led approach to skill acquisition (see, for example, Davids, Button and Bennett 2008).

The establishment of a regular series of international conferences from 2001 (Plymouth, New Hampshire, US) convened by Joy Butler contributed to growing interest in TGfU. Subsequent conferences were convened in Australia (2003 at the University of Melbourne), Hong Kong (2005 at the Hong Kong Institute of Education), Canada (2008 at the University of British Columbia) and most recently in the UK (2012 at Loughborough University). The global promotion of TGfU was first managed by a TGfU Task Force set up at the 2002 AIESEP (Association Internationale des Ecoles Superieurs d'Education Physique) World Congress in La Coruña, Spain and its membership evolved into a special interest group operating within AIESEP. Attendance at the TGfU symposia held at AIESEP World Congresses has also been strong in Finland (2006), Japan (2008) and Spain (2010) and there have also been conferences convened with a more regional focus such as the 'Asia-Pacific Conference on Teaching Sport and Physical Education for Understanding' at the University of Sydney in 2006.

The international TGfU conferences have generated a significant literature that includes peer-reviewed conference proceedings (see, for example, Light, Swabey and Brooker 2004; Light 2007; Liu, Li and Cruz 2006) and edited books (see, for example, Griffin and Butler 2005). Authored books have been published on the American tactical games approach (see, for example, Griffin *et al.* 1997) and the French tactical-decision learning model (see Gréhaigne *et al.* 2005).

There has also been a spike in the publication of books drawing on approaches that resonate with the key intentions of Game Sense pedagogy aimed at practitioners in the past few years (see, for example, Breed and Spittle 2011; Pill 2007; Slade 2010) and a recent research-based book focused specifically on Game Sense by Light in 2013. Interest in GBA is also suggested by the publication of special issues of *Physical Education and Sport Pedagogy* on TGfU in 2005 and *The Journal of Physical Education New Zealand* on the games approach to coaching in 2006.

There is significant writing on games teaching in Western settings and in Anglo cultures in particular but developments in Asia, apart from publications on the Singapore GCA (games concept approach), have received less attention to date. GCA was developed to meet the expectations of the Singapore Ministry of Education that physical education teaching contribute toward high-quality learning as part of its Thinking Schools, Learning Nation policy. Over the past decade researchers in Singapore have conducted a sustained programme of research on GCA and its implementation that Fry and McNeill draw on in Chapter 3 to reflect upon a decade of research on GCA in Singapore.

More recently, the Japanese Ministry of Education, Culture, Sports, Science and Technology (MEXT) implemented a new primary (2011) and secondary (2012) physical education curriculum that mandates a games and inquiry-based teaching approach influenced by international developments and by Game Sense in particular. Prior to Suzuki's chapter in this book there had been nothing written on this in English. At the same time new physical education curricula have been introduced in China and Taiwan that seem to encourage student-centred, inquiry-based approaches to teaching games but which face similar challenges to Japan (Jin 2011). Developments in games teaching in France have been made available in English through the publication of *Teaching and Learning Team Sports and Games* (Gréhaigne *et al.* 2005). There has also been some innovative research conducted on the subjective dimensions of play in team sports in France that have only just begun to emerge in the English literature (see, for example, Light, Harvey and Mouchet 2012). Some of this work is presented in Chapter 10 by Alain Mouchet.

The book

The book is divided into three sections that are briefly outlined below. They focus on (1) recent pedagogical and policy developments in games teaching, (2) research on the implementation of game-based approaches, and (3) issues in teaching game-based approaches.

Part I: Recent pedagogical and policy developments in games teaching

This section comprises chapters that present new ideas, innovations in pedagogy and recent policy developments in game-based approaches. It begins by examining some of the philosophic and epistemological underpinnings of game as 'context', especially given our focus on the localised, social and cultural contexts in which teaching and coaching occur. Too often lacking in the literature are philosophical groundings or foundations for the development of, and research into, GBAs and, as such, this valuable chapter presents epistemological issues of what counts as valued knowledge and how we acquire it as central themes to any thinking about learning and pedagogy. In particular, John Quay and Steve Stolz focus on the notion of context as a pivotal concept in the development of GBA and in research on it in Chapter 1. As they point out, it was 30 years ago when Bunker and Thorpe (1982) argued that traditional methods of teaching and coaching tended to emphasise motor techniques while overlooking the contextual nature of games. Taking this as their starting point, Quay and Stolz provide a philosophical perspective on the nature of context and the forms of inquiry designed to explore and adapt contextually through Game Sense pedagogy that draws primarily on the work of John Dewey and Martin Heidegger.

In Chapter 2 Richard Light uses Game Sense as an example of what he calls positive pedagogy and which he argues offers a way of using Game Sense pedagogy beyond games and team sports. Light suggests that, while TGfU has drifted away from Thorpe's original ideas, Game Sense has remained largely committed to these ideals and that its looser approach offers a framework for delivering high-quality teaching across the broader physical education curriculum. Light suggests that all student-centred, inquiry-based approaches to games teaching can provide positive pedagogy that can not only enrich games teaching but also inform other aspects of the curriculum.

Chapter 3 examines GBA development in Asia through the work of Joan Fry and Mike McNeill, who examine a decade of research into the development, and implementation, of the Games Concept Approach (GCA) in Singapore. The Singaporean GCA is a hybrid of TGfU and the North American Tactical Games Approach (see, for example, Griffin, Mitchell and Oslin 1997). Not only does this chapter provide us with an understanding of the development of GBA in Asian settings but it also gives an account of the most extensive, sustained programme of research on the implementation of GBA that has been conducted anywhere in the world to date. Fry and McNeill review research on teaching a conceptual approach to games pedagogy to specialist physical education student teachers.

Over the past 12 years a series of investigations into learning to teach and learning to play in Singapore have revealed the difficulties encountered by university faculty, student teachers and school-based mentors in teaching using the GCA. On the other hand, it also suggests that those learning to play this way (student teachers and school students) see these games lessons as being 'value-added'. Set against published studies, this chapter considers the perspectives of university faculty on their current approaches to games teaching and their reflections on the take-up of the GCA in school physical education.

In Chapter 4 Naoki Suzuki considers significant changes in the Japanese physical education curriculum and their implications for the development of

GBA in Japan. This discussion provides valuable understanding of the specific cultural and institutional factors shaping the development of GBA in Japan and the opportunities offered for its development by curricula development. Specifically, Suzuki's chapter focuses on an examination of radical curricula change in the teaching of ballgames in Japan. The '2008 national course of study for physical education' mandated by the Ministry of Education, Culture, Sports, Science and Technology (MEXT) specifies a focus on ballgames taught using a student-centred, tactical approach. However, because Japanese teachers are not particularly well versed in adopting student-centred and/or tactical approaches a major focus of the reform effort centres on curricular issues as they relate to learning theory. Suzuki outlines that behaviourist, constructivist and situated learning theories are being considered by Japanese educationalists who draw heavily from Western literature to guide curriculum development for teaching ballgames.

This section concludes with Wendy Piltz's overview of Play Practice and offers some background on its development by Alan Launder, its key principles and some suggestions for how it can be used to guide professional practice. While Play Practice has been around for a decade it is still an innovative approach to coaching sport and one that is applied to physical education. In this chapter, Piltz outlines the principles, processes and advantages of Play Practice as an innovative model for teaching and coaching sport. Tracing its origins back to 1957 she highlights the significance of deep and extended participation in reflective practice as the foundation for the Play Practice model and its value for teachers and coaches. She then explains the key principles of the approach with attention directed to using the 'power of play' to engage the learner. Focusing on the complexity of skilled performance in sport, she suggests the elements of skilled play including the critically important notion of 'Game Sense'.

Part II: Research on the implementation of game-based approaches

Part II begins with a review of the literature on empirical research conducted on GBA. In Chapter 6, Kendall Jarrett and Stephen Harvey identify new trends in GBA research that suggest increased interest in the affective dimensions of learning in and through GBA. They also identify key challenges that arise in the implementation of GBA and the utilisation of a diverse range of research designs and methodologies in response to the performative culture so often embedded within physical education and youth sport programmes. The following three chapters in this section provide localised and contextually relevant examples of the empirical research being conducted on GBA, specifically in rural schools and sports clubs in Victoria, Australia, an elite independent school in Sydney and the use of Game Sense by elite-level rugby unions coaches.

Chapters 7 and 8 report on research that involved interventions in quite different settings. In Chapter 7 Amanda Mooney and Meghan Casey examine the ways in which physical education teachers and community sports coaches responded to a curriculum intervention designed to enhance school–community sporting links in rural Victoria, Australia. Their research examines a collaborative partnership with Tennis Victoria and Football Federation Victoria that drew on the principles of games sense to reinvigorate adolescent girls' participation in the sports of tennis and soccer.

In Chapter 8 Christina Curry and Richard Light draw on a recent study conducted in an elite independent secondary school that inquired into the implementation of a TGfU approach to games teaching. They report on the ways in which the context of the school influenced the implementation of the TGfU approach with a focus on teacher experience. They identify how contextual factors such as the school's traditional emphasis on competitive team sports (rugby and rowing in particular) and the implementation of a teaching for understanding approach across the whole school shaped PE teachers' experiences of the implementation of TGfU.

The use of small-sided, modified games and questioning are two distinctive features of Game Sense that present challenges for teachers and coaches. Communication is also very different. Where 'traditional' approaches emphasise a monologue of instruction from coach/teacher to players/students, Game Sense emphasises productive dialogue between players/students and between players/students and the coach/teacher, which requires, and builds, very different relationships between them.

There has been some attention paid to specific aspects of Game Sense, TGfU and other game-based approaches (GBA) that present challenges for coaches and teachers, such as meeting the challenges of effective questioning (see, for example, Roberts 2011; Wright and Forrest, 2007) and the issue of game design (addressed by Adrian Turner in this book in Chapter 13). There has, however, been little attention paid to the significant change in relationships involved in implementing Game Sense and other GBA. In Chapter 9 John Evans attempts to redress this oversight by drawing on a study that investigated the interpretation and use of Game Sense by elite-level rugby coaches in Australia and New Zealand. It explores the nature of relationships developed by the coaches with their players and how they related to both the coaching approaches used and the coaches' perspectives on good coaching.

Part III: Issues in adopting game-based approaches

Part III comprises four chapters written by authors from France, Australia, the UK and the US that consider issues in the implementation of GBA. In Chapter 10 Alain Mouchet exposes us to some of the innovative research being conducted in sport coaching in France but which has primarily been published in French to suggest how understanding the subjective elements of thinking and decision making in team sports can be used to improve performance. Greg Forrest then draws on his research on pre-service teachers' experiences of using GBA (referred to by him as game-centred approaches) with a focus on the challenges of questioning, with Stephen Harvey, Edward

Cope and Ruan Jones drawing on some of the Francophone literature to make suggestions for implementing authentic assessment that considers embodied knowledge and knowledge inaction. In Chapter 13 Adrian Turner provides suggestions for meeting the challenge of designing effective modified or practice games.

Chapter 10 builds upon French research on the relationship between embodied (non-reflective) and conscious (reflective) thinking in decision making in team sports. Within this work psycho-phenomenology has helped in understanding the links between embodied and conscious thinking and subjectivity. In this chapter Alain Mouchet proposes the pragmatic utility of psycho-phenomenology for facilitating the coaching of decision making in team sports. He suggests that consideration of players' subjective experience is an important way of improving the co-construction of the team identity and game style and the flexibility between strategy and tactical adaptations in action. He also outlines an innovative use of this work in elite ruby clubs by linking these interviews to player's subjective experience in competitive matches. In Chapter 11 Greg Forrest draws on a study of pre-service teachers' experiences of learning to use game-centred approaches, with a focus on the development and use of questions as a key component to effective teaching in games and sports.

Authentic assessment is an important issue in the implementation of GBA and this forms the focus of Stephen Harvey, Edward Cope and Ruan Jones in Chapter 12. The importance of authentic assessment for GBA cannot be understated as it provides a way of assessing *knowledge-in-action* (Schön 1983) and the body thinking (Light and Fawns, 2003). This chapter examines why this is the case and outlines various strategies to overcome the challenges for authentic assessment in game-centred pedagogies. One strategy suggested is the infusion of Francophone research and perspectives on games teaching and assessment (see, for example, Gréhaigne *et al.* 2005). 'Getting the game right' (Thorpe and Bunker 2008) is probably the most important task facing a teacher or coach when taking a game-based approach (Light 2013) and this is the focus of Chapter 13. In 'Learning games concepts by design' Adrian Turner focuses on the design and development of modified games for learning in the invasion games category. His chapter covers both intra-game and inter-game development of sport concepts and uses a learner-centred approach within which modified games are used to highlight specific tactics that facilitate players' Game Sense and enable them to play more effectively by learning to read the game. It provides teachers and coaches with pedagogical structures to enhance player understanding during game development.

Using this book

Whilst this book is intended to engage any undergraduate or postgraduate student in physical education and coaching studies, the contributions in this collection, taken together or drawn upon separately, provide insights and learnings for practitioners and researchers interested in fostering student centred, inquiry-based approaches to games and team sports, and to their broader pedagogical practices. Each contribution brings up issues that can resonate with any professional's practice in the teaching and coaching of games and team sports. As such, they provide examples that can be drawn on to make sense of, or seek a deeper understanding of, their reflections on their own practice.

Questioning is central to all GBAs as a valuable tool for promoting student inquiry, generating dialogue and stimulating thinking and learning. Yet, as Wright and Forrest (2007) point out, many of the current resources on games teaching and coaching present and model questioning techniques more closely akin to a 'closed Initiation – Response – Evaluation (IRE) pattern' (p. 276). This, they argue, can lead to teachers and coaches expecting one right answer to the questions posed and can close off opportunities to construct and negotiate meaning with students, an approach that may more accurately reflect a 'student-centred' approach. In teaching, questions should generate thinking, dialogue and action in the development of knowledge and a positive disposition toward learning and moving.

For the same reasons, at the conclusion of each chapter the authors pose three discussion questions. These are not offered in an attempt to control the direction conversation about the ideas presented in the chapter will take, but rather to stimulate and encourage readers to think deeply and broadly and control the direction of their own conversations, reflections and learning   without boundaries and limits.

References

Breed, R. and Spittle, M. (2011) *Developing Game Sense through Tactical Learning: A Resource Book for Teachers and Coaches*, Melbourne: Cambridge University Press.

Bunker, D. and Thorpe, R. (1982) 'A model for the teaching of games in secondary school', *Bulletin of Physical Education*, 18: 5–8.

Davids, K. W., Button, C. and Bennett, S. (2008) *Dynamics of Skill Acquisition: A Constraints-led Approach*, Champaign, IL: Human Kinetics.

Deci, E. L. and Ryan, R. M. (2000) 'The "what" and "why" of goal pursuits: Human needs and the self-determination of behavior', *Psychological Enquiry*, 11: 227–268.

Den Duyn, N. (1997) *Game Sense: Developing Thinking Players*, Canberra: Australian Sports Commission.

Evans, J. R. (2012) 'Elite rugby union coaches' interpretation and use of Game Sense in New Zealand', *Asian Journal of Exercise and Sport Science*, 9(1), 85–97.

Gréhaigne, G.-F. and Godbout, P. (1998) 'Observation, critical thinking and transformation: Three key elements of a constructivist perspective of the learning process in team sports', in R. Feingold, R. Rees, G. Barette, I. Fiorentino, S. Virgilio and E. Kowalski (eds) *Education for Life*, New York: Adelphi University, pp. 490–505.

Gréhaigne, G-F., Richard, J-F. and Griffin, L. L. (2005) *Teaching and Learning Team Sports and Games*, London and New York: Routledge.

Griffin, L. L. and Butler, J. I. (eds) (2005) *Teaching Games for Understanding: Theory, Research and Practice*, Champaign, IL: Human Kinetics.

Griffin, L. L., Mitchell, S. A. and Oslin, J. L. (1997) *Teaching Sport Concepts and Skills: A Tactical Games Approach*, Champaign, IL: Human Kinetics.

Holt, N., Strean, W. and Bengoechea, E. G. (2002) 'Expanding the Teaching Games for Understanding model: New avenues for future research and practice', *Journal of Teaching in Physical Education*, 21(2): 162–177.

Jin, A. (2011) 'Challenges facing Chinese PE curriculum reform', paper presented at the Australian Association for Research in Education annual conference, Hobart, Australia, 27 November–2 December.

Kirk, D. and Macdonald, D. (1998) 'Situated learning in Physical Education', *Journal of Teaching in Physical Education*, 17: 376–387.

Launder, A. G. (2001) *Play Practice: The Games Approach to Teaching and Coaching Sports*, Champaign, IL: Human Kinetics.

Lave, J. and Wenger, E. (1991) *Situated Learning: Legitimate Peripheral Participation*, Cambridge: Cambridge University Press.

Light, R. (2004) 'Australian coaches' experiences of Game Sense: Opportunities and challenges', *Physical Education and Sport Pedagogy*, 9(2): 115–132.

Light, R. (ed.) (2007) *Proceedings for the 2006 Asia Pacific Conference on Teaching Sport and Physical Education for Understanding*, Sydney: University of Sydney, available at: www.proflearn.edsw.usyd.edu.au/proceedings_resources/index.shtml (last accessed 3 June 2012).

Light, R. (2008) '"Complex" learning theory in physical education: An examination of its epistemology and assumptions about how we learn', *Journal of Teaching in Physical Education*, 27(1): 21–37.

——(2013) *Game Sense: Pedagogy for Performance, Participation and Enjoyment*, London and New York: Routledge.

Light, R. and Fawns, R. (2003) 'Knowing the game: Integrating speech and action through TGfU', *Quest*, 55: 161–177.

Light, R. and Wallian, N. (2008) 'A constructivist approach to teaching swimming', *Quest*, 60(3): 387–404.

Light, R. L., Harvey, S. and Mouchet, A. (2012) 'Improving "at-action" decision-making in team sports through a holistic coaching approach', *Sport, Education and Society*, DOI:10.1080/13573322.2012.665803.

Light, R., Swabey, K. and Brooker, R. (eds) (2004) *Proceedings for the Second International Conference: Teaching Sport and Physical Education for Understanding*, Melbourne, Australia: University of Melbourne, available at: www.conferences.unimelb.edu.au/sport/proceedings.htm (last accessed 29 April 2013).

Liu, R. and Chung, L. (eds) (2006) *Teaching Games for Understanding in the Asia-Pacific Region*, Hong Kong: Hong Kong Institute of Education.

Liu, R., Li, C. and Cruz, A. (2006) *Teaching Games for Understanding in the Region*, Hong Kong Asia Pacific: Hong Kong Institute of Education.

Mahlo, F. (1974) *Acte Tactique en Jeu* [Tactical Action in Play], Paris: Vigot.

Mitchell, S., Oslin, J. and Griffin, L. L. (1995) 'The effects of two instructional approaches on game performance', *Pedagogy in Practice-Teaching and Coaching in Physical Education and Sports*, 1: 36–48.

Oslin, J. and Mitchell, S. (2006) 'Game-centred approaches to teaching physical education', in D. Kirk, D. Macdonald and M. O'Sullivan (eds) *The Handbook of Physical Education*, London: Sage, pp. 627–651.

Oslin, J., Mitchell, S. and Griffin, L. L. (1998) 'The Game Performance Assessment Instrument (GPAI): Development and preliminary validation', *Journal of Teaching in Physical Education*, 17(2): 231–243.

Pill, S. (2007) *Play with Purpose: A Resource to Prepare Teachers in the Implementation of the Game-centred Approach to Physical Education*, Hindmarsh, SA: ACHPER Australia.

Richard, J.-F. and Godbout, P. (2000) 'Formative assessment as an integral part of the teaching-learning process', *Physical and Health Education Journal*, 66(3): 4–10.

Roberts, S. J. (2011) 'Teaching Games for Understanding: the difficulties and challenges experienced by participation cricket coaches', *Physical Education & Sport Pedagogy*, 16: 33–48.

Rovegno, I. and Dolly, J. P. (2006) 'Constructivist perspectives on learning', in D. Kirk, D. Macdonald and M. O'Sullivan (eds) *The Handbook of Physical Education*, London: Sage.

Slade, D. (2010) *Transforming Play: Teaching Tactics and Game Sense*, Champaigne, IL: Human Kinetics.

Schön, D. A. (1983) *The Reflective Practitioner: How Professionals Think in Action*, New York: Basic Books.

Thorpe, R. and Bunker, D. (2008) 'Teaching Games for Understanding – Do current developments reflect original intentions?', paper presented at the fourth Teaching Games for Understanding Conference, Vancouver, BC, Canada, May 14–17.

Turner, A. P. and Martinek, T. J. (1992) 'A comparative analysis of two models for teaching games: Technique approach and game-centered (tactical focus)', *International Journal of Physical Education*, 29(4): 15–31.

Wade, A. (1967) *The FA Guide to Training and Coaching*, London: Heinemann.

Wallian, N. and Chang, C.-W. (2007) 'Language, thinking and action: Towards a semio-constructivist approach in physical education', *Physical Education and Sport Pedagogy*, 12(3): 289–311.

Williams, K. and Kentel, J. (in press) 'Risky pedagogy: Reconceptualizing gymnastics education through collaborative inquiry in an Irish primary school', *Asian Journal of Exercise and Sports Science*.

Wright, J. and Forrest, G. (2007) 'A social semiotic analysis of knowledge construction and game-centred approaches to teaching', *Physical Education and Sport Pedagogy*, 12(3): 273–287.

Wright, J., Macdonald, D. and Burrows, L. (eds.) (2004) *Critical Inquiry and Problem-solving in Physical Education*, London: Routledge.

Part I

Recent pedagogical and policy developments in games teaching

1 Game as context in physical education
A Deweyan philosophical perspective

John Quay and Steven Stolz

The issue of context and physical education

It was 30 years ago when Bunker and Thorpe (1982: 5) made the claim that 'traditional methods' of teaching physical education 'have failed to take into account the contextual nature of games'. Their aim was to problematise the teaching of particular techniques *before* these techniques had been contextualised within a specific game. They understood that when the game as context is missing, questions of what to do with a technique and when to apply it emerge for students, along with the broader question of why one needs to learn the technique in the first place. As a response to this problem they envisaged a model for teaching in physical education that 'starts with a game and its rules which set the scene for the development of tactical awareness and decision making, which, in their turn, always precede the response factors of skill execution and performance' (p. 8). In other words, the game contextualises the tactics or strategies, and the strategies contextualise the skills. Their model is widely known as teaching games for understanding (TGfU), which contrasts with more traditional technique-orientated models, the traditional methods, which are known in this way as the technical approach or the 'skills approach' (Brooker, Kirk, Braiuka and Bransgrove 2000: 20), or sometimes as fundamental motor skills (FMS).

In this paper we focus first on the shift in context between these two models, FMS and TGfU, and the ramifications for physical education. This is the shift from learning techniques before a game to learning techniques, tactical awareness and decision making in the context of a game. We then explore the notion of the game itself as context by questioning who is involved in the creative development of the game, referring to Almond's (1983) work on 'games making'. In addition we investigate the further contexts within which the game itself sits. In a physical education setting games are usually considered to be competitive to some degree, thereby positioning a game within an aspect of the context of sport (but not necessarily labelling a game as a *particular* sport). We understand sport as context through the model of 'sport education' designed by Siedentop (1994). And then sport itself is part of the broader social context, for which Hellison's (1995) model of taking personal and social responsibility in physical education (TPSR) provides a widely known approach.

Our purpose in this paper is therefore to examine the notion of context as it influences games-based teaching in physical education. We are cognisant that other authors have approached the notion of context in physical education via concepts such as 'the naturalistic context' (Brooker, Kirk, Braiuka and Bransgrove 2000: 9) and 'situated learning' (Kirk and MacPhail 2002), however, our understanding of context is, we believe, different. We would argue that this term – context – has largely been taken for granted by physical educators and thereby left unquestioned as to its deeper meaning. Without being clear about what is meant by context, especially as this relates to education, our analyses remain open to misunderstanding. To provide this increased level of clarity we specifically turn to the educational philosophy of John Dewey. Here we note, like Armour (2010: 5), the 'sobering' fact that 'Dewey got there before us' in the consideration of many educational issues, including those of physical education. Dewey's work illuminates many of the issues we face in physical education today. Awareness of Dewey's important contribution to physical education stretches back at least 40 years, when Park (1969: 55) identified three significant aspects of Dewey's educational philosophy – 'the assumed historical dualisms', 'experience' and 'the play-work-recreation complex' – that he believed could assist physical educators in better comprehending their work. Of these three it is *experience* which we wish to focus on in this paper, and how context is understood through this lens. We begin with Dewey's account of environment as another way of considering context, always aware that environment must itself be understood via experience. And as we shall show, it is experience itself that provides the sense of context, which we wish to embrace.

Context as experience: a Deweyan perspective

Dewey considers 'every experience in its direct occurrence' to be 'an interaction of environing conditions and an organism' (1939: 544). This may sound fairly simple, and it is, however, it should not be perceived simplistically. What Dewey means by environment here needs further explication in order to adequately convey the richness he perceives in this term, a term that offers a way into understanding the notion of context. One possible misunderstanding concerns the contemporary use of the term environment to mean the natural environment: the natural world that is considered to exist separate from human beings, although effected by us. Dewey (1938a: 33) acknowledges that 'a natural world ... exists independently of the organism', but he also stipulates that 'this world is *environment* only as it enters directly and indirectly into life-functions'. But these life functions are not merely physical. 'Environment ... is not equivalent merely to surrounding physical conditions. There may be much in the physical surroundings to which an organism is irresponsive; such conditions are no part of its *true* environment' (Dewey 1911: 487, italics added).

For Dewey there is a 'true environment' that does not simply equate to the natural physical environment. But how is one environment truer than another? The key to understanding what Dewey means by a true environment lies in his emphasis on interaction. However, this is not to be understood such that 'organism and environment' are 'given' as independent things and 'interaction is a third independent thing which finally intervenes' (Dewey 1938a: 33). Instead, interaction has the deeper sense of transaction or integration. 'Integration is more fundamental than is the distinction designated by interaction of organism *and* environment' (p. 34). For 'the organism brings with it through its own structure, native and acquired, forces that play a part in the interaction' (Dewey 1934: 246). And correspondingly 'the processes of living are enacted by the environment as truly as by the organism; for they *are* an integration' (Dewey 1938a: 25).

> An experience is always what it is because of a transaction taking place between an individual and what, at the time, constitutes his environment, whether the latter consists of persons with whom he is talking about some topic or event, the subject talked about being also a part of the situation; or the toys which he is playing with; the book he is reading (in which his environing conditions at the time may be England or ancient Greece or an imaginary region); or the materials of an experiment he is performing.
>
> (Dewey 1938b: 43–44)

Thus 'even when a person builds a castle in the air he is interacting with the objects which he constructs on fancy' (Dewey 1938b: 44). So interaction, integration, transaction, is not merely between an individual organism and physical conditions or surroundings, as if a person is 'in' the environment. For 'an organism does not live *in* an environment', like an object contained in a box; instead, 'it lives by means of an environment' (Dewey 1938a: 25). In other words, an organism is *involved* with an environment; it doesn't just sit amongst a collection of things. A person and his or her environment are in this sense 'involved' with each other in an integrated way. Hence 'the words "environment", "medium" denote something more than surroundings which encompass an individual. They denote the specific *continuity* of the surroundings with his [sic] own active tendencies' (Dewey 1916: 13).

> Some things which are remote in space and time from a living creature, especially a human creature, may form his environment even more truly than some of the things close to him. The things with which a man *varies* are his genuine environment. Thus the activities of the astronomer vary with the stars at which he gazes or about which he calculates. Of his immediate surroundings, his telescope is most intimately his environment.
>
> (Dewey 1916: 13)

Environment, in other words, cannot be understood in isolation from organism or person. Environment, true environment, is a factor *within* experience, not something that exists outside of experience. Thus a more complete description of experience suggests that 'experience is a matter of interaction of organism with its environment, an environment that is human as well as physical, that includes the materials of tradition and institutions as well as local surroundings' (Dewey 1934: 246).

Importantly, this means that 'no complete account of *what* is experienced ... can be given until we know *how* it is experienced or the mode of experiencing that enters into its formation' (Dewey 1930: 417, italics added). And educationally speaking, 'when we give names to this distinction [between what and how] we have subject matter and method as our terms' (Dewey 1916: 196).

Therefore, the entities that we contend with in experience, be they solid objects, other persons, knowledge concepts or flights of fancy, are contended within a particular mode of experiencing. *What* is experienced as environment cannot be separated from the mode of experiencing the *how*. Environment and organism are integrated in experience. In educational terms *what* is subject matter, content or curriculum, and this is integrated with *how* as method, process, pedagogy. Curriculum as what is therefore an aspect of the environment, while pedagogy as how is the mode of experiencing.

Dewey (1916: 361) encapsulates this integration in his understanding of 'education *through* occupations'. A *what* experienced and a *how* of experiencing sit within an occupation, describable via the pronoun *who*. Here an occupation, as who, is not merely an adult job, in the way we would tend to interpret this term in its more mundane or everyday meaning. An occupation for Dewey, in this sense of *who*, is holistic, it is qualitative, and it cannot be separated from his understanding of interest (a term perhaps more easily understood educationally as 'engagement') as this connects deeply with self. For 'the genuine principle of interest is the principle of the recognized identity of the fact to be learned or the action proposed with the growing self' (Dewey 1913: 7). Thus 'wholes for purposes of education are not ... physical affairs. Intellectually the existence of a whole depends upon a concern or interest; it is qualitative, the completeness of appeal made by a situation' (Dewey 1916: 232). A whole for the purposes of education is an occupation (Figure 1.1).

Who circumscribes *how* and *what*. In this way how and what are also occupational. As *how*, 'an occupation is a continuous activity having a purpose' (Dewey 1916: 361). As *what*, an occupation is 'an organizing principle for information and ideas; for knowledge and intellectual growth' (p. 362). This has ramifications for our understanding of the notion of context and contextualisation in physical education. When we are dealing with the entities of physical education (such as other people, physical objects, knowledge concepts, or even flights of fancy) as *what* is experienced (subject matter, curriculum) this always occurs within a *how* or mode of experiencing (method, pedagogy). This integration *is* experience. Context is thus not merely environment, it is experience itself, encapsulated in its various wholes as occupations.

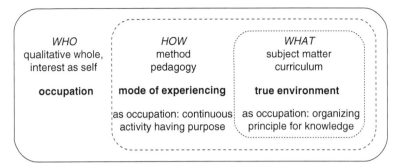

Figure 1.1 The who (occupation), how (mode of experiencing) and what (true environment) of education *through* occupations. Here the occupation as who is
holistic, embracing particular activities and knowledge

This rich understanding of context as experience feeds into Dewey's (1916: 89–90) 'technical definition of education'. In this definition Dewey characterises education as 'that reconstruction or reorganization of experience which adds to the meaning of experience, and which increases ability to direct the course of subsequent experience'. Education works to reconstruct experience. It does this by manipulating *how* (experiencing) and *what* (experienced), but at the same time this affects the transaction understood holistically, as *who*, as occupation. Experientially, context is occupation. Education works *through* occupations.

The experiential contexts of physical education

Skills/techniques first: game as appendage

Bunker and Thorpe's awareness of the importance of understanding the game as context can be illuminated by Dewey's views on experience. Bunker and Thorpe had concerns about the physical education setting wherein techniques were taught *before* the game, and therefore in isolation of the game. So in this traditional setting the game is not the 'true environment' in the sense in which Dewey meant this term. Rather, in this setting the technique is the central aspect of the true environment; the technique is the major *what* that is experienced. And drawing on Dewey's view of experience – that there is always a *how* or mode of experiencing involved in transaction with *what* is experienced – there is in this traditional setting a particular (usually teacher centred) mode of experiencing, a way of learning, a pedagogy. Curriculum (content, subject matter) as what, and pedagogy (process, method) as how, are involved in transaction. Both of these together, holistically, describe an occupation.

In the occupation engendered by this how and what, this traditional pedagogy and curriculum, the underlying rationale for learning the technique is generally teacher centred: the primary incentive involves doing what the teacher requires. This occupation could perhaps be described as that of 'one who is engaged not in having fruitful experiences but in absorbing knowledge directly' (Dewey 1916: 164). So while there is a general understanding that a game exists within which the technique can be contextualised, this game is distanced from the technique to the extent that the reason for learning the technique must be provided in some other way. As such, 'the game is a mere appendage to technique teaching' (Thorpe and Bunker 1982: 9). This is especially so for those who may not have played the (yet to be played) game before, and who may have no real interest in playing this game at all, beyond having to do so as part of the physical education class. As Dewey points out, experience here is not necessarily fruitful.

Many students will, in such a situation, be clamouring for the game, for a broader sense of true environment and a mode of experiencing within which the techniques have a different sense: for a different occupation. This is well illustrated in an example provided by Berenstain and Berenstain (1964), which some readers may be familiar with. In this book the young bear receives a new bike as a present and of course immediately wishes to try to ride it, but is not allowed to until he has received a series of six lessons from his father. 'First come the lessons, then the fun' (p. 6), says the father bear – a statement that could readily be made by a teacher focused primarily on techniques. The young bear attends to his father's lessons, during which his chief task is to indulge his father's efforts to teach him. But his continual refrain, following each lesson, is: 'May I ride it now? May I ride it now?' (p. 50). Yet he waits until all the lessons are complete. This situation is similarly described in an example from philosopher Gilbert Ryle (1972), which also focuses on a child learning to ride a bike for the first time.[1] 'No child can ride a bicycle at first go', claims Ryle, 'he [sic] has to learn how to balance, steer, propel and brake the machine' (p. 46). But such learning cannot be achieved through mere lecturing. 'The father cannot just lecture his son into mastery of the bicycle' (p. 46). For the child, learning the techniques of riding a bike requires trying out everything 'time and time again' (p. 46). And this trying, the effort applied, is part of a much broader context – one that could be equated to a game in our current discussion.

When the techniques are introduced before they are understood in their connection with the game, then the primary concern becomes 'the problem of meeting the peculiar requirements set by the teacher … of finding out what the teacher wants, what will satisfy the teacher in recitation and examination and outward deportment' (Dewey 1916: 183). Thus 'learning here means acquisition of what already is incorporated in books and in the heads of the elders' (Dewey 1938a: 19). The teacher's requirement for acquisition (prior to a game) of particular techniques (what) necessitates a specific mode of learning or experiencing (how), which sets up an occupation (who) that is not the ideal occupation through which to educate in physical education.

Strategies/tactics first: the teacher's game

The development that Bunker and Thorpe introduced, of beginning with the game, offers the possibility of contextualising the skills/techniques by way of their application within a game. And more than this, of understanding the game by way of tactics and the decisions they engender. As mentioned previously, TGfU 'starts with a game and its rules which set the scene for the development of tactical awareness and decision making, which, in their turn, always precede the response factors of skill execution and performance' (Bunker and Thorpe 1982: 8). Here the game is a central feature of the true environment. But this development cannot be understood in its fuller sense without attending to the mode of experiencing, the way of learning and hence the occupation.

The TGfU approach 'starts with a game but it must be simplified to be readily understood, with the minimum of rules necessary to retain the essential elements of the game' (Thorpe and Bunker 1982: 10). Thus this approach actually *begins* with the teacher modifying the game, in order to have an appropriately modified game as environment through which to approach tactics, decision making and skills. This is the 'framework' of TGfU: 'an appropriate game, tactical awareness, decision-making and skill execution', where 'the order' as presented here 'is vital' (p. 11). This order expresses a way of learning, a mode of experiencing, which is integrated with the true environment. The game is presented by the teacher as a modification of, usually, an adult sport, such that this modification is easier for students to understand and play than the full adult version of the game. The TGfU approach then 'requires the teacher to highlight the problems raised by the game and for pupils, using their experience of playing the [modified] game, to find solutions to them' (p. 11). In other words, 'a teaching progression is presented as a series of problems set to the children' (p. 11).

Thorpe and Bunker see the presentation of these problems achieved via teacher questioning. This is a key aspect of the mode of experiencing: the how or pedagogy. In other words, TGfU comprises not just a shift to a broader 'true environment' (the what or subject matter content) but it also incorporates a different mode of experiencing. Using appropriate modifications of badminton as an example, they suggest possible teacher questions:

Teacher question: How do we win a point?
Predictable student answer: By getting the shuttle onto the floor of our
    opponents' court.
Teacher question: What do we need in order to achieve this?
Predictable student answer: A space to hit into.
[Now] play the game and look carefully to see where the spaces are.
Teacher question: Where are the spaces on a long and narrow court?
Predictable student answer: At the front and back, not down the sides
    (the shuttle travels slowly making it very difficult to pass the opponent).
                                    (adapted from Thorpe and Bunker 1982: 11)

Such a way of learning as a mode of experiencing suggests a particular understanding of the true environment. The game – with its tactics, decision making and skills – is now central to the true environment. But it is important to recognise that this game is the teacher's modification of an adult game. TGfU thus promotes understanding of *this* game, the teacher's game, via questioning and problem solving, building up via a series of sequential modifications towards an adult game. Questioning (how) is always integrated with the teacher's game (what). This *how* and *what* describe the *who* of TGfU, an occupation that is quite different from that espoused when techniques are the primary focus. But can we broaden the true environment (curriculum) even further, and thereby shift the occupation again?

Game appreciation first: the students' game

A central tenet of TGfU as expressed by Bunker and Thorpe (1982: 6) is 'game appreciation'. Game appreciation emphasises student understanding of the rules of the game, 'as the rules give the game its shape' (p. 6). For example, 'increasing the height of a net slows the game down and increases the duration of rallies; reducing the number of fielders in a striking game increases the chances of scoring runs' (p. 6). Yet in the TGfU framework, such game appreciation is to be understood *following* the modifications made by teachers. TGfU does not usually involve students *suggesting* these modifications and so the game remains the teacher's game.

We can, therefore, broaden the context of game-based teaching beyond that expressed within TGfU (as usually understood) by changing the mode of experiencing, as integrated with the true environment, such that the game is open to modification by the students. Being a student, as a physical education occupation, is concomitantly affected.

This opening up of the game to student input was championed by Almond, who noticed how 'our preoccupation with major team games has constrained our thinking in such a way that we have given our pupils little opportunity to devise and develop their own games' (1983: 32). This preoccupation with major team games seems to underpin TGfU, as the modified games employed in TGfU are appropriate modifications of adult games, usually major team games. In contrast, Almond suggests that through making games students can:

1. Construct a game, which is theirs, something that they have made and created.
2. Find out for themselves why rules are important and what purpose they serve.
3. Be involved in their own learning.
4. Share their ideas and work cooperatively.
5. Communicate and explain how their game developed.
6. Teach others including the teacher.

(Almond 1983: 32)

Evident here is a shift in the physical education occupation beyond TGfU. It is noteworthy that this approach – involving students making or creating their own games – enables game appreciation to be achieved at a deeper level, where students 'learn the relevance and value of rules in the context of having to create a rule to solve a problem that arises in a developing game' (Almond 1983: 35). The experiential context, the occupation, has thus been broadened by broadening the true environment beyond that of a focus on tactical awareness, decision making and skill execution, to involve the game itself, a real appreciation of games and how they work.

But in his promotion of students creating games, Almond (1983: 35) stresses the need to give 'careful thought' to 'the context in which you put pupils'. This is not a matter of simply giving students access to equipment and asking them to get to it. For, 'the teacher must learn how to intervene to support pupils doing things for themselves' (p. 35). Additionally, Almond believes that 'using games as a problem solving experience requires a detailed knowledge of games' (p. 35). Both of these points highlight the importance of understanding how games themselves work, the variables that are to be manipulated in supporting students who are creating their own games. And these variables are not the rules themselves. The rules emerge from consideration of a range of more foundational factors, including:

Every game has a level of *enjoyment*.
Every game has a level of *participation*.
Every game has a level of *safety*.
Every game requires *skills*.
Every game has *equipment*.
Every game has a period of *time*.
Every game has a *space*.
Every game has a method for *umpiring or refereeing*.
Every game has a method for *scoring*.

(Quay and Peters 2012: 17)

The teacher can think of these variables as setting the parameters for game creation. The teacher can then predetermine these variables and in so doing construct a 'true environment' and mode of experiencing within which students can more effectively discuss and develop the rules that will characterise their game. This enables students to engage with a far deeper sense of game appreciation. And when games are being developed in this way, tactics and skills can also be discussed, as games are tested by being taught to and played with others. Tactics and skills are also part of the true environment in this physical education occupation. As Almond (1983: 34) suggests, 'once a game has been developed, each group should be given the opportunity of explaining it to others in the class, demonstrating it, and allowing other groups to try it out, and evaluate it'. Teaching and evaluating games engages students directly in game appreciation, at a level deeper than that achieved by just playing the game.

Involving students in creating games shifts the experiential context; it shifts the holistic physical education occupation, who the young people are asked to *be*. The developing game is the students' game, rather than the teacher's, although the teacher will have specified the foundational variables. This is a different mode of experiencing in relation to games, a different way of learning (achieved via a different way of teaching: pedagogy). The true environment (curriculum) takes a step beyond the usually accepted teacher modification of adult games and the strategies and skills within, to incorporate the nature of the game itself.

Sport first: the season of games

Up to this point we have been focused primarily on the game as context, whether the teacher's game or the students' game. Yet there is a broader context within which the game itself sits: that of sport. However, as Siedentop points out, 'sport in physical education has typically been decontextualized' (1994: 7). By this, Siedentop means that the idea of sport as applied in physical education has come to be chiefly identified with the sets of skills/techniques and strategies/tactics that can be distilled from major team sports. In other words, a sport in physical education has become little more than the teaching of the skills and strategies associated with a particular adult sport. As exemplary of this situation, Siedentop argues that in physical education 'the rituals, values, and traditions of a sport that give it meaning are seldom ever mentioned, let alone taught in ways that students can experience them' (p. 7). As a response to this issue, he draws out 'six primary features' that characterise 'the typical context for sport' (p. 8). These are 'seasons, affiliation, a formal schedule of competition, a culminating event, records, and a festive atmosphere' (p. 9).

When these features of sport are experientially incorporated within physical education, the true environment (the curriculum) expands, the mode of experiencing (the pedagogy) changes, and thus the physical education occupation shifts. The student-developed game, as a stand-alone entity, is no longer the true environment of physical education. Instead, by situating the game within the features of sport, the game itself actually becomes much more. The game now sits in a season of games with a formal schedule of competition, a culminating event, records and a festive atmosphere. But perhaps most importantly there is now affiliation with a team, an ongoing team. Being a team member becomes a significant aspect of the physical education occupation.

Teams are a common feature of physical education, however, the traditional physical education team is usually very short lived. The physical education team may exist for one lesson, or perhaps not even that. This means that the team is not, in the usual sense of sport, a team. In fact in most instances, success experienced by a (very temporary) physical education team can be attributed to this team being a 'team of champions', of gifted individual performers. This contrasts markedly with a 'champion team', a team that has gelled as a team, which can take quite a while to develop. But there is no capacity to develop a champion team in physical education because the team will be disbanded at the end of the lesson (or before).

Development, improvement, is central to sport in physical education. Yet improvement takes time, time through which interest must be maintained so that effort will be sustained. A season can provide this by offering a fixed number of games (a fixture), leading to a culminating event, all held within a festive atmosphere. And another significant aspect of a sport season is that if your team loses a game, there is another game on which to focus: the next game. This next game functions as a motivating factor, a purpose or 'end-in-view' (Dewey 1929: 86), which enables frustration to be channelled into team improvement via practice. Such team development, as practice, can take account of strategies/tactics and skills/techniques. So, by expanding the experiential context to include the features of sport, the physical education occupation has again changed.

Social responsibility first: the team

There is another element of team improvement, which we have not yet stressed. Siedentop (1994: 7) notes that 'affiliation with a team or group that provides the context for personal growth and responsibility in sport is noticeably absent in physical education'. Membership of a team engenders much more than merely strategies and skills. The team is a social entity. In this way being a team member is crucial to our sense of a physical education occupation. But as physical educators we often ignore this point, or at best pay lip service to it.

If we wish to assist students to improve their performance as a team we must focus on issues of personal and social responsibility that add up to being a team member (MacPhail, Kirk and Kinchin 2004). Hellison's (1995) model of taking personal and social responsibility in physical education (TPSR) helps us to do this by articulating a hierarchical framework, each level of which can be described as a different way of understanding and expressing one's being a team member. Hellison describes five levels of which level one is the lowest:

Level 1: Respecting the rights and feelings of others.
Level 2: Participation and effort.
Level 3: Self-direction.
Level 4: Caring about and helping others.
Level 5: Outside the gym.

(adapted from Hellison 1995: 14)

When Hellison's levels are aligned with notions of team membership, a rationale for moving through the levels is more clearly pronounced. As a team member moves through the levels, towards level three or four, their contributions to the team generally improve, and thus the team improves.

Hellison's fifth level describes transfer of this understanding to other contexts, other occupations beyond physical education. Learning *through* occupations thus involves not only learning within one occupation, but importantly brings this learning (in its holistic sense as an occupation) into juxtaposition with other occupations. This is not mere transfer of knowledge concepts or skill techniques (as *what*), but rather translation of meaning from one occupation to another, which involves *who*, *how* and *what*.

Conclusion: integrating contexts through team, game, season and practice

So far our presentation appears as a progression that moves through a range of different experiential contexts that has led first from the narrow focus on techniques (FMS) to the broader sense of a teacher's game (TGfU); then passing ownership for the game to students (games making); then situating the game in the features of sport (sport education); and finally emphasising the importance of the social nature of the team (TPSR). This progression appears as an ever-widening set of concentric circles, each of which encompasses a broader true environment (curriculum) and a different mode of experiencing (pedagogy) such that through this progression the physical education occupation has been significantly altered. In other words, this is not simply a change from a teacher-centred to a student-centred pedagogy. Rather it involves changes in physical education curriculum (true environment) integrated with changes in mode of experiencing (pedagogy). And together these changes reveal a continuous shift in the holistic occupation espoused for physical education.

We are aware that it is more usual for each of these models of physical education to be considered as separate, such that they appear as books on a bookshelf that the teacher may select from. But we hope that our presentation of the ever-widening experiential contexts of physical education highlights how they can all work together. Such integration has been described in some detail by Quay and Peters (2008, 2012). This integration builds on an awareness of the importance of Dewey's sense of education *through* occupations.

Here, rather than beginning with the narrowest parts of the true environment where curriculum is concerned (the techniques), the beginning is with the broadest (the team). Being a team member is an essential aspect of a physical education occupation because it is at the heart of the meaning of physical education for students. But a team must also have a game, and so involving the teams in game creation is an important part of this physical education occupation; thus students learn game appreciation in a much deeper way. The development of one class game then requires a season for its more meaningful expression: a schedule of games, a culminating event, all within a festive atmosphere. And for the sake of team improvement through the season there must be opportunities for practice of strategies and skills, as well as fitness, all together with taking on the personal and social responsibilities that are central to being a team member.

In this way, by focusing as Dewey did on the holistic experiential context as occupation, we have turned physical education upside down and around about. The team, as an element of sport, is the experiential context that provides the reason for engaging with the game. Here the game is not a modified adult game, it is the students' game. And it is within this game, played by a team through a season, that dealing with strategies and skills makes sense. This integration espouses a physical education occupation, one different to that ascribed by FMS, TGfU, making games, sport education and TPSR, when each of these is considered separately. But bringing them together through a Deweyan understanding of experiential context as holistic occupation provides us with a broader physical education curriculum and richer pedagogies, especially where games are involved.

Discussion questions

1. Why do you think context is an important issue in physical education?
2. How does context change across the different models of teaching in physical education from technical or skills-based approaches (FMS), to TGfU, to making games, to sport education and to TPSR?
3. How does changing context effect teaching and learning in physical education?

Note

1 We are cognisant of the fact that Ryle is employing this example – of a child learning how to ride a bike – to make a point about the problems he perceives with teaching virtues, which are not normally directly taught. Our purpose is different to Ryle's but we draw on his example as it also challenges the problems and supports thinking about teaching the same issue with traditional forms of education wherein the learning context is markedly different to that in which the knowledge and skills being learnt are to be more meaningfully employed.

References

Almond, L. (1983) 'Games making', *Bulletin of Physical Education*, 19(1), 32–35.

Armour, K. M. (2010) 'The physical education profession and its professional responsibility... or... why "12 weeks paid holiday" will never be enough', *Physical Education and Sport Pedagogy*, 15(1), 1–13.

Berenstain, J. and Berenstain, S. (1964) *The Bike Lesson*, New York: Beginner Books, Random House.

Brooker, R., Kirk, D., Braiuka, S. and Bransgrove, A. (2000) 'Implementing a Game Sense approach to teaching junior high school basketball in a naturalistic setting', *European Physical Education Review*, 6(1), 7–26.

Bunker, D. and Thorpe, R. (1982) 'A model for the teaching of games in secondary schools', *Bulletin of Physical Education*, 18(1), 5–8.

Dewey, J. (1911) 'Environment and organism', in P. Monroe (ed.) *An Encyclopedia of Education, Vol. II*, New York: Macmillan, pp. 486–487.

——(1913) *Interest and Effort in Education*, Cambridge, MA: The Riverside Press.

——(1916) *Democracy and Education*, New York: The Free Press.

——(1929) *Experience and Nature* (second edition), Chicago, IL: Open Court Publishing.

——(1930) 'Conduct and experience', in C. Murchison (ed.) *Psychologies of 1930*, Worcester, MA: Clark University Press, pp. 409–422.

——(1934) *Art as Experience*, New York: Capricorn Books.

——(1938a) *Logic: The Theory of Inquiry*, New York: Holt, Rinehart and Winston.

——(1938b) *Experience and Education*, New York: Collier Books.

——(1939) 'Experience, knowledge and value: A rejoinder', in P. A. Schilpp (ed.), *The Philosophy of John Dewey*, Evanston, IL: Northwestern University Press, pp. 515–608.

Hellison, D. (1995) *Teaching Responsibility through Physical Activity*, Champaign, IL: Human Kinetics.

Kirk, D. and MacPhail, A. (2002) 'Teaching games for understanding and situated learning: Rethinking the Bunker–Thorpe model', *Journal of Teaching in Physical Education*, 21(2), 177–192.

MacPhail, A., Kirk, D. and Kinchin, G. (2004) 'Sport education: Promoting team affiliation through physical education', *Journal of Teaching in Physical Education*, 23(2), 106–122.

Park, R. J. (1969) 'The philosophy of John Dewey and physical education', *The Physical Educator*, 26(2), 55–57.

Quay, J. and Peters, J. (2008) 'Skills, strategies, sport and social responsibility. Reconnecting physical education', *Journal of Curriculum Studies*, 40(5), 601–626.

——(2012) *Creative Physical Education: Integrating Curriculum through Innovative PE Projects*, Champaign, IL: Human Kinetics.

Ryle, G. (1972) 'Can virtue be taught?', in R.F. Dearden, P.H. Hirst and R.S. Peters (eds), *Education and Reason: Part 3 of Education the Development of Reason*, London: Routledge and Kegan Paul, pp. 44–57.

Siedentop, D. (1994) *Sport Education: Quality PE through Positive Sport Experiences*, Champaign, IL: Human Kinetics.

Thorpe, R. and Bunker, D. (1982) 'From theory to practice: Two examples of an "understanding approach" to the teaching of games', *Bulletin of Physical Education*, 18(1), 9–15.

2 Positive pedagogy for physical education and sport

Game Sense as an example

Richard L. Light

Introduction

Student-centred, inquiry-based approaches to teaching games are effective for improving game playing ability, increasing student motivation and providing positive affective experiences of learning (see, for example, Kirk 2005; Mitchell, Oslin and Griffin 1995; Pope 2005). Consistent with social constructivist theories of learning (see, for example, Fosnot 1996; Gréhaigne, Richard and Griffin 2005; Wallian and Chang 2007), the central role that dialogue, reflection and purposeful social interaction play in facilitating learning in these approaches can promote deep understanding (Light, Curry and Mooney in press) and make learning meaningful. Through these experiences students/ players/athletes not only learn the content of the lesson or practice session but also learn how to learn and develop a positive inclination toward learning. The modes of learning employed in Game Sense and other game-based approaches (GBA) can generate positive intellectual and affective experiences of learning that foster an enjoyment of learning, confidence in the learners' ability and inclination to learn as they develop into independent learners: not just in sport and physical education but also in most areas of life.

Games-based pedagogy

The different approaches used in game-based teaching vary in detail but can all provide consistently positive learning experiences that enhance learning and promote both the ability and the inclination to learn. This is largely due to them being student-centred, inquiry-based approaches that emphasize learner reflection upon experience and social interaction. The oldest and most established of these approaches is Teaching Games for Understanding (TGfU – Bunker and Thorpe 1982) with later variations of this GBA developed in Australia as Game Sense (den Duyn 1997; Light 2013a), in the US as tactical games (Griffin, Mitchell and Oslin 1997) and in Singapore as the games concept approach (GCA) (see, for example, McNeill, Fry, Wright, Tan, Tan and Schempp 2004). Similar approaches have also been developed that are not direct derivatives of TGfU but do share similar pedagogy such as the tactical-decision learning model (Gréhaigne *et al.* 2005) in France and Play Practice (Launder 2001) in Australia. While these approaches focus on developing better games players the process of learning involved can generate positive experiences that are enjoyable, satisfying and facilitate learning how to learn (Light 2003; Pope 2005). The learning experiences provided by this pedagogy can also contribute toward positive social, moral and personal development (see, for example, Dyson 2005; Light 2013b; Sheppard and Mandigo 2005) due to the nature of learning involved. However, these should not be seen as automatic outcomes of taking these approaches.

A range of programmes or 'instructional models' have been developed for specifically promoting positive personal, social and moral development through sport and other physical activity over the past three decades such as positive youth development through sport (see, Holt, Sehn, Spence, Newton and Ball 2012), sport education (Siedentop 1994) and teaching responsibility through physical activity (see Hellison 2003). More recently, there has been something of a positive turn in the social sciences. In addition to positive youth development (PYD – Learner *et al.* 2005), positive psychology (Seligman and Csikszentmihalyi 2000) has had a significant impact in schools as have approaches to redressing student behaviour problems that emphasize positive experiences (see, for example, Roffey 2011). This includes positive parenting (see, for example, Latham 1994) and a positive approach to health that focuses on the positive social features of the conditions within which good health flourishes (Antonovsky 1979, 1987).

Antonovsky's (1979, 1987) salutogenic theory and sense of coherence (SoC) model focus on the socially constructed 'resources' that allow people to achieve and maintain good health. In this chapter I draw on Antonovsky to provide a framework for understanding what is needed to make pedagogy positive. Atonovsky (1979) developed the concept of 'salutogenesis' as a reference to *the origins of health* to take a positive, holistic approach by emphasizing what supports health and wellbeing rather than what causes disease or the 'lifestyle' approach that focuses on identifying risk factors (Antonovsky 1996). He rejects the dichotomy of health and disease with his SoC model offering a useful way of identifying the ways in which pedagogy can produce positive learning experiences. He is primarily concerned with the affective and social dimensions of life rather than with its cognitive aspects and with a focus on experience. His model comprises three elements necessary for good health: (a) comprehensibility, (b) manageability and (c) meaningfulness that can also be used to identify conditions that promote positive experiences of learning.

Comprehensibility is developed through experience and refers to the extent to which things make sense for the individual in that events and situations are ordered and consistent. Very relevant to this concept is the emphasis on deep understanding and game awareness that is achieved through experience in the Game Sense approach. *Manageability* is the extent to which an individual feels s/he can mange stress and challenge by having the resources at hand. Resources can be objects such as tools and equipment, skills, intellectual ability, social and cultural capital and so on. In a Game Sense lesson or training session this means that the challenges set by the teacher are seen to be manageable when the student feels s/he has adequate skill and understanding and has the support of teammates, the class and the teacher in order to meet these challenges; with the collective, social element of prime importance here. *Meaningfulness* refers to how much the individual feels that life makes sense and that its challenges are worthy of commitment. According to Antonovsky, meaningfulness promotes a positive expectation of life and the future. It encourages people to see challenges as being interesting, relevant and worthy of emotional commitment. When positive pedagogy is employed *engagement* gives meaning to tasks and experiences.

Positive pedagogy for physical education and sport

The literature and the media are full of examples of the negative learning that can occur through playing youth sport such as violence (see, for example, White 2012). There is also well-justified concern with physical education teaching that marginalizes the less skilled and the less confident and reduces self-esteem by highlighting what they cannot do (see, for example, Ennis 1999). The teacher-centred, sports skills, multi-activity approach has much to answer for in regard to the host of negative experiences that it fosters for many learners, how it marginalizes the less skillful and how it dis-empowers young learners (Ennis 1999). Even for the confident and experienced students who have the necessary skills to meet expectations of performance in this approach the learning involved is not necessarily positive. It may be enjoyable for them because it allows them to demonstrate competency but it does not help them learn to learn. Neither will it encourage or foster positive personal or psychological attributes. Indeed it can promote selfishness, egotism and a lack of empathy or compassion for other learners (teammates) while also failing to teach real teamwork, which is a core focus of Game Sense.

Traditional sport skills approaches are based upon the belief that learning to play team games requires reaching a level of competence in performing techniques seen to be fundamental to the game *before* playing it. Assuming that there is one ideal form of technical execution that learners must strive to master, teaching in this approach focuses upon reducing errors and moving the student closer to the 'correct' performance of the technique. While the extent to which this de-contextualized practice can be applied in the dynamic context of games is questionable (see, Light, Harvey and Mouchet 2012) this is not my focus here. Instead, my focus is on the essentially negative nature of these learning experiences that too often highlight what learners *cannot* do, sometimes exacerbated by attempting to perform these skills in front of their peers and teacher(s). The positive pedagogy provided in games-based teaching such as Game Sense is devoid of this essentially negative, corrective feedback and this sense of being under the 'critical gaze' of peers and teachers due to learning being based in and focused on games and its learner-centred pedagogy.

Positive psychology sets out to redress a preoccupation of psychology with pathologies and repairing the 'worst aspects' of life by promoting its positive qualities (Seligman and Csikszentmihalyi 2000). It focuses on wellbeing and satisfaction in the past, on happiness and the experience of 'flow' in the present and on hope and optimism in the future (Jackson and Csikszentmihalyi 1999). It aims at building 'thriving individuals, finding and nurturing talent and making normal life more fulfilling', drawing on the concepts of *flow* and *mindfulness* as positive states that generate learning (Seligman and Csikszentmihalyi 2000: 5). Flow has also been proffered to explain the experiences possible when learning through sport and practice/modified games that provide appropriate challenges (Jackson and Csikszentmihalyi 1999) and which can be experienced through GBA such as TGfU (Lloyd and Smith 2010). It refers to a state of being absorbed in the experience of action through intense concentration as the athlete is 'lost' in the flow of experience. It provides a positive affective experience through which deep learning occurs.

Both concepts suggest a circumvention of the problematic relationship between mind and body embedded in the dualism that dominates Western philosophic traditions. The Japanese cultural concept of *mushin* is very similar to flow and has also been drawn on specifically to deal with the limitations placed upon understanding learning as a whole-person experience by Western dualism when coaching decision making in team sports (Light *et al.* 2012). Western interpretations of mindfulness (see, for example, Seligman and Csikszentmihalyi 2000; Varela, Thompson and Rosch 1991) see it as an intentionally focused awareness of immediate experience, thoughts, emotions and surroundings grounded in the present moment. With its roots in Buddhist philosophic traditions, others such as Varela and colleagues (1991) also draw upon mindfulness to deal with the problematic relationship between mind and body in Western thinking and theories of learning.

Making learning positive

Positive pedagogy provides consistently positive learning experiences that enhance intended learning, foster positive attitudes toward learning and contribute toward the positive whole-person development of the learner. Although it does not specifically focus on developing wellbeing or happiness all five elements of Seligman's (2012) PERMA (positive emotions, engagement, relations, meaning and achievement) model are evident in Game Sense as an example of positive pedagogy. It generates positive emotions such as enjoyment or delight (Kretchmar 2005), engagement in learning, the building of relationships and a sense of belonging (Light 2008), meaning, and opportunities for achievement, both individually and collectively. Positive pedagogy emphasizes what the learner can do and how s/he can draw on existing individual and social resources to meet learning challenges through reflection and dialogue.

In taking a positive pedagogy approach to teaching piano George (2006) suggests that it provides positive learning experiences that can foster a love of learning, imagination, problem-solving skills and can develop active, inquisitive learners instead of passive receivers of knowledge. She argues that taking an approach to teaching that focuses on 'fixing' mistakes deprives learners of the positive experience of the joy of self-discovery that can build self-confidence and autonomy. She contends that basing learning on the teacher correcting mistakes leads to a lack of learner focus, engagement and motivation, which are significant problems associated with the directive, teacher-centred, sport-skills approach (see, for example, Ennis 1999; Kirk 2005, 2010). George's positive approach to teaching piano is evident in GBAs as examples of positive pedagogy.

Positive pedagogy is informed by theories of learning, including social contructivism (see, for example, Vygotsky 1978) and enactivism (see, for example, Varela *et al.* 1991) as well as concepts such as situated learning (Lave and Wenger 1991) that can be included under the umbrella term of complex learning theory (CLT), first proposed by Davis and Sumara (2003). The broad principles common to all these perspectives and that underpin positive pedagogy approaches are that learning is:

- a process of adaptation (transformation/change);
- a social process;
- an interpretative process.

Antonovsky's SoC model

Appropriating Antonovsky's SoC model provides a means of identifying how positive pedagogy generates positive experiences of learning that allow learning to 'flourish'. For learning to be *comprehensible* it should help learners know, not only how to do something, but also when, where and why. It should also foster deep learning that typically involves understanding the 'big ideas' (Fosnot 1996) that underpin learning. Comprehensive understanding involves not only rational, conscious and articulated knowing, but also a practical sense (Bourdieu 1986) developed through experience and engagement in a process of learning as the unfolding of knowledge that includes learning how to learn.

Learning is manageable when the challenges set extend the learner but can be met by drawing on individual resources (for example, skill, physical capacity, intelligence) and/or social resources such as social interaction with peers and the teacher/coach. The provision of a supportive socio-cultural environment assists in making challenges manageable and rewarding. Learning is meaningful when its comprehensibility gives meaning to tasks and learning activities because they make sense within the 'big picture' and can be related to the end aims of learning – not just cognitively, but also in an affective way. When activities engage learners affectively and socially as well as physically and intellectually they are likely to be meaningful.

Game Sense as an example of positive pedagogy

This section of the chapter examines the ways in which the four core features of Game Sense pedagogy (Light 2013a) provide for consistently positive learning experiences. They are that: (1) it emphasizes engagement with the learning environment; (2) the teacher asks questions that generate dialogue and thinking instead of telling students what to do; (3) it provides opportunities for students to formulate, test and evaluate solutions to problems; and (4) it provides a supportive socio-moral environment in which making mistakes is accepted as an essential part of learning.

Designing the learning environment (modified games)

Game Sense focuses on the game as a whole rather than on discrete components of it such as technique (den Duyn 1997). The game is seen as a complex phenomenon within which learning to play involves adapting to its dynamics with tactical knowledge, skill execution and decision making all interconnected as knowledge-in-action (Light 2013a). Learning is located within modified games or game-like activities based on the assumption that learning occurs through engagement with the learning environment and not through direct instruction (Dewey 1916/97). This is also initially learning that largely takes place as a process of adaptation at a non-conscious level and forms the basis of ensuing learning experiences as attempts are made to bring it to consciousness through dialogue. This means that 'getting the game right' is of pivotal importance (Thorpe and Bunker 2008).

As students adapt to the Game Sense approach they take on more autonomy and ownership to participate in practice-game modification (Almond 1983) as well as the formulation and testing of tactical solutions. This leads to the empowerment of them as learners achieved through a growing understanding in and about games and of how to learn. As students become more independent learners, and more prepared to engage in purposeful social interaction, they take more responsibility for their own learning as an important and positive learning experience. Learning through games occurs at a non-conscious level through participating in practice games where players respond to the dynamics of the game in a process of adaptation as emphasized by Piaget and suggested as a core principle of CLT (Davis and Sumara 2003). While some practice games are designed to focus on particular aspects of the full game they provide a holistic experience and are always social in nature, even when there is no verbal interaction (see Chapter 13 by Turner for a more detailed discussion of game design).

Ask questions to generate dialogue and thinking

Questioning is one of the central mechanisms employed for promoting student-centred learning in Game Sense (see Chapter 11 by Forrest). It aims to stimulate dialogue, reflection and the conscious processing of ideas about playing the game as 'the debate of ideas' (Gréhaigne *et al*. 2005). The questions asked strive to stimulate thinking by being open and generating dialogue, to promote a sense of inquiry and lead to the construction of new knowledge and understandings. They aim to generate possibilities and a range of answers or solutions rather than lead to predetermined answers that are deemed to be correct or incorrect. Wright and Forrest (2007) identify this problem through their criticism of the sequencing of questions suggested in some TGfU texts and the ways in which it limits the possible responses instead of expanding them.

To promote creativity and enjoyment of meeting challenges and the joy of discovery (George 2006) the Game Sense teacher avoids being critical or telling learners they are wrong. Although they will invariably find that some of their tactical solutions do not work they will collectively modify them or seek a different solution. Within this debate of ideas (Gréhaigne *et al*. 2005) there will clearly be some disagreement, because this is the nature of debate, but there is a need here for teachers to shape and facilitate the development of students' debating skills and abilities to negotiate, compromise and arrive at outcomes without making any participants feel 'wrong' or excluded. As with handling debate in classrooms in other subjects, this is an important teaching skill. The Game Sense teacher's contribution here is typically to promote a positive enjoyment of inquiry and ask questions about what options or strategies might be appropriate to guide inquiry. This should help students learn that making mistakes is an essential part of learning with these learning experiences promoting resiliency, creativity, social learning, collective effort and an enjoyment of inquiry and discovery (see Chapter 11 by Forrest for a more detailed treatment of questioning).

Provide opportunities for formulating, testing and evaluating solutions

When complex practice games are used in Game Sense the teams should have opportunities to have 'team talks' at appropriate times (Light 2013a). This would be introduced after the players develop a feel for the game or *game appreciation* (Bunker and Thorpe 1982). In these team talks the students formulate strategies through group dialogue that they implement in the game. After this they gather again to critically reflect upon how the strategy worked. If it didn't work they are asked to identify why it didn't work and formulate a new strategy or plan and test it (Light 2013b). Even if they don't have time to try it again this is a positive experience in terms of affective experience, the depth and breadth of learning and learning how to learn because they come to understand why it did not work.

While the more confident and experienced players may initially dominate proceedings, the less experienced players can make valuable contributions when encouraged by the coach through participation in dialogue and the 'debate of ideas' (Gréhaigne *et al*. 2005). Students learn to be better game players while developing confidence in their ability to become independent learners and problem solvers. The productive social interaction involved in this process can also lead to students understanding each other as more than objects on the field or court. It encourages empathy, compassion, meaningful relationships, a sense of connection and care for each other as well, both on and off the field. This was a very strong theme to arise from a study I conducted on the capacity for Game Sense pedagogy to engender more positive attitudes toward cricket among year-six primary school children. The pedagogy used promoted interpersonal relationships and understanding, and consideration of other students within the class (Light 2008).

Develop a supportive environment

To get students to speak up, formulate ideas or strategies and take risks teachers have to build a supportive environment where they feel secure enough to do so. This requires the socio-moral environment that DeVries and Zan (1996) recommend for supporting learners when adopting constructivist-informed teaching approaches. Teachers also need to make it clear that making mistakes is an essential part of learning in physical education classes: and in any other aspect of their lives. This not only provides positive learning experiences but also makes them relevant and meaningful beyond games and physical education. It helps develop an awareness of the process of learning and its meaningfulness as suggested in Antonovsky's (1979) sense of coherence (SoC) model to see it as being worthy of emotional commitment.

Discussion

Just as words are given meaning in language by their context, effective skill execution is dependent upon the context within which it is done and how it meets the demands of the situation. This is discussed in detail by Quay and Stolz in Chapter 1. There is, thus, no one ideal 'correct' form of a technique and little point in pursuing 'mastery' of technique through a process that necessarily requires providing negative feedback as the player attempts to reproduce it. Locating learning within games is one feature of the Game Sense approach that helps avoid the constant correction of 'errors' in technique, provides for positive affective experiences such as 'delight' (Kretchmar 2005), and increased motivation at all levels, up to the most elite levels of sport (see, for example, Evans 2012). It provides the *meaningfulness* that makes learning a challenge 'worthy of investment and engagement' (Antonovsky 1987: 19) because the learners understand the game as a whole and how different aspects of the game fit in and make sense.

The learning that arises from playing practice games as a process of adaptation occurs at a non-conscious level as students develop a practical sense of the game (Bourdieu 1986). This is then enhanced by bringing it to consciousness through dialogue in team talks and whole class discussions between students and the teacher and between students. Over time this leads to the development of what Antonovsky (1979) refers to as comprehensibility, as students make sense of games through affective and intellectual experiences that are perceived to be coherent and structured.

In Game Sense and TGfU learning involves social interaction that has been strongly linked to joyful experiences in research I have conducted myself in universities and schools (see, for example, Light 2002, 2008; Light and Georgakis 2005). Large-scale research in psychology also suggests strong links between happiness and social interaction (see, for example, Fowler and Christakis 2008). Recent work on student behaviour in schools stresses the importance of good relationships between teacher and students, feelings of belonging and connectedness, engagement (giving meaning) and of the emotional and social aspects of learning as a positive approach (see, for example, Roffey 2011). The social nature of learning emphasized in Game Sense and its inclusive nature facilitates this sense of belonging (see, for example, Light 2002). Self-determination theory (Deci and Ryan 2000) suggests that, along with *autonomy* and *competence*, the similar notion of *relatedness* is a psychological requirement for human growth and the promotion of wellbeing. This is further emphasized in Seligman's Positive Psychology model as 'relationships', which is a reference to the importance of supportive personal connections for wellbeing.

The learner-centred nature of Game Sense pedagogy and the way in which it empowers learners can be seen to provide more autonomy while the deep understanding developed in Game Sense could be seen to encourage a feeling of competence emphasized in self-determination theory. Games are enjoyable for people of all ages because they are social activities in which humans interact verbally and in corporeal ways (Light 2002). Game Sense pedagogy extends this social interaction into collective discussion about, and reflection upon, experience and the formulation of ideas and strategies. In any game, players also communicate through movement and gestures as well as verbal communication during play. When the right level of challenge is provided through modifications to practice games they can produce the enjoyable experience of *flow* (Csikszentmihalyi 1990) or *mushin* (Light *et al.* 2012) as a positive state of wellbeing and learning in which the player is 'lost in the game' as experience; the mind and body become one.

Questioning forms a key tool in Game Sense to stimulate thinking and learning through the dialogue and debate it generates among learners (Gréhaigne *et al.* 2005). It can vary from a quick question to one student 'on the run'; to collaboration in team meetings during complex practice games to an end of lesson evaluation of learning (Light 2013a). Questioning is used to structure and shape thinking and understanding through productive dialogue, as opposed to the monologue used in directive 'command' style instruction (Mosston and Ashworth 1986) in the pursuit of correct technique. The questions do not seek yes or no answers with the teacher asking more probing, generative questions instead of telling the students they are wrong. In Game

Sense teaching questions should stimulate the exploration of possibilities rather than leading learners to one predetermined answer (see, for example, Wright and Forrest 2007). This can build confidence and self-esteem within a supportive environment in which students feel confident enough to offer ideas and possible solutions without fear of being embarrassed or drawing attention to what they can't express or do. It can encourage creativity and promote a collective sense of team as something stronger and more meaningful than the mere sum of its parts (players) in sport and other aspects of social life.

Conclusion

Game Sense pedagogy can foster an enjoyment of learning and learning how to learn while contributing toward achieving its core aim of developing better games players, and this is its focus. This can, however, include encouraging the development of many of the same positive personal traits that Positive Psychology aims to develop such as compassion, resilience, self-confidence, creativity or the competence, coping ability, health, resilience, and wellbeing that Positive Youth Development through Sport aims at achieving (Holt *et al.*, 2012: 98). It can also facilitate the positive social learning and social skills that participation in sport and physical education is commonly assumed to deliver but which merely playing games will not necessarily teach (see, for example, De Martelaer, De Bouw and Struyven 2012; Light 2013c). It is the specific characteristics of the pedagogy used in Game Sense that can foster positive personal and social learning and facilitate the development of social skills and not just the content of the lesson. This is, of course, enhanced when the teacher has an explicit focus on promoting this learning.

Positive pedagogy in physical education and sport emphasizes the holistic, social nature of learning, and the role of experience and the body in it. It encourages the development of the social skills involved in engaging in purposeful dialogue, a willingness and ability to negotiate and compromise and an understanding of the democratic processes involved in making and enacting collective decision making, while making learning enjoyable. Viewed from this perspective, the pedagogy used in Game Sense, TGfU, Play Practice and similar approaches offers great potential for delivering high-quality learning across the physical education, practical, curriculum (Light *et al.* in press). Most importantly, the positive nature of the pedagogy employed helps learning to flourish. Learning to learn and the positive inclinations toward learning it can generate, and some of the social learning that can accompany it, is more likely to transfer into life outside schools than improved sport technique and fitness are. For physical education teaching it highlights the important role that the body and physical experience can play in learning when appropriate pedagogy is adopted. The way in which it can develop active, inquiring and reflective learners and the contribution it can make toward wellbeing provides a more positive rationale for physical education than seeing it as a tool in the fight against obesity or of merely 'skilling up' students.

Discussion questions

1. Explain how the author suggests the positive pedagogy proposed in this chapter makes learning positive.
2. In what ways does the author suggest a focus on technique can promote negative experiences of learning in comparison to the Game Sense focus on the game?
3. What claims are made about the capacity of Positive Pedagogy to encourage positive moral and social learning and what limitations are suggested?

References

Almond, L. (1983) 'Games making', *Bulletin of Physical Education*, 19(1), 32–35.

Antonovsky, A. (1979) *Health, Stress and Coping*. San Francisco: Jossey-Bass.

——(1987) *Unraveling the Mystery of Health*. San Francisco: Jossey-Bass.

——(1996) 'The salutogenic model as a theory to guide health promotion', *Health Promotion International*, 11(1), 11–17.

Bourdieu, P. (1986) *Distinction*. London: Routledge and Kegan Paul.

Bunker, D. and Thorpe, R. (1982) 'A model for teaching games in secondary school', *Bulletin of Physical Education*, 10, 9–16.

Csikszentmihalyi, M. (1990) *Flow: The Psychology of Optimal Experience*. New York: Harper and Row.

Davis, B. and Sumara, D. (2003) 'Why aren't they getting this? Working through the regressive myths of constructivist pedagogy', *Teaching Education*, 14(2), 123–140.

Deci, E. L. and Ryan, R. M. (2000) 'The "what" and "why" of goal pursuits: Human needs and the self-determination of behavior', *Psychological Enquiry*, 11, 227–268.

De Martelaer, K., De Bouw, J. and Struyven, K. (2012) 'Youth sport ethics: Teaching pro-social behaviour', in S. Harvey and R. Light (eds) *Ethics in Youth Sport: Policy and Pedagogical Applications*. Abingdon: Routledge, pp. 55–73.

den Duyn, N. (1997) *Game Sense: Developing Thinking Players*. Canberra: Australian Sports Commission.

DeVries R. and Zan, B. (1996) 'A constructivist perspective on the role of the sociomoral atmosphere in promoting children's development', in C. T. Fosnot (ed.) *Constructivism: Theory, Perspectives and Practice*. New York: Teachers College, Columbia University, pp. 103–119.

Dewey, J. (1916/97) *Democracy in Education*. New York: Free Press.

Dyson, B. (2005) 'Integrating cooperative learning and tactical games models: Focusing on social interactions and decision-making', in L. L. Griffin and J. I. Butler (eds) *Teaching Games for Understanding: Theory, Research, and Practice*. Champaign, IL: Human Kinetics, pp. 149–168.

Ennis, C. (1999) 'Creating a culturally relevant curriculum for disengaged girls', *Sport, Education and Society*, 4(1), 31–50.

Evans, J. R. (2012) 'Elite rugby union coaches' interpretation and use of Game Sense in New Zealand', *Asian Journal of Exercise and Sport Science*, 9(1), 85–97.

Fosnot, C. T. (ed.) (1996) *Constructivism: Theory, Perspectives and Practice*. New York: Teachers College, Columbia University.

Fowler, J. H. and Christakis, N. A. (2008) 'Dynamic spread of happiness in a large social network: longitudinal analysis over 20 years in the Framingham heart study', *British Medical Journal*, 337(768): doi:10.1136/bmj.a2338.

George, M. G. (2006) 'The power of positive pedagogy', *Music Learning Community. com Newsletter*, October–November. Available at: www.musiclearningcommunity. com/NewsletterArchive/2006October.The%20Power%20of%20Positive%20Pedagogy. htm (last accessed 29 April 2013).

Gréhaigne, J.-F., Richard, J.-F. and Griffin, L. L. (2005) *Teaching and Learning Team Sports and Games*. London: Routledge.

Griffin, L. L., Mitchell, S. A. and Oslin, J. L. (1997) *Teaching Sport Concepts and Skills: A Tactical Games Approach*. Champaign, IL: Human Kinetics.

Hellison, D. R. (2003) *Teaching Responsibility through Physical Activity* (second edition). Champaign, IL: Human Kinetics.

Holt, N. L., Sehn, Z. L., Spence, J. C., Newton, A. S. and Ball, G. D. C. (2012) 'Physical education and sport programs at an inner city school: exploring possibilities for positive youth development', *Physical Education and Sport Pedagogy*, 17(1), 97–113.

Jackson, S. A. and Czikszentmihalyi, M. (1999) *Flow in Sports*. Champaign, IL: Human Kinetics.

Kirk, D. (2005) 'Future prospects for Teaching Games for Understanding', in L. Griffin and J. Butler (eds) *Teaching Games for Understanding: Theory Research and Practice*. Champaign, IL: Human Kinetics, pp. 213–226.

——(2010) 'Towards a socio-pedagogy of sports coaching', in J. Lyle and C. Cushion (eds) *Sport Coaching: Professionalisation and Practice*. Edinburgh: Elsevier, pp. 165–176.

Kretchmar, S. (2005) 'Understanding and the delights of human activity', in L. Griffin and J. Butler (eds) *Teaching Games for Understanding: Theory Research and Practice*. Champaign, IL: Human Kinetics, pp. 199–212.

Latham, G. I. (1994) *The Power of Positive Parenting: A Wonderful Way to Raise Children*. North Logan, UT: P & T Ink.

Launder, A. G. (2001) *Play Practice: The Games Approach to Teaching and Coaching Sports*. Champaign, IL: Human Kinetics.

Lave, J. and Wenger, E. (1991) *Situated Learning: Legitimate Peripheral Participation*. Cambridge: Cambridge University Press.

Learner, R.M., Lerner, J.U., Almerigi, J.B., Theokas, C., Phelps, E., Gestdottir, S., Naudeau, S., Jelicic, H., Alberts, A., Lang, M., Smith, L.M., Bobeck, D.L., Richman-Raphael, D., Simpson, I., Christeansen, E.D. and von Eye, A. (2005) 'Positive youth development, participation in community youth development programs, and community contributions of fifth grade adolescents: Findings from the fifth wave of the 4-H Study of Positive Youth Development', *Journal of Early Adolescents*, 25, 17–71.

Light, R. L. (2002) 'The social nature of games: Pre-service primary teachers' first experiences of TGfU', *European Physical Education Review*, 8(3), 291–310.

——(2003) 'The joy of learning: Emotion, cognition and learning in games through TGfU', *New Zealand Journal of Physical Education*, 36(1), 94–108.

——(2008) *Sport in the Lives of Young Australians*. Sydney: University of Sydney Press.

——(2013a) *Game Sense: Pedagogy for Performance, Participation and Enjoyment*. London: Routledge.

———(2013b) 'O Game Sense como pedagogia positiva para treinar o desporto juvenil [Game Sense as positive pedagogy for coaching youth sport]', in C. Congalves (ed.) *Educação Pelo Desporto e Associativismo Desportiva* [*Youth Sport: Between Education and Performance*], Instituto do Desporto de Portugal/IDP (national institute of sports): Lisbon, Portugal, pp. 111–131.

Light, R. L. and Evans, J. R. (2010) 'The impact of Game Sense pedagogy on elite level Australian rugby coaches' practice: A question of pedagogy', *Physical Education & Sport Pedagogy*, 15(2), 103–115.

Light, R. and Fawns, R. (2003) 'Knowing the game: Integrating speech and action through TGfU', *Quest*, 55, 161–177.

Light, R. and Georgakis, S. (2005) 'Integrating theory and practice in teacher education: The impact of a Games Sense unit on female pre-service primary teachers' attitudes toward teaching physical education', *Journal of Physical Education New Zealand*, 38(1), 67–80.

Light, R. L., Curry, C. and Mooney, A. (in press) 'Game Sense as model for delivering quality teaching in physical education', *Asia-Pacific Journal of Health, Sport & Physical Education*.

Light, R. L., Harvey, S. and Mouchet, A. (2012) 'Improving "at-action" decision-making in team sports through a holistic coaching approach', *Sport, Education & Society*, DOI:10.1080/13573322.2012.665803.

Lloyd, R. J. and Smith, S. S. (2010) 'Feeling flow motion in games and sports', in J. I. Butler and L. L. Griffin (eds) *More Teaching Games for Understanding: Moving Globally*. Champaigne, IL: Human Kinetics, pp. 89–104.

McNeill, M., Fry, J., Wright, S., Tan, C., Tan, S. and Schempp, P. (2004) '"In the local context": Singaporean challenges to Teaching Games on practicum', *Sport, Education & Society*, 9(1), 3–32.

Mitchell, S.A., Oslin, J.L. and Griffin, L.L. (1995) 'The effects of two instructional approaches on game performance', *Pedagogy in Practice – Teaching and Coaching in Physical Education and Sports*, 1, 36–48.

Mosston, M. and Ashworth, S. (1986) *Teaching Physical Education* (third edition). Columbus, OH: Merrill.

Pope, C. (2005) 'Once more with feeling: Affect and playing with the TGfU model', *Physical Education and Sport Pedagogy*, 10(3), 271–286.

Roberts, J. (2011) 'Teaching Games for Understanding: the difficulties and challenges experienced by participation cricket coaches', *Physical Education and Sport Pedagogy*, 16(1), 33–48.

Roffey, S. (2011) *Children's Behavior in Schools*. Thousand Oaks, CA: Sage.

Seligman, M. E. P. (2012) *Flourish: A Visionary New Understanding of Happiness and Wellbeing*. Sydney: Random House.

Seligman, M. E. P. and Csikszentmihalyi, M. (2000) 'Positive Psychology: An introduction', *American Psychologist*, 55(1), 5–14.

Sheppard, J. and Mandigo, J. (2005) 'PlaySport: Teaching life skills for understanding through games', in T. Hopper, J. L. Butler and B. Storey (eds), *TGfU … Simply Good Pedagogy: Understanding a Complex Challenge*. Toronto: HPE Canada, pp. 73–86.

Siedentop, D. (1994) *Sport Education: Quality PE through Positive Sport Experiences*. Champaigne, IL: Human Kinetics.

Thorpe, R. and Bunker, D. (2008) 'Teaching Games for Understanding – Do current developments reflect original intentions?', paper presented at the fourth Teaching Games for Understanding conference, Vancouver, BC, Canada, 14–17 May.

Varela, F. J., Thompson, E. and Rosch, E. (1991) *The Embodied Mind: Cognitive Science and Human Experience.* Cambridge, MA: MIT Press.

Vygotsky, L. S. (1978) *Mind in Society: The Development of Higher Psychological Processes.* Cambridge, MA: Harvard University Press.

Wallian, N. and Chang, C. W. (2007) 'Language, thinking and action: Towards a semio-constructivist approach in physical education', *Physical Education and Sport Pedagogy*, 12(3), 289–311.

White, A. (2012) 'Youthful violence', *Sunday Herald Sun*, 3 June, p. 17.

Wright, J. and Forrest, G. (2007) 'A social semiotic analysis of knowledge construction and games centred approaches to teaching', *Physical Education and Sport Pedagogy*, 12(3), 273–287.

3 Teaching how to play and teach games in Singapore

A decade in the field

Joan Marian Fry and Michael Charles McNeill

Introduction

It is now over a decade since the Singapore Ministry of Education (MOE) introduced an education policy (*Thinking Schools, Learning Nation* [TSLN], Goh 1997) that, through subsequent national curriculum revisions (Curriculum Planning and Development Division [CPDD] 1999, 2005), has had local ramifications for the teaching of games within physical education. Given that there has been a recent teacher education curriculum review at the National Institute of Education (NIE), it would seem timely to consider the approaches to games teaching in operation among the current physical education pedagogy team and the extent that these might be congruent with the intentions of the national physical education curriculum.

We and/or our colleagues (McNeill, Fry, Wright, Tan, Tan and Schempp 2004; McNeill, Sproule and Horton 2003; Tan and Tan 2001) have written elsewhere about the socio-political context into which this uniquely Singaporean[1] slant on games teaching made its debut. Since full independence in 1965, the national government has taken a pragmatic approach to education: initially to achieve literacy and numeracy for the masses; next to provide technical skills for productivity; and more recently to diversify the competencies of the populace. Needless to say, the purpose of physical education has been similarly pragmatic: essentially to prepare a fit cohort of young men for the compulsory national service that follows their schooling and to provide young people with practical skills in physical activities, which will enable them to engage in an active lifestyle (Fry and McNeill 2011). These ends are not dissimilar to those defined in the 1999 physical education syllabus and affirmed in the 2006 revision. However, until that juncture, Singapore's teachers had traditionally employed direct teaching methods that sought to develop physical fitness and basic sports skills that would facilitate specialization in particular sports. In physical education such methods and purpose are driven by values that Jewett, Bain and Ennis (1995) would define as 'discipline mastery' in orientation.

In contrast, the new syllabus (CPDD 1999), reinforced in a subsequent revision (CPDD 2005), called for a 'learning process' philosophical orientation.

That these two perspectives might be built on assumptions that are not complementary was earlier identified by Tan and Tan (2001) who, from interviews with physical education heads of department (HODs), noted a number of other challenges to implementation including: teacher complacency, games concept approach (GCA) pedagogical competency, inadequate resources, curriculum emphasis on physical fitness, and marginalization of physical education. Indeed these have been instrumental in the way the GCA has been taken up (Fry and McNeill 2011; McNeill and Fry 2010). In order to overcome the personnel issues, there were content and pedagogical changes within physical education teacher education (PETE) programmes at the NIE. Similarly, the MOE conducted workshops led by overseas experts in tactical games teaching. These initiatives were intended to influence the way in which the GCA was implemented.

GCA research and development

In the intervening years, the NIE's physical education pedagogy team, which includes the authors of this chapter, has conducted a number of studies into using the GCA in local schools. Investigations have focused on the perspectives of student teachers and their practicum mentors, and experienced teachers as well as their pupils. From the collective results a number of emerging ideas have subsequently influenced the pedagogy of games teaching. Mostly these were dimensions of a large investigation funded by the MOE. The following review on studies into the use of the GCA is a prelude to an evaluation of GCA-pedagogy in both school and teacher education.

Research on GCA teaching in Singapore

Given that the key responsibility at NIE is physical education teacher training, our preliminary investigation engaged us in studying student teachers who were learning to use the GCA from two perspectives. The first view (McNeill *et al.* 2004) was drawn from a small cohort of specialist primary physical education student teachers (n = ten) who were completing their final practicum (ten weeks) and the second (Fry, Tan, McNeill and Wright 2010) was of their pupils who were learning to play through the approach. Each student teacher was mentored and interviewed about their perspectives on learning to use the GCA by a research team member who made observational visits for the study in addition to the NIE's supervisory requirements. A significant finding was that the student teachers had developed different constructions of the approach. The GCA was viewed as (a) structure, as (b) outcome and/or as (c) process, with these meanings implicated in the ways in which these beginning teachers used the GCA. First, the dominant view was that the GCA was seen simply as the three-part lesson plan (game with question and answer, practice, then game) introduced to the student teachers during their coursework. In the little more than 20 minutes instructional time for physical education and with limited space and modifiable equipment, the student teachers often struggled to implement the small-sided tasks planned for the three phases. Second, the student teachers were challenged by what lies at the heart of game-centred teaching – a focus on teaching games concepts rather than on techniques. The neophytes were evidently products of their own schooling – locked in a technical mindset and most generally unconvinced by the teaching games for understanding (TGfU) rationale to teach skill only as a necessary element to improve the quality of games play. Third, all generally struggled with teaching in context. Not only was designing a situated task difficult but, even if identified, teachable moments for probing 'what to do' and 'how to do it' were not easily taken up with their pupils who were themselves novices in learning to learn how to play through the GCA.

Furthermore, many of the student teachers reported that several children seemed disinterested in learning to play this way. That all three conceptions of the GCA were problematic to the student teachers is an indication that the GCA was requiring a significant change in mindset for these young people whose games learning experiences from their own schooling had been traditional. (Time allocated for physical education in those days was short: it was mainly spent in physical fitness training and testing, because physical education here has played an important pragmatic role in producing a fit cohort of young men for the annual national service intake; and furthermore, lessons devoted to games and sports activities were most likely spent in warming up, refining technique with little time for skill application. Thus, both fitness and games teaching, with their emphasis on 'how?', would be categorized by Habermas as raising a technocratic consciousness [in Kirk 1988: 24].)

As Fullan (1993) has argued, *real* change requires participants to self-assess and readjust. Action emerging for PETE from this study was a restructuring of games teaching. A new games-learning/games-teaching course, itself employing a conceptual approach, was included in all PETE programmes. In addition, some faculty members explicitly taught specialist games courses, such as basketball and volleyball, through a game-centred rather than a technique-focused approach.

In the parallel dimension of the investigation (Fry *et al.* 2010), perceptions of the primary school pupils (n = 297) were garnered through an open-ended survey. Framed around Fullan's (1982, 1991) four images of students and curriculum change, the content analysis revealed that, contrary to their student teachers' understandings of them, the children were responding very favourably to their 'new' games pedagogy: (a) the majority (90 per cent) reported heightened interest in learning to play and clearly identified aspects of their learning that can be defined as 'value-adding' dimensions to their physical education lessons. Less than 10 per cent of the children reported experiencing all or aspects of their GCA lessons less favourably: for them the GCA was seen as (b) only a temporary escape from the boredom of the routine of their usual skill-based physical education or the intensity of the academic classroom.

While a small group of children were (c) indifferent to what others had described as either the 'fun' or 'excitement' of their GCA lessons, there were others who, (d) confused by the change in pedagogical approach through poorly timed or misdirected questioning, were unsure of their teacher's purpose. Our analysis suggested that (student) teacher qualities (their content knowledge and/or pedagogical content knowledge [Shulman 1987]) were implicated in the ways pupils experience GCA pedagogy. Action emerging for PETE from this study was a need to reinforce to student teachers the motivational qualities of small-group games play that Bunker and Thorpe (1982) maintained were at the heart of the rationale for TGfU. Also necessary were opportunities for student teachers to develop strategies for introducing pupils to learning through the GCA, a constructivist approach rather than a direct, traditional approach.

Given the key findings of the initial study, with colleagues (McNeill, Fry, Wright, Tan and Rossi 2008) we subsequently undertook an intensive study of how student teachers (n = 49) structured time and questioning during their GCA lessons. Systematic quantitative analysis of lessons captured on videotape toward the end of their practicum revealed an encouraging finding: pupil time (53 per cent) exceeded teacher time (47 per cent). However, across programmes (diploma, degree and postgraduate diploma) little learning time was spent in contextualized practice, which is consistent with earlier findings (McNeill *et al.* 2004). Of serious concern was the student teachers' general inability to frame open questions: 76.3 per cent of those asked were classified as simple recall, 'yes'/'no', or rhetorical, while only 6.7 per cent probed the higher order, tactical thinking of pupils.

Analysis of practice time found that only 2.1 per cent was spent in contextualized practice: primary lessons included more de-contextualized drills, while secondary lessons offered pupils more game time. Action emerging for PETE from these findings was directed toward student teachers learning to pose a situational problem through the conditions of the opening lesson game, and then considering a number of possible player response scenarios that offered opportunities for teacher intervention with situated questioning. Student teachers were exposed to such situations that were modelled in the general games principles course and given situated practice in authentic school settings, a component of the physical education pedagogy courses, and the equivalent of a 'lab' school (Garrett, Wrench and Piltz 2007).

It is understandable that practical knowledge accruing from these studies would inevitably influence the games pedagogy of us as researcher-pedagogues. A comparative case study (Wright, McNeill, Fry and Wang 2005) was undertaken to investigate the impact of GCA principles on teaching within PETE. The responses of student teachers (n = 15) taught how to teach and how to play basketball through a tactical approach were compared with those (n = 15) taught through a technical approach. In spite of the basketball tutor's initial misgivings (documented in his reflective journal) about the efficacy of the GCA approach, statistical analysis revealed that the tactically taught group fared better in terms of their games-playing abilities, self-ratings of perceived abilities to teach tactics and strategies and using their skills in games situations.

Ninety per cent of all student teachers (100 per cent of the tactically taught group, 80 per cent of the technically taught group) preferred to take a tactical approach in associated lesson-planning tasks. However, there was no sought explanation for their choice. Action emerging for PETE from this study was a need to strengthen further the teaching of games courses through tactical approaches as well as to emphasize effective pedagogical strategies such as using small-group work, developmentally appropriate practices, and lead-up games in those courses taught through a technical approach.

During the initial study (McNeill *et al.* 2004), interviews with the student teachers' cooperating teachers (CTs) revealed that many of these experienced teachers were concerned about their role in supporting the novices who were learning to contextualize their campus-based coursework in the 'real world' of local primary schools. Thus, a professional development course on GCA-focused mentoring was established for potential CTs. The initial concerns of these school-based personnel (n = 58) were documented and monitored (Wright, McNeill and Fry 2009; Wright, McNeill, Fry, Tan, Tan and Schempp 2006) during subsequent teaching practices when student teachers were matched with such 'expert' mentors.

As might be anticipated, self-reported presage (Duncan and Biddle 1974) expectations were best met through the practical aspects of the course. The future GCA mentors saw case-study analysis, systematic coding of videotaped teaching behaviours and role-playing post-lesson observation conferences as most relevant. Almost a third of the trained mentors (n = 17) were interviewed following their experience of working with a mentee on a 'GCA-practicum': overall this personal experience was reported as enjoyable and various practical aspects of their mentor training had been useful. A small proportion (18 per cent) perceived the practicum as professionally renewing.

From the research team's perspective, there was potentially less conflict for student teachers, because the views on games teaching of cooperating teachers who were 'GCA-trained' were in greater congruence with those of the university supervisors than were the views of those cooperating teachers who were not 'GCA-trained'. From informal conversations, those non GCA-trained CTs tended to be more custodial of technical approaches to games teaching than they were open to student teachers using constructivist approaches. Action emerging for PETE from this study was a need to press the MOE and NIE to institutionalize GCA-mentor training for all future cooperating teachers.

Wright, McNeill and Butler (2004) wrote about the strong effects that presage socialization has on novice teachers. They highlighted four key issues (marginalization of physical education, role conflict, reality shock and wash-out effect [Solmon, Worthy and Carter 1993]), which beginning teachers face as they assume their professional roles on completion of their initial teacher education. Hopeful that the heavy investment in the initial cohort, the mentoring programme and revisions to the games pedagogy courses within PETE would pay off, the research team supervised and/or undertook several small studies of novice teachers in their early years. These attempts documented the perspectives and/or detail GCA-pedagogy of beginning teachers as they took up their initial postings.

Although their foci differed, all these studies revealed the struggles of beginning teachers as they face the dominant culture in Singapore schools – the hegemony of academic over practical learning – and within physical education, the hegemony of physical fitness training findings. Lam (2002), for example, interviewed seven of the original GCA cohort during their initial year after graduation. His findings were not encouraging: given the MOE regulations that physical education teachers must also teach their second subject, no one was teaching physical education full-time and all reported that institutional pressures to provide 'healthy' pupil fitness test results steered the direction of their various school physical education programmes.

We would conclude that none of this batch seemed to be gaining extensive experience in GCA teaching. Action emerging for PETE practice was that during this period we introduced a Masters degree level course with the self-explanatory title, 'Constructivist approaches to teaching physical education', in order to support in-service teachers in the expansion of their pedagogical repertoire to incorporate the GCA and other allied approaches.

In another follow-up investigation, Leow (2004) undertook an in-depth study of what might be seen as a bellwether case (Merriam 1991) – a novice teacher who had earned the highest practicum grade and had been appointed to a school, privileged with more than adequate indoor and outdoor facilities. Although the lessons were appropriately structured with an opening situational game problem, followed by practice tasks then opportunities to replay the game, there was unfortunately little documented evidence to support a developing pedagogical maturity in terms of variability. The teacher reported having little time for preparation and was consumed with administrative responsibilities. More encouraging results were found by Tan (2005), who was also able to track four teachers from the initial cohort of his case study that self-identified as having found the traditional approach less than satisfying in their own learning experience as students. This group was keen to make curriculum changes at the school level.

All reported personal cost in being innovative, but found that their tenacity had rewards through observable changes in student learning. They revealed during interview a change in their value system – a newly felt strong belief in GCA efficacy. Similarly, Light and Tan (2006) undertook a comparative study of the social meanings about games and games teaching derived from schooling and pre-service PETE in Australia and Singapore. In this study none of the four Singaporean student teachers interviewed had been highly successful games players. Indeed some reported being turned off by the over-emphasis on technique in the physical education of their own school days, thus all were somewhat receptive to the GCA, and especially reported coming to value the approach as an inclusive pedagogy. Furthermore, all four seemed to concur with, even value, its intention – to develop games understanding through an emphasis on probing students' thinking – and process.

Other work within our research team has captured the views and GCA teaching characteristics of experienced teachers (Rossi, Fry, McNeill and Tan 2007; Wright, Reimer and McNeill 2005) as they make a shift from a technical to constructivist approach in teaching games. Wright *et al.* (2005) used interviews and reflective journals to monitor the responses of a mature primary school physical education teacher who was attempting to reconfigure (Fullan 1993) from technical to tactical games teaching. With 20 years games teaching experience this teacher described himself, and was described by others, as 'successful', yet in the early days of the project his concerns mirrored those of the beginning teachers we have already reported on.

He felt that his pupils were initially unsure of the new learning process while he lacked confidence that he could sustain a focus on tactical, rather than skill, development. However, once the children's interest was captured in the increased games-play that was central to his pedagogy, he was able to focus his attention once more on meeting their learning needs, rather than on implementing his lesson plan. He reported shared enjoyment with the children in the intensity of their engagement in the lessons. This also seems to have formed an important factor for the Australian teachers adopting a positive approach to TGfU in Curry and Light's study reported on in Chapter 8. Reflecting on the findings, we researchers considered motivation to develop new pedagogical skills as a key driver of successful pedagogical change.

Given the key element of increased interest and excitement that children (Fry *et al.* 2010) report experiencing in GCA lessons, members of our team (Low 2006; McNeill, Fry and Hairil 2011) have also undertaken detailed case studies of students' responses to the GCA as taught by expert teachers. McNeill *et al.*'s study (2011) of experienced GCA teachers (n = 3) focused on the motivational climate that they generated as well as children's (n = 115) motives for participating. A strong mastery (learning orientation) and moderate performance climate was found and children reported personal success as their prime motivator, followed by learning and affiliation. Low (2006) used videography, interviewing and student journals to investigate the personal meanings that secondary students derived from the GCA compared with direct instruction, and reflected these against their teacher's purpose.

Although sometimes the teacher's intentions did not always translate into purposeful GCA/TGfU practice in terms of Metzler's (2000) benchmarks for TGfU teaching, these Singapore high school students (n = 40) clearly reported that their GCA lessons provided them with opportunities to satisfy their desire to play, build teamwork, learn motor skills and experience the challenge of learning to play. On the other hand, these teenagers reported that when their teacher reverted to direct teaching they found it disruptive and drew similarities with 'unfavourable' pedagogies characteristic of the academic classroom. While the former study suggests that children might find some games categories more motivating as an alternative learning context than others, the latter is a clear indication that the motivational impact of the GCA is well received by adolescents in their physical education lessons.

As previously reported (Light and Tan 2006; McNeill *et al.* 2004; Wright *et al.* 2004), the GCA is mandated practice. Our early research suggests, however, that for several contextual reasons, Singapore's physical education teachers have been slow to progress in developing this constructivist pedagogical expertise. Rossi and colleagues (2007) analysed the implementation concerns expressed in interviews with 22 experienced teachers who attended the mentoring workshops (Wright *et al.* 2006). Notable in the findings was that when experienced teachers regard the GCA as meaningful they are more likely to change their pedagogy. Four constructed personal histories were representative of those in the study. Each represented a particular perspective on the challenge of GCA teaching: (a) a personal career turning point; (b) going with the flow of meeting system technocratic demands; (c) developmentally appropriate pedagogy for mid-secondary pupils; or (d) confusion given that we, 'GCA experts', who presented at the workshops were not unified in our interpretation of the pedagogy. Five years on from that study, we sought to determine the emphasis on the GCA in Singapore school physical education programmes, in terms of the perceptions of physical education head teachers on the extent that the GCA had taken hold in the practice of physical education. The views of the PETE faculty were also solicited on school-based support for student teachers' use of the GCA on teaching practice.

Method

Participants

A short survey on individual use of the GCA and colleagues' use of the GCA was distributed to participants (n = 28 Singapore nationals) in a course for physical education HODs at the NIE, Singapore. These MOE-identified leaders (equally from either a primary or secondary school) were drawn from across the four school regions of Singapore. All participants were in full-time employment in their respective role of physical education pedagogue or physical education teacher and were consenting volunteers to the study.

Data collection

In order to determine views on the extent to which the GCA was being used in schools a short survey was constructed and assessed for readability by a local pedagogical expert. On five-point Likert scales it aimed to determine: (a) 'personal familiarity' with the GCA (1 = 'not at all' to 5 = 'highly familiar'), 'personal expertise' (1 = 'none' to 5 = 'expert'), 'use' of the GCA in own games pedagogy (1 = 'never' to 5 = 'all the time'); and (b) 'fraction of your

PE department' using the GCA ('none', '1/4', '1/2', '3/4', 'all'), 'use of GCA' within school's games lessons (1 = 'never' to 5 = 'all the time') and 'overall quality' of GCA teaching within own department (1 = 'not at all competent' to 5 = 'highly competent'). The respondent was also asked if the amount of GCA teaching within the department had increased or decreased over time. Unidentified returns (100 per cent) were collected in an envelope by a course participant and given to the course lecturer.

Information also was gathered from PETE faculty members about their perceptions of the support for student teachers in their use of the GCA on teaching practice. The second author conducted informal conversations with PETE faculty members (n = 11) who were currently teaching games-related courses in the PETE curriculum and who had been university supervisors in the recent teaching practice. Given that all student teachers in their final teaching practice (ten weeks) were required to use the GCA, and those in their first teaching practice could choose to use the GCA, the faculty members were asked about GCA teaching observed during their visits to the school teaching practice sites. In particular, they were also asked about their perceptions of the quality of school-based support the student teachers had in their use of the GCA. In order to provide additional context to the study, PETE games pedagogues were also asked about their own games play and games teaching experience.

Data analysis

Numerical data from the HOD survey were calculated using Microsoft Office Excel © (2007 version). The second author undertook content analysis of the open-ended survey items and coding results were checked by the non-coding author. Coding discrepancies were discussed and final results are reported below.

Findings

The return rate for the school GCA survey was 100 per cent (n = 28). The summary data are shown in Table 3.1. The HOD candidates as a collective reported themselves, in terms of the GCA, as being very familiar (M = 4.18 ± 0.55), beyond a moderate expert (M = 3.89 ± 0.57) as well as beyond a moderate user (M = 3.86 ± 0.76). However, in terms of the GCA practice in their own school, they reported just above moderate quality of lessons

Table 3.1 Perspectives on GCA familiarity, use and expertise in schools of PE HODs (n = 28)

Personal			Departmental	
Familiarity	*Expertise*	*Use*	*Quality*	*Use*
4.18 (0.55)	3.89 (0.57)	3.86 (0.76)	3.33 (0.71)	3.71 (0.85)

(3.33 ± 0.71) and above moderate use (M = 3.71 ± 0.85) by two-thirds (66.96 per cent) of their faculty. On reflection, over 71 per cent (n = 20) reported that GCA use had increased over time, less than 20 per cent (n = six) reported GCA use as having been constant across time, whereas only two participants (7.1 per cent) reported a decrease of GCA use in their school.

The informal conversations with the PETE staff members revealed that, from their perspective, most of their student teachers were competent in using the GCA within the teaching practice guidelines and the contextual constraints of their school. However, they indicated that there was some variance in the observed practice of the student teachers whom they had supervised. By way of explanation, they suggested that the range of GCA-teaching competence (content knowledge and pedagogical content knowledge [Shulman 1987]) was, in the main, derived from the student teachers' prior games experience. Those PETE members, who supervised at both the primary and secondary levels, also contended that the primary school context was not always as conducive for GCA teaching as was the situation in most secondary schools. Explanations that they put forward were (a) shorter lesson time (usually 30 minutes compared with one-hour lessons in most secondary schools), (b) a relative lack of resources (the MOE's up-grade of school sports facilities is still ongoing), and (c) a relative shortage of primary school specialist physical education teachers.

Summary

There is convincing evidence that the GCA is widely operationalized at both school levels – primary and secondary. According to the data from both PETE teaching practice supervisors and physical education HODs, the GCA (in various forms) was being practised in schools, although the quality of pedagogy reportedly observed in schools varies according to student teachers' games play experience and games teaching/coaching biographies. Thus, our findings refute Tan and Tan's (2001) expectations that contextual factors would place serious limitations on the uptake of the GCA as an innovative pedagogy in the 1999 revised physical education syllabus. Given that many of the contextual factors such as large class size and limited space, highlighted as serious limitations, are still in evidence (albeit the MOE is very active in policy change and resource upgrade) it would seem that student teachers on teaching practice still offer an intensive GCA experience to school physical education students.

Although the following suggestions are specific to teaching how to teach and how to play games in the Singapore context, they are relevant to strengthening the implementation of innovative pedagogy elsewhere. From the findings reported above, we make the following recommendations:

1. Mentoring courses are needed for school-based personnel who supervise student teachers on teaching practice. Such courses should focus on recent developments in game-centred pedagogy as well as general mentoring skills.

2. In order to continue to have strong support for student teachers using the GCA during their teaching practice, induction courses are needed for new faculty without a pedagogical background. These should help them to understand the range of teaching/coaching approaches (especially the GCA) to developing games and games pedagogical expertise.
3. Prior to their block teaching practice experiences, opportunities are still needed for student teachers who are learning 'new' games pedagogies to apply their developing content knowledge and pedagogical content knowledge. Incorporating school-based experiences into campus-based courses whereby novice teachers build their developing competencies within the constraints of authentic school settings is an important component of ongoing implementation of the innovation.
4. Professional development courses are important for extending the scope of GCA-development beyond the coursework Masters degree at NIE.
5. For practising teachers, formal and informal networking is essential. Regional clusters would provide an ideal setting for further teacher development in the national growth of our Southeast Asian version of games-based pedagogy.

Discussion questions

1. In the Singapore experience of introducing tactical games teaching in schools student teachers and their students presented two different perspectives on the same lessons. Compare the student teachers' understanding of their students' learning and the students' own perspectives on what they learnt. What might explain the difference in these two perspectives?
2. The research reported in the chapter revealed that Singapore student teachers had great difficulties in promoting games sense among their students who were learning to play. Reflect on your own experiences in learning to teach games. What issues have you faced in using a tactical approach in your lessons?
3. The studies reported in this chapter investigated a range of issues associated with tactical games teaching in the Singapore context. If you were to undertake a small investigation on the effectiveness of your own games teaching, what would be the focus? Outline the approach you would take to the study.

Note

1 Known locally as 'the GCA', the games-concept approach is a local mix of teaching games for understanding philosophy, developed by faculty members at the United Kingdom's Loughborough University (Bunker and Thorpe 1982, 1986), to

which Singapore physical education has strong allegiance, through Loughborough's role in establishing Singapore's College of Physical Education 1985 (later incorporated into NIE, since 1991 within Nanyang Technological University), and the teaching sport concepts and skills model of United States-based professors (Griffin, Mitchell and Oslin 1997) who have conducted several workshops for teachers at the invitation of the Ministry of Education, NIE or the Singapore Physical Education Association.

References

Bunker, D. and Thorpe, R. (1982) 'A model for the teaching of games in secondary schools', *Bulletin of Physical Education*, 18(1): 5–8.

——(1986) 'The curriculum model', in R. Thorpe, D. Bunker and L. Almond (eds) *Rethinking Games Teaching*, Loughborough: University of Technology, Loughborough.

Curriculum Planning and Development Division (CPDD) (1999) *Revised Physical Education Syllabus for Primary, Secondary and Pre-university Levels*, Singapore: Ministry of Education.

——(2005) *Physical Education (Primary, Secondary, Pre-university) Syllabus 2006*, Singapore: Ministry of Education.

Duncan, M. and Biddle, B. (1974) *The Study of Teaching*, New York: Holt Reinhart and Winston.

Fry, J. M. and McNeill, M. C. (2011) '"In the Nation's good": Physical education and school sport in Singapore', *European Physical Education Review*, 17(3): 287–300.

Fry, J. M., Tan, W. K. C., McNeill, M. C. and Wright, S. C. (2010) 'Children's perceptions of conceptual games teaching: A value-adding experience', *Physical Education & Sport Pedagogy*, 15(2): 139–158.

Fullan, M. (1982) *The Meaning of Educational Change*, New York: Teachers College Press.

——(1991) *The New Meaning of Educational Change*, New York: Teachers College Press.

——(1993) *Change Forces: Probing the Depths of Educational Reform*, London: Falmer.

Garrett, R., Wrench, A. and Piltz, W. (2007) 'Lab school as a teaching strategy in physical education teacher education', *ACHPER Healthy Lifestyles Journal*, 54(2): 19–24.

Goh, C. T. (1997) *Shaping our Future: Thinking Schools, Learning Nation*, Speech presented at the opening of the 7th International Conference on Thinking, 6 June, Singapore.

Griffin, L. L., Mitchell, S. A. and Oslin, J. L. (1997) *Teaching Sport Concepts and Skills: A Tactical Games Approach*, Champaign, IL: Human Kinetics.

Jewett, A. E., Bain, L. L. and Ennis, C. D. (1995) *The Curriculum Process in Physical Education*, second edition, Dubuque, IA: Brown and Benchmark.

Kirk, D. (1988) *Physical Education and Curriculum Study: A Critical Approach*, London: Croom Helm.

Lam, B. S. (2002) *Experiences Using the Games Concept Approach among Beginning Physical Education Teachers*, BSc honours dissertation, Singapore: Nanyang Technological University.

Leow, C. S. (2004) *A Portraiture of GCA Teaching Strategies: A Singapore Case Study*, unpublished BA honours dissertation, Singapore: Nanyang Technological University.

Light, R. and Tan, S. (2006) 'Culture, embodied experience and teachers' development of TGfU in Australia and Singapore', *European Physical Education Review*, 12(1): 99–117.

Low, Y. M. D. (2006) *Students' Perceptions towards a GCA Unit*, unpublished MA thesis, Singapore: Nanyang Technological University.

McNeill, M. C. and Fry, J. M. (2010) 'Physical education and health in Singapore schools', *Asia-Pacific Journal of Health, Sport and Physical Education*, 57(1): 13–18.

McNeill, M. C., Fry, J. M. and Md Hairil, B. J. (2011) 'Motivational climate in games concept lessons', *The ICHPERD-SD Journal of Research in Health, Physical Education, Recreation, Sport and Dance*, 6(1): 34–39.

McNeill, M. C., Fry, J. M., Wright, S., Tan, C., Tan, S. and Schempp, P. (2004) '"In the Singapore context": Challenges to teaching games on practicum', *Sport, Education & Society*, 9(1): 3–32.

McNeill, M. C., Fry, J. M., Wright, S. C., Tan, W. K. C. and Rossi, T. (2008) 'Understanding time management and questioning strategies used in a games concept approach to develop "Game Sense"', *Physical Education and Sport Pedagogy*, 13: 231–239.

McNeill, M. C., Sproule, J. S. and Horton, P. H. (2003) 'The changing face of sport and physical education in post-colonial Singapore', *Sport, Education & Society*, 8: 35–56.

Merriam, S. (1991) *Case Study Research in Education: A Qualitative Approach*, San Francisco: Jossey-Bass.

Metzler, M. (2000) 'Direct instruction: Teacher as instructional leader', in *Instructional Models for Physical Education*, Boston: Allyn & Bacon, pp. 161–184.

Rossi, T., Fry, J. M., McNeill, M. and Tan, W. K. C. (2007) 'The games concept approach (GCA) as a mandated practice: Views of Singaporean teachers', *Sport, Education & Society*, 12: 93–111.

Shulman, L. (1987) 'Knowledge and teaching: foundations of the new reform', *Harvard Educational Review*, 57: 1–22.

Solmon, M. A., Worthy, T. and Carter, J. A. (1993) 'The interaction of school context and role identity of first year teachers', *Journal of Teaching in Physical Education*, 12: 313–328.

Tan, S. (2005) 'Implementing teaching games for understanding: stories of change', in L. L. Griffin and J. K. Butler (eds), *Teaching Games for Understanding: Theory, Research, and Practice*, Champaign, IL: Human Kinetics, pp. 207–224.

Tan, K. S. S and Tan, E. K. H. (2001) 'Managing change within the physical education curriculum: issues, opportunities and challenges', in J. Tan, S. Gopinathan and W. K. Ho (eds), *Challenges Facing the Singapore Education System Today*, Singapore: Prentice Hall.

Thorpe, R. D. (1982) 'The psychological factors underpinning the "teaching for understanding games" Movement', in T. Williams, L. Almond and A. Sparkes (eds), *Sport and Physical Activity: Moving Toward Excellence*, Proceedings of the AIESEP World Convention, Loughborough, UK, London: Spon, pp. 209–218.

Wright, S. C., McNeill, M. C. and Butler, J. (2004) 'The role socialization can play in promoting teaching games for understanding', *JOPERD*, 75(3): 46–52.

Wright, S., McNeill, M. and Fry, J. M. (2009) 'The tactical approach to teaching games from the perspective of student teachers, cooperating teachers and pupils', *Sport, Education & Society*, 14: 223–244.

Wright, S., McNeill, M., Fry, J. and Wang, J. (2005) 'Teaching teachers to play and teach games', *Physical Education and Sport Pedagogy*, 10(1): 61–82.

Wright, S., McNeill, M., Fry, J. M., Tan, S., Tan, C. and Schempp, P. (2006) 'Implications of student teachers' implementation of a curricular innovation', *Journal of Teaching in Physical Education*, 25: 310–328.

Wright, S., Reimer, M. and McNeill, M. (2005) 'Curricular innovation for an elementary teacher's perspective', *Journal of ICHPERD-SD*, XLI(1): 19–24.

4 Innovation in the Japanese games curriculum

Naoki Suzuki

Introduction

Since the proposal by Bunker and Thorpe (1982) for a radical change in teaching games there has been ongoing innovation in games teaching across the world. This has included developments in Asia where traditional approaches to education, including physical education, and the philosophic traditions they sit on can make the adoption of student-centered teaching in physical education challenging. This has been identified in a decade of research on the implementation of the games concept approach (GCA) in Singapore schools (see, for example, McNeill, Fry, Wright, Tan, Tan, and Schempp 2004; Rossi, Fry, McNeill, and Tan 2007). For many decades there has been little change in either the games curriculum or in games pedagogy in Japan but it is now undergoing what can be seen as radical change driven by a push for lifelong engagement in sport over recent years. In this chapter I outline the direction of the new games curriculum of Japan and the ways in which game-based approaches (GBA) such as Game Sense have a place in physical education teaching in Japan in both primary and secondary schools. I provide some detail on the changes that have taken place in the Japanese physical education curriculum with a focus on games teaching as a distinct component of the curriculum.

Traditional games teaching in Japan

Traditional game teaching in Japan has followed one of two approaches. One is the 'roll out the ball' approach (Graham 2008) in which there was no teaching provided at all with the students given a ball and the rules of the game and then asked to play the game. The other was the military drill approach that emphasized endless repetitive drills aimed at perfecting technique out of context but with little actual game play. These are two extremes of games teaching that involve either no teaching or structured learning or over teaching aimed at developing discipline and the perfection of technique unrelated to the game. In both approaches there was little consideration of students' differences in skill, confidence, experience and motivation: it was a one-size-fits-all approach. As has been shown in research on games in other countries, the practice of isolated skills that lacked connection to the game caused many students to struggle with transferring techniques learned in drills to a game environment (see, for example, Bunker and Thorpe 1982; Brooker and Abbot 2001), when practice games are not only more effective in transferring the learning of skill and tactical knowledge to the game (see, for example, Holt, Ward, and Wallhead 2007) but also much more fun. As Light, Harvey, and Mouchet (2012) argue, skill (technique performed in game contexts), tactical knowledge, decision-making ability, game awareness and other aspects of game play form aspects of games as complex phenomena and cannot be separated from each other without losing meaning and application.

Traditional teaching for games in Japan took a 'skill-centered approach' that Bunker and Thorpe (1982) were critical of. This is based on behaviorist theories of learning (Light 2008) and influenced by structuralism and essentialism. It followed the process of drill-drill-drill-main game, based on the assumption that technique had to be mastered *before* being able to play the game. In each lesson the vast majority of learning time was devoted to drills with sometimes only a few minutes left to play a game at the end of the lesson. PE teachers intended to teach students how to play the official, full game and did not consider changing the game to make it easier to learn or scaffolding on previous learning by moving from simple games to more complex games as is practised in Game Sense (Light 2013). This learning was much like the production line in a factory, which transfers techniques and knowledge using a conveyor belt entirely, and assembling them into the finished product at the end of the line. Some students were satisfied with it, others were not satisfied with it, but few felt the pleasure of playing a good game.

Contemporary developments in Japan

There has been significant international interest in GBA across the world for the last two decades. There has also been growth in variations and different developments in approaches to teaching games shaped by cultural contexts (Light 2013). Several variations of teaching games for understanding (TGfU – Bunker and Thorpe 1982) have been developed in different countries such as Game Sense in Australia (Light 2013), the Tactical Games Model (TGM – Mitchell, Oslin, and Griffin 2006) in the US and the games concept approach (GCA) developed for Singapore (Rossi *et al.* 2007). There are also other similar approaches that are not developed directly from TGfU such as Play Practice (Launder 2001), and the tactical-decision learning model (Gréhaigne, Wallian, and Godbout 2005). These are learner-centered, game-based approaches to teaching that are consistent with a constructivist theories of learning (Griffin and Patton 2005). One of the features of TGfU that is now universally adopted is the game classification system proposed by Almond (1986). These four categories of games were developed to allow teaching to promote the growth of tactical understanding within specific game categories where all games shared similar tactical problems.

Tactical approaches to teaching games are going to become a fixed part of teaching ballgames in Japan and replace the outdated approaches I have earlier outlined. This is because of a very major change in view on the place of physical education in schools and its aims. These changes involve a major shift from teacher-centered to student-centered learning and an emphasis on the intellectual and social aspects of learning in and through games. As such, there is a need to better understand the nature of tactical learning and relevant outcomes. A prominent focus of student learning within tactical models of instruction is the ability to make appropriate decisions in game play situations. Over recent years the traditional technical approach in Japan is being abandoned to adopt an approach that aims to have every student learn to play games joyfully regardless of skill level, with the new national curriculum based on this idea.

The new Japanese curriculum

In Japan compulsory education is undertaken for nine years and includes six years of elementary school and three years of junior high school (first three years of secondary school). High school (second three years of secondary school) is optional but 98 per cent of students complete high school. In this article, I focus on the compulsory education years – elementary school and junior high school (grade one to grade nine). Public Schools open five days a week but some private schools have six school days in a week. On Saturday and Sunday, public schools close. This system came to be adopted from 2002 before which public schools opened on Saturdays. Each school level requires the teacher certification/qualification with certifications

Table 4.1 The education system in Japan

Option	High school	3 years	PE teacher teaches PE
Compulsory education	Junior high school *3 times PE in a week (50 minutes per lesson)	3 years	PE teacher teaches PE
	Elementary school1-4 Grade*3 times PE in a week (45 minutes per lesson)	6 years	Classroom teacher teaches PE
	5–6 Grade*3 times PE in a week (45 minutes per lesson)		
Option	Preschool	3 years (3, 4, 5 years old)	Gymnastic instructor trains students (they may not have a certification)

for pre-school students, elementary school students, junior high school students, high school students and special needs students. In elementary schools, classroom teachers teach all subjects but, recently, specialist teachers of PE have been increasing in number. On the other hand, in junior high school and high school, teachers change for each subject and PE is taught by specialist PE teachers.

In Japan, the Ministry of Education, Culture, Sports, Science and Technology issues a curriculum that is standard across the country and all teachers must follow it and this includes physical education. It is revised approximately every ten years with the current curriculum set up in March 2008. Overall objectives of the new curriculum are described below (MEXT; Ministry of Education, Culture, Sports, Science and Technology 2008a, 2008b).

Overall objectives for elementary school

To help pupils – through proper exercise experience and understanding of health and safety, and by considering physical and mental aspects in an integrated manner – develop basic qualities and the ability to participate in enjoyable physical activity throughout their lives, maintain and improve their health and fitness and cultivate an appropriate attitude toward leading a pleasant and happy life.

Overall objectives for junior high school students

Overall objectives for junior high school students include enabling students to engage in physical activity sensibly, by cultivating an understanding of

Table 4.2 Contents of learning in 2008 (Ministry of Education, Culture, Sports, Science and Technology 2008a, 2008b)

Grade		1–2	3–4	5–6		7–8	9		
Contents	A	Physical fitness			Requirement	Physical fitness	Requirement	A	Contents
	B	Play with apparatus and equipment	Apparatus gymnastics			Apparatus gymnastics	Two contents are selected from B, C, D, G	B	
	C	Playing with running and jumping	Running and jumping	Track and field		Track and field		C	
	D	Playing in water	Floating and swimming	Swimming		Swimming		D	
	E	Games		Ball games		Ball games	One content is selected from E, F.	E	
						Budo (Martial arts)		F	
	F	Expression and rhythm play	Expressive activity			Dance	Two contents are selected from B, C, D, G	G	
						Theory of sport and physical education	Requirement	H	
	G			Health		Health	Requirement		

physical activity, health and safety, and by considering physical and mental aspects in an integrated manner. Another objective is to develop the qualities and abilities to enjoy physical exercise throughout their lives, and to help them cultivate practical abilities for the maintenance and improvement of health and the improvement of physical fitness, as well as cultivate an appropriate attitude toward leading a happy and fulfilling life.

The physical education curriculum contents are influenced by the play theory of Huizinga (1938) and Callois (1958), and the exercise/sport classification ideas of Loy (1980) and McIntosh (1963). The exercise domains of physical education in Japanese elementary and junior high school are shown in Table 4.2.

Table 4.3 shows the transition of the contents of the game. In previous versions of the curriculum, the name of the full official sport was used to indicate learning content and, in particular, with the three big sports of soccer, basketball and volleyball. However, the broader term, 'type', came to be used for the notation of the contents from the revision in 1998 to broaden possibilities for modified, small-sided games. In the curriculum in 2008 this tendency was increasingly emphasized with a move to using the game categories used in TGfU. As a result, all learning contents were described as a type and a full sport name is only shown to provide guidelines. Thus, it seems that the game curriculum has been increasingly shaped by the tactical approach as is evident in the transition of the contents.

The new curriculum considers it to be important to carry out instruction according to the stage of development. For example, in teaching ball games, the official sport typically has rules that are too complicated for elementary school students to understand and play. In addition, it can be too hard for them to perform the skills required in the official sport. For example, if you incorporate the official rules of soccer into third graders' game lessons some students will not be able to engage in the game and can be excluded. Modifying the rules and the configuration of the games and emphasizing students tackling the tactical aspects of games in groups or teams can make the game more enjoyable for them. It allows them to feel the pleasure of competing as a team through cooperation and collaboration, making up rules and battle plans (strategies for the game) in a ball-game lesson. This is recognition of the social nature of games (Light 2002), of the intellectual aspects of games and the importance of interaction for learning. To enable every student to have these experiences teacher planning must be undertaken according to the stage of the students' development and abilities. This means it is necessary for teachers to modify the rules of the games, the space used, the number of players and the ensuing skills required to provide the appropriate level of challenge that enables students to feel the satisfaction of meeting these challenges as a team.

The learning contents shown in the 2008 curriculum that were revised based on these ideas are as follows.

Table 4.3 History for games content in course of study

Year	Grade 1 and Grade 2	Grade 3 and Grade 4	Grade 5 and Grade 6	Grades 7, 8 and 9
2008	*Ball games with throwing *Ball games with shooting	*Invasion games *Net/wall-type games *Striking/fielding-type games	*Invasion games *Net/wall-type games *Striking/fielding-type games	*Invasion games *Net/wall-type games *Striking/fielding-type games
1998	*Ball games with throwing *Ball games with shooting	*Basketball-type games *Soccer-type games *Baseball-type games	*Basketball *Soccer *Softball or soft volleyball	*Basketball or handball * Soccer *Volleyball *Tennis, table tennis or badminton *Softball
1988	*Dodge ball *Ball games with shooting	*Port ball *Line soccer *Hand baseball	*Basketball *Soccer	*Basketball or handball *Soccer *Volleyball *Tennis, table tennis or badminton *Softball
1977	*Ball games with throwing *Ball games with shooting	*Dodgeball (Grade 3) *Port Ball (Grade 4) *Line soccer	*Basketball *Soccer	*Basketball *Volleyball *Soccer

Table 4.3 (continued)

Year	Grade 1 and Grade 2	Grade 3 and Grade 4	Grade 5 and Grade 6	Grades 7, 8 and 9
1968 (Grade 1–6) 1969 (Grade 7–9)	Grade 1 *Delivering a ball by hand *Dodge ball with rolling a ball *Ball-toss game, in which balls are thrown into a basket on a high pole *Kicking a ball in parallel Grade 2 *Delivering a ball by pass *Circular dodge ball *Throwing *Kicking a ball in parallel	Grade 3 *Square dodge ball *Hand baseball *Foot baseball *Line soccer Grade 4 *Port ball *Hand baseball *Foot baseball *Line soccer	Grade 5 *Port ball *Hand baseball *Simple soccer Grade 6 *Port ball *Softball *Simple soccer	*Basketball *Handball *Volleyball *Soccer (boys)
1958	Grade 1 Delivering a ball by hand Dodge ball with rolling a ball Ball-toss game, in which balls are thrown into a basket on a high pole Kicking a ball in parallel Grade 2 Delivering a ball by pass Circular dodge ball ThrowingKicking a ball in parallel	Grade 3 *Square dodge ball *Hand baseball *Foot baseball *Line soccer Grade 4 *Port ball *Hand baseball *Foot baseball *Line soccer	Grade 5 *Port ball *Hand baseball *Simple soccer Grade 6 *Port ball *Softball *Simple soccer	*Volleyball *Basketball *Soccer (boys) *Softball

Learning content in elementary school course of study (Ministry of Education, Culture, Sports, Science and Technology 2008a, 2008b)

Grade 1 and Grade 2

E. Games:

(1) To enable pupils to acquire the relevant motor skills by enjoying the following activities:

   a. Ball games, including games involving hitting a target and offensive/ defensive transition with simple on-the-ball skills and off–the-ball movements.
   b. Tag games, including escaping, chasing and gaining/protecting territory within a fixed area.

(2) To enable pupils to actively engage in activities while observing rules in a friendly manner, to accept victory and loss and to pay attention to the safe use of place.
(3) To enable pupils to devise simple rules and decide on offensive formation.

Grade 3 and Grade 4

E. Games:

(1) To enable pupils to acquire the relevant motor skills by enjoying the following activities:

   a. Invasion games, including easy modified game transition with basic on-the-ball skills and off-the-ball movements.
   b. Net/wall-type games, using easy modified game transitions that promote basic continuing rallies and ball passing.
   c. Striking/fielding-type games, including easy modified game transition with basic involving such movements as kicking, hitting, catching and throwing.

(2) To enable pupils to actively engage in activities while observing rules in a friendly manner, to accept victory and loss and to pay attention to the safe use of place and equipment.
(3) To enable pupils to devise rules, and to make simple operations in accordance with the type of game.

Grade 5 and Grade 6

E. Ball games:

(1) To feel the fun and pleasure of the following activities and to enable pupils to acquire the relevant motor skills:

    a. In invasion games, including offensive and defensive plays in modified transition with on-the-ball skills and off-the-ball movements.

    b. In net/wall-type games, including offensive and defensive plays in modified transition through coordinated team attack and defense.

    c. In striking/fielding games, including offensive and defensive plays in modified transition through attacks of hitting the ball and defense formation.

(2) To enable pupils to actively engage in activities while observing rules and helping each other and to pay attention to the safe use of place and equipment.

(3) To enable pupils to devise rules and make operations in accordance with the characteristics of the team.

Learning content in junior high school course of study (Ministry of Education, Culture, Sports, Science and Technology 2008a, 2008b)

Grade 7 and Grade 8 (Grade 1 and Grade 2 in junior high school)

E. Ball games:

(1) With regard to the following activities, to enable students to experience the fun and pleasure of competing over wins and losses, and to enable the students to engage in games by using basic motor skills and coordinated movements with their teammates.

    a. For goal-type games, to enable students to engage in offense and defense in front of the goal via on-the-ball skills and off-the-ball movements such as running into open spaces.

    b. For net-type games, to enable students to engage in offense and defense surrounding open areas via on-the-ball skills and off-the-ball movements such as returning to a base position.

    c. For baseball-type games, to enable students to engage in offense and defense such as by going on the offensive via basic bat manipulation and base running, and defending via on-the-ball skills and positioning at a base position.

(2) To enable students to actively engage in ball games. To enable students to strive to observe fair play, fulfill one's own responsibilities, and take part in discussions on game plan, as well as to enable the students to mind health and safety.

(3) To enable students to understand the characteristics and origin of ball games, the names of techniques and how to perform them and the physical fitness components expected to be improved in conjunction with this, while also enabling the students to devise ways of solving problems according to their own tasks.

Grade 9 (Grade 3 in junior high school)

E. Ball games:

(1) With regard to the following activities, to enable students to experience the fun and pleasure of competing over wins and losses, and to enable the students to engage in games by coordinating with their teammates through skills according to a strategy.

    a. For goal-type games, to enable students to engage in offense and defense such as by penetrating to in front of the goal via steady on-the-ball skills and off-the-ball movements such as creating open spaces.

    b. For net-type games, to enable students to engage in offense and defense surrounding open areas by steady on-the-ball-skills according to one's role, and coordinated movements with others.

    c. For baseball-type games, to enable students to engage in offense and defense such as by going on the offense via steady bat manipulation and base running, and manipulation of the ball and a coordinated defense with others.

(2) To enable students to independently engage in ball games. To strive to hold fair play in high esteem, fulfill one's own responsibilities and contribute to discussions on game play, as well as to enable the students to maintain health and safety.

(3) To enable students to understand the names of techniques and how to perform them, how to enhance physical fitness and methods for observing exercise, while also enabling the students to devise ways of solving problems according to their own tasks.

Trends in strategies for teaching: the battle plan

In Japan, the traditional approach to teaching PE sometimes looks like a military drill with most of the 'good' students faithfully reproducing the teacher's movements. In this approach students are passive learners and are seen to receive knowledge from the teacher, but in the new approach to games teaching they are seen as being very active learners. In this approach teachers focus on the game as a whole instead of on separate parts of the game such as technique as is the case in Game Sense (Light 2013). This is a game-based approach.

While it is clear that drilling technique out of context does not produce good games players or typically generate much pleasure for learners, just letting students play the full game without any structure or aim on the part of the teacher will not necessarily produce good games players either. With the new curriculum, Japanese teachers want students to acquire both knowledge and skills but within the modified games. So, they ask their students to implement 'battle plans' for each modified game as an agreed strategy for the team. A battle plan is a tactical plan developed by the teams in the game.

Table 4.4 Comparison among approaches

Skill-centered approach	Battle-plan-centered approach	Game-centered approach
Drill	Skill practice	Game
↓	↓	↓
Drill	Meeting for making a battle plan	Game appreciation
↓	↓	↓
Drill	Game	Tactical awareness
↓	↓	↓
Drill	Meeting for reflection and practice	Game
↓	↓	↓
Game	Game	Tactical understandings
	↓	↓
	Game	Skill practice
	↓	↓
	Meeting for reflection	Game

The battle-plan-centered approach is used to dissolve the differences between players in skill and confidence by allowing all players to contribute to the battle plan and share in the team effort. It focuses on the social interaction involved in the collective design of battle plans as an intellectual activity and a means of improving game performance by the team. The process thus involves collective discussion and the formulation of a battle plan that is then tested in the game. This is followed by group reflection and evaluation of the plan leading to modification and further testing in the game. This is very similar to the framework for Game Sense outlined by Light (2013), which describes the need to provide opportunities for learners to collectively formulate strategies, test them in the game, reflect upon and evaluate them, and test again in the same process of inquiry asked for in the battle plan approach.

Conclusion

The current physical education curriculum in Japan aims to guide students toward achieving the ideal of lifelong participation in sport and leading an active lifestyle. In games teaching it is thus important to make learning enjoyable and meaningful as Light suggests in the positive pedagogy approach he promotes in Chapter 2. The influence of tactical approaches such as TGfU, Game Sense and Play Practice on the games curriculum in Japan has made a significant contribution toward achieving this aim by moving away from the outdated skill-drill approach and bringing games learning to life for Japanese students. The teaching strategies for games teaching in Japan are changing to learner-centered and game-centered approaches that ask students to think, to interact and to intellectualize learning in games. Students' learning experience in this approach can make games fun and educationally valuable. The games curriculum in Japan is now at a turning point in the move from military drilling of de-contextualized technique (or just rolling out the ball and not teaching, see, for example, Graham 2008). The new curriculum and its focus on inquiry and student-centered learning can produce learning that is fun and promote a fascination with games for young people by giving the game(s) back to children (Light 2004) and allowing them to enjoy and learn through structured play, reflection and social interaction.

This is all good news but it is also a huge challenge for Japanese teachers to move from a teacher-centered, technical approach to a student-centered, inquiry-based approach. As research shows elsewhere, this is quite a difficult challenge across a range of different cultural settings (see, for example, Butler 1996; Li and Cruz 2008; Roberts 2011; Rossi *et al.* 2007; Chapters 8 and 3 in this volume). The new games curriculum is exciting and offers great possibilities for the quality of student learning in physical education but this is only the start. The real turning point will be when teachers across the country can implement this change. It is the creation of the curriculum that is the starting point for changing the game but there can be no actualization of this curriculum without teachers understanding the idea of this curriculum, believing in it and being able to develop it through reflective practice, as Chapter 8 by Curry and Light suggests. From now on, the spread of this curriculum policy and development of the strategy accompanying it are important for the positive development of games teaching and learning in Japan.

This is a good opportunity for the transformation of physical education teaching in Japan but will require an ongoing commitment from the Ministry of Education, Culture, Sports, Science and Technology to ensure that this significant curriculum change is realized in practice and in the learning experiences of Japanese students through effective professional development programmes. As suggested in Chapter 8 by Curry and Light, extended time and support is needed for teachers to attempt to implement such innovation, to have opportunities to share experiences with other teachers and to reflect upon experiences of implementing innovation in an extended process of change and the transformation of their teaching.

Discussion questions

1. What have been the two traditional approaches to teaching games in Japan and how would this make it difficult for physical education teachers to implement authentic learner-centered, inquiry-based approaches to teaching?
2. Identify and discuss the opportunities provided by the new Japanese curricula in secondary and primary schools for the development and uptake of GBAs such as Game Sense?
3. Discuss the suggestions Suzuki makes for meeting the expectations of the new Japanese games curricula and add any suggestions you might have for meeting this significant challenge.

References

Almond (1986) 'A games classification', in R. Thorpe, D. Bunker and L. Almond (eds) *Rethinking Games Teaching*, Loughborough: University of Technology, Loughborough, Department of Physical Education and Sports Science, pp. 71–72.

Brooker, R. and Abbott, R. (2001) 'Developing intelligent performers in sport: Should coaches be making more sense of Game Sense?', *Journal of Sport Pedagogy*, 7(2), 67–83.

Bunker, D. and Thorpe, R. (1982) 'A model for the teaching of games in secondary schools', *Bulletin of Physical Education*, 18, 5–8

Butler, J. (1996) 'Teacher responses to Teaching Games for Understanding', *Journal of Physical Education, Recreation and Dance*, 67, 28–33.

Caillois, R. (1958) *Les Jeux et les Hommes*, Paris: Gallimard.

Graham, G. (2008) *Teaching Physical Education: Becoming a Master Teacher* (third edition), Champaign, IL: Human Kinetics.

Gréhaigne, J.-F., Godbout, P. and Bouthier, D. (2005) 'Tactical-decision learning model and student practices', *Physical Education and Sport Pedagogy*, 10, 255–269.

Gréhaigne, J.-F., Richard, J.-F. and Griffin, L. L. (2005) *Teaching and Learning Team Sports and Games*, London and New York: Routledge.

Gréhaigne, J.-F., Wallian, N. and Godbout, P. (2005) 'Tactical-decision learning model and students' practices', *Quest*, 47, 490–505.

Griffin, L. and Patton, K. (2005) 'Two decades of teaching for understanding: Looking at the past, present, and future', *Teaching Games for Understanding: Theory, Research and Practice*, Champaign, IL: Human Kinetics.

Holt, J. E., Ward, T. and Wallhead, T. (2007) 'The transfer of learning from Play Practices to game play in young adult soccer players', *Physical Education and Sport Pedagogy*, 11(2), 101–118.

Huizinga, J. (1938) *Homo Ludens, a Study of the Play Element in Culture*, Boston, MA: Beacon Press.

Launder, A. G. (2001) *Play Practice: The Games Approach to Teaching and Coaching Sports*, Champaign, IL: Human Kinetics.

Li, C. and Cruz, A. (2008) 'Pre-service PE teachers' occupational socialization experiences on teaching games for understanding', *New Horizons in Education*, 56 (30), 20–30.

70   *Naoki Suzuki*

Light, R. (2002) 'The social nature of games: Pre-service primary teachers' first experiences of TGfU', *European Physical Education Review*, 8(3), 291–310.

——(2004) 'Coaches' experiences of games sense: opportunities and challenges', *Physical Education and Sport Pedagogy*, 9(2), 115–131.

——(2008) '"Complex" learning theory in physical education: An examination of its epistemology and assumptions about how we learn', *Journal of Teaching in Physical Education*, 27(1), 21–37.

——(2013) *Game Sense: Pedagogy for Performance, Participation and Enjoyment*, London: Routledge.

Light, R. L., Harvey, S. and Mouchet, A. (2012) 'Improving "at-action" decision-making in team sports through a holistic coaching approach', *Sport, Education and Society*.

Loy, J.W. (1969) 'The nature of sport', in J. W. Loy and G. S. Kenyon (eds) *Sport, Culture and Society*, London: Macmillan.

McIntosh, P. C. (1963) *Sport in Society*, London: C.A. Watts and Co., Ltd.

McNeill, M., Fry, J., Wright, S., Tan, C., Tan, S. and Schempp, P. (2004) '"In the local context": Singaporean challenges to Teaching Games on practicum', *Sport, Education & Society*, 9(1), 3–32.

Mitchell, S. A., Oslin, J. L. and Griffin, L. L. (2006) *Teaching Sport Concepts and Skills: A Tactical Games Approach* (second edition), Champaign, IL: Human Kinetics.

Monbukagaku-sho (Ministry of Education, Culture, Sports, Science and Technology) (2008a) Shougakkou Gakushuu Shidou Youryou (Course of Study in Elementary School), www.mext.go.jp/component/a_menu/education/micro_detail/__icsFiles/afield file/2009/04/21/1261037_10.pdf (last accessed 13 May 2013).

Monbukagaku-sho (Ministry of Education, Culture, Sports, Science and Technology) (2008b) Chuugakkou Gakushuu Shidou Youryou (Course of Study in Junior High School), www.mext.go.jp/component/a_menu/education/micro_detail/__icsFiles/ afieldfile/2011/04/11/1298356_8.pdf (last accessed 13 May 2013).

Roberts, S. (2011) 'Teaching Games for Understanding: the difficulties and challenges experienced by participation cricket coaches', *Physical Education and Sport Pedagogy*, 16(1), 33–48.

Rossi, T., Fry, J., McNeill, M. and Tan, C. (2007) 'The Games Concept Approach (GCA) as a mandated practice: views of Singaporean teachers', *Sport, Education & Society*, 12(1), 93–111.

5 Play Practice

An innovative model for engaging and developing skilled players in sport

Wendy Piltz

> But careful study has shown that creative innovation follows a very precise pattern; like excellence itself, it emerges from the rigors of purposeful practice.
>
> (Syed 2010: 98)

Alan Launder developed the foundations of Play Practice from his experience as a player, teacher, coach, physical education teacher, educator and coach educator. Since *Play Practice* (Launder, 2001) was published there has been a continued refinement of these ideas and ongoing application to professional practice, resulting in a comprehensive framework to support professional learning; one that can be easily understood and broadly applied to the teaching and coaching of any sports activity (Launder and Piltz, in press). This chapter will include a brief history detailing the origins of ideas, the key principles and operating models together with the main theoretical underpinnings. In addition, it will discuss the efficacy of this approach for novice educators informed by practice-based studies.

Research investigating the characteristics of 'expertise' in a range of fields suggests the expert acquires a refined set of capabilities, including deeper levels of understanding of their specific domain and rich stores of personal knowledge, which can be drawn on seamlessly to solve problems. This deeply layered expertise enables insight, breadth in vision, and affords flexibility with changing circumstance and the capacity for creative innovation (Berliner 1994; Côté, Baker and Abernethy 2007; Ericsson 2006). Syed (2010: 98) suggests creativity emerges from the 'rigours of purposeful practice' and it is the consequence of experts deeply immersing themselves in their chosen field over a period of time that enables them to experience 'transformed insight' and be able to contribute innovative approaches. The combined depth of accumulated expertise of the contributing authors of the second edition of *Play Practice* provides an example of how a prolonged immersion in purposeful experience has enabled the emergence of creative insight and innovative practice.

Play Practice is a comprehensive approach for engaging and developing skilled players in sports and a framework for facilitating the improvement of teaching and coaching practice. Inherent in the overall framework of Play Practice is the recognition of the complexity of the teaching and learning

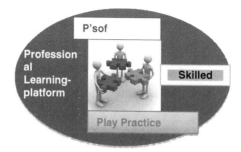

Figure 5.1 This diagram shows the models and their connectivity

processes. The framework is comprised of four models that, when drawn together, capture the complexity of learning and succinctly present a volume of information, practical experience and wisdom, to facilitate the development of players, teachers and coaches across all experience levels. In this chapter the key ideas of Play Practice will be explored through a reflection of the origins and evolution of the approach and through a review of the models central to Play Practice. This includes the '*Ps of perfect pedagogy*', a guide to developing teaching and reflective capabilities, the '*model of skilled play*', a tool for comprehensive analysis of the activity and the '*process for implementing*' Play Practice – a guide for teaching/coaching. The fourth model is a '*structure for professional learning*' featuring a progressive series of key experiences, applicable to a variety of contexts, to facilitate professional learning. This is the foundation for the other models to be embedded. Information drawn from practice-based studies of pre-service teachers learning in HPE at the University of South Australia will be included to highlight the efficacy of the framework.

History and evolution

The roots of Play Practice stem back to 1957 in England when Launder commenced teaching PE at Wymondham Secondary Modern School in Norfolk and then at Dr Challoner's Grammar School in Buckinghamshire (1960–7). A significant challenge for Launder, as a beginning teacher, was finding a way to introduce 'disinterested' learners to cross-country running. This was overcome by using *individual challenges* and *recording personal performances* that fostered engagement, intrinsic motivation and helped build learner commitment. Another key strategy was to establish a class climate that acknowledged personal effort and improvement; an environment where no single student 'won' and no one finished 'last'. Launder extended these ideals to track and field athletics, expanding concepts further by using '*working technical models*' to promote *early and continuing success.* A working technical model focuses on the most simplistic movement form, ensuring inclusivity and ensuring all participants could participate successfully in a range of athletic events. Launder's role as field event coach at Western Kentucky University (WKU) from 1967 to 1973 and national pole vault coach for Australia from 1973 to 2000 lead to the Play Practice mantra 'what is technically desirable must be physically possible' and highlighted the place of learner 'understanding' in the effective development of technique. It also reinforced the importance of the learner making a self-determined commitment to mastery in order to extend and progress performance. Launder's influence in schools and in coaching led to flourishing participation and achievement resulting from the provision of opportunity for all participants, encouragement, acknowledgement of effort, feedback and involvement in culminating events, tournaments and competitions.

Coaches providing professional development courses for their organizations influenced the early evolution of Play Practice. The most significant single contribution came from Alan Wade, Director of Coaching for the English Football Association. Launder was introduced to Wade in 1959 and was influenced by his ideas for teaching football through the use of small-sided games and the 'tactical principles of play', which presented a clear solution to the problem of teaching tactical positioning and decision making in games. This understanding, combined with experience in teaching the principles of play to a diversity of learners, allowed two important pedagogical insights to emerge. First, the technical demands of a game could be reduced through intelligent application of the principles of play. Second, there is a tight relationship between a player's technical ability and the tactical possibilities open to them. These insights led to the development of the Play Practice mantra – 'What is tactically desirable must be technically possible'.

A second major influence in the evolution of Play Practice has been the popularity of *pick-up* games. These games are played with minimal equipment, in any available space, with no officials, uniforms, time limits or prizes. Not only do they provide everyone and anyone with a chance to play, but also promote a climate of innovation where mistakes are accepted. An analysis of pick-up games lead to a key precept relating to the place of failure in learning, which is an idea also discussed by Light in Chapter 2 on Positive Pedagogy. For any learning situation to be valuable, failure is significant, mistakes are a part of learning and they must be accepted and even legitimized. Berry, Abernethy and Côté (2008) also identify the value of these games for learning. They emphasize the value of deliberate play, typified by activities like the neighbourhood pick-up games, as a key experience in building player expertise. In these games participation is less formalized, play is small sided, intrinsically motivated and developed by the playing group.

Whilst undertaking graduate studies at WKU in 1967, Launder taught elementary children movement education, dance, drama and introductory games. These experiences confirmed the importance of early success and enjoyment as the key for motivation and learning. The period of time at WKU was a time of deep levels of reflection on Launder's accumulated teaching and learning experiences. This lead to the creative design of a course of study introducing pre-service elementary education majors at WKU to teaching and learning in physical education. This course was the beginnings of the '*P's model of instruction*' in physical education and it also generated ideas for a '*model for teacher education*', in physical education. In September 1973, Launder accepted a position in curriculum and teaching studies at the University of South Australia (formerly Adelaide Teachers College), which provided the opportunity to refine the Ps of pedagogy model further and to create an innovative programme for pre-service physical education teacher education.

Models to guide professional practice

The Ps of perfect pedagogy, a working model of instruction, has been used to introduce generations of pre-service teachers in HPE at the University of South Australia to the complexities of teaching (Launder 1989, 2001) with research suggesting that the model positively impacts on the personal confidence and professional competence of pre-service teachers (Piltz 2006, 2008b). It serves as a framework to assist in planning, reflective evaluation and in the provision of feedback. Pre-service teachers report on the efficacy of the model to facilitate their understanding of quality teaching and learning practice and to enable them to self-monitor the development of their teaching capabilities. They express feelings of empowerment as they learn to teach in a simplified 'lab school' learning environment, utilizing this model as a tool for development and creating a self-determined cycle of success.

The *model of skilled performance* evolved to assist teachers and coaches to improve their understanding of sports and to inform their analysis of the activity they are teaching. Based on observation and interaction with teachers/coaches and an analysis of the literature in the field, it became evident that a guiding framework would be beneficial. It also became evident that much of the confusion relating to effective sports pedagogy arose from the careless use of key terms associated with skilled performance and an assumption that teachers and coaches clearly understand the complex nature of skilled play. In a review of the original teaching games for understanding (TGfU) model (Bunker and Thorpe 1983) it is suggested that 'the activity' and 'the learner' require consideration before starting in a modified game form. This is an important starting point, however, there is no guiding framework provided to help teachers and coaches understand what the activity is about, or how to appraise what the learner is capable of doing. In other publications on games teaching a review of the terminology of sport performance highlights the haphazard use of key terms and the lack of definition or clarification of the meaning of these terms. For example, in Butler and Griffin (2010) the terms 'skill', 'skilled', 'basic skill', 'basic skill movement', 'skill technique', 'technique', 'tactical skills of throwing', are all used in a variety of contexts, without clarification of meaning, which can be confusing and misleading for sport educators. Other key terms such as 'tactics' and 'strategy' are also used synonymously without clarification of either term or discussion of the relationship that exists between them. The term 'Game Sense' provides another example of a term requiring clarification. Game Sense was originally used as the title of a series of workshops undertaken by Rod Thorpe with the Australian Sports Commission in 1994 and this subsequently evolved into the name for the TGfU approach in Australia. The term is also implicitly used to describe expert players with advanced decision-making capabilities and it is referred to as something that players can learn. Game sense is defined by Launder (2001: 36) as 'the ability to use an understanding of the rules, tactics, strategy and of oneself (and of one's teammates) to overcome the problems posed by the sport or by one's opponents in the game'. This definition emphasizes the contextual nature of this element, it identifies key elements, draws together *understanding and action* and incorporates the decision-making process. Once key terms are defined and clarified, it enables better understanding of the concept, consistent communication and coherent application to professional practice. With game sense defined in this way, it is possible for teachers and coaches to begin to facilitate learning of this capability through the design of relevant and challenging situations.

One of the major advantages of Play Practice is that it provides a detailed analysis of skilled performance in sport presented in the *model of skilled play*. This analysis, subsequently confirmed with practice-based data from pre-service teachers, suggests that teachers and coaches would benefit if the following terms and definitions were to be accepted and used. *Technical ability* enables players to control and direct the object. *Agility* enables players to get into good positions, at the right time. *Endurance* ensures players can keep on getting into good positions, to maintain high levels of concentration and technical ability throughout the game. *Courage* ensures players can take on any of the specific challenges presented by the sport and *communication* improves team work. *Game sense* is the ability to use an understanding of the rules, tactics, strategy and of oneself (and of one's teammates) to overcome the problems posed by the sport or by one's opponents in the game. *Resilience* enables players to focus and to respond positively to setbacks, and this, together with *fair play*, forms the foundation underlying participation enjoyment and a sense of achievement.

The model clearly highlights how all elements of skilled performance are inter-related and suggests that in games, tactics often depend on the technical ability of the players. It enables teachers and coaches to determine which elements of skilled play to emphasize as they plan learning experiences for a specific group of students or players. In addition, it helps them to understand the relationships among different sports and to appreciate the way in which good ideas and methods can be transferred from one to another. Importantly, it exposes the limitations of out-dated methods that focus almost exclusively on the development of technical ability – commonly termed *ball skills* or *the basics* – and which can leave novices completely unprepared for the complexities of games. The model also raises serious questions about the value of approaches that solely emphasize tactics over technical ability when teaching games. Finally, and most importantly, it redirects the focuses back to a reasoned and holistic analysis of what is actually required to play a specific sport well, as the basis for teaching and learning.

Practice-based studies (Piltz 2006, 2008a, 2008b) indicate the efficacy of this model in helping pre-service teachers to teach games effectively. Pre-service teachers indicated how the clarification of terminology improved their understanding of sports performance and assisted their ability to analyze activities. This in turn led to an increase in confidence and understanding of how to structure relevant game-like learning experiences, improved understanding of the process of progressing learning and increased ability to provide authentic feedback. The model also helped pre-service teachers to observe and identify what the learners are able to do as a basis for the students' learning. Pre-service teachers also discovered that while using the model to guide the focus for teaching and learning, it freed up cognitive space and enabled more time to be available for increased interaction with individuals in the class. More recent evaluations of students who were introduced to this framework as a part of a course of study on teaching and learning games reported similar findings (Piltz and Launder 2012). Students indicated they gained an increased confidence in their ability to analyse sports, an improved understanding of the complexities of different activities and a better appreciation of how all components interact and influence each other. The model also impacted on their perceptions and understanding of the differences existing between beginner and elite performers and provided them with strategies for simplifying learning tasks to enable early success for novice participants. Many students had not considered *fair play* and *resilience* as key aspects of skilled play. The model helped them to develop a deeper understanding of these elements and a better appreciation of the significance of foregrounding fair play and resilience when introducing children to games and sport.

The *process for implementing* Play Practice is continuously evolving. The purpose of this model is to provide a guiding framework to support professional practice. It is easy to understand and relatively easy for teachers and coaches to employ when planning and facilitating learning. This model reflects the perspective of learning as a complex social process where engagement and the power of play feature significantly in establishing an intrinsic, self-determined motivation for participation. The process begins with an analysis of the activity by identifying which elements of skilled play are important in a particular sport. In addition, educators must determine which elements should be emphasized with a specific group of players, especially if they are beginners. The process of simplifying, shaping, focusing and enhancing the play can then be undertaken to facilitate learning.

Simplifying the activity is a critical process for engaging beginners and ensuring they have early success. The process begins with the teacher introducing the activity safely, and in a way that emphasizes the sheer joy of playing or of meeting a challenge. By doing this and maximizing participation, it is likely to minimize management issues and foster a positive class climate. There are a variety of strategies for '*simplifying*', depending on the nature of the activity. The agility demands can be minimized by adjusting the playing space or by including a particular target score zone for racquet activities. It is possible to eliminate the need for physical courage and toughness by modifying the rules so as to minimize physical contact, reduce the risk of injury and foster safe participation. The importance of endurance can be minimized by controlling the dimensions of the playing area and the time allocated to a practice. The technical demands can be minimized to enable beginners to begin playing as soon as possible. This can be done by modifying the rules, altering the equipment and introducing the notion of working technical models. Tactical demands can be minimized by playing with small teams in relatively large spaces as this makes decision making easier and provides players with more time to be skilful. Large goals can be used to make scoring easier and an emphasis on the primary rules also assists in reducing tactical complexity. Both the technical and tactical demands of a game can be minimized by giving attackers a numerical advantage in three against one or five against two game play.

Simplifying the activity is a specific example of *shaping* the play involving the manipulation of key variables to create a specific learning environment for beginners. At the elite level shaping is used to create realistic practice situations to improve specific elements of skilled play with a particular group of players. At this level, practice should be structured to stretch players, up to and beyond the edge of failure in order to challenge their continued improvement.

Shaping the play is an important process for teachers and coaches to master, as it is the *foundation for facilitating and differentiating learning*. It is referred to as teaching 'through the game', as the variables of the game dynamic are manipulated to create opportunities for engagement and learning for a diversity of learners, from novice to elite. Hopper (2009) refers to the concept of 'game as teacher' in a similar way, to illustrate the importance of designing game-centred environments to enable players to self-regulate, adapt and learn. A game-centred environment is advocated for facilitating learning by Slade (2010) as he demonstrates how variables can be manipulated in tactical game challenges to engage and transform learners' capabilities.

It is important to remember that in many games the critical variable in skilled performance is time. Teachers and coaches must therefore continually monitor the variables that impact the time a player has to be skilful as they shape the play. The equation space = time = skilled play (good decisions and sound execution) has been found to be of value when designing these learning settings.

When shaping the learning environment in court and field invasion games, it is possible to manipulate a range of variables including, but not limited to, the number of players involved, the dimensions of the playing area and the ratio of attackers to defenders as particularly important considerations. Good players must learn to play in limited space whilst novices require plenty of space to enable them to pass the ball and begin to develop both technical ability and game sense. Beginning attackers must always be given a numerical advantage so in basketball, netball or korfball, where the ball is easily controlled in the hands and it is possible to scan the environment, a single player advantage is enough. However, in games such as soccer, hockey and lacrosse, where controlling the ball is more difficult and where the ball player must continually switch their focus from ball to opponent, it may be necessary to begin with four attackers against a single defender or possibly five against two.

The primary and secondary rules can be considered when shaping the practice, together with specific 'conditions' that can be applied to the game. With beginners it is important to start with as few rules as possible to allow play to flow, and introduce new rules as they are needed. Conditions of play, which take on the power of rules for the duration of a practice, can be applied to attain specific outcomes. For example in lacrosse, the condition that the ball must go behind the goal before attempting a shot, helps to focus players on using this important space in the game. The nature of the goal, choice in equipment, differential scoring and personalized play are other possible considerations when shaping the play.

In racquet sports, games can be shaped to maximize individual opportunity to hit the ball, while minimizing the importance of agility and tactics. An example is 'target table tennis' where points can never be lost, they can only be won. This immediately shapes and focuses consistent stroke play and facilitates the improvement of technique. In addition, playing games in which points can only be won but never lost allows participants to build their confidence. Then as players improve, games can be shaped to demand increasing levels of tactical and technical ability while at the same time putting pressure on their agility.

The principles and practices of Play Practice are underpinned by theory from a range of multidiscipline areas. Of significance is the connection to the conception of learning as a complex, dynamic process that draws on information from motor learning in dynamical systems theory and ecological psychology (Abernethy 1986; Clark 1995; Davids, Button and Bennett 2008; Bernstein 1967 as cited in Chow *et al.* 2007) and from educational theory on complexity (Davis, Sumara and Luce-Kapler 2008). In recent times, this perspective has been used to inform game-centred approaches to teaching and coaching of which Play Practice is one practical example. The theory highlights the complexity of factors that influence learning and suggest learning emerges through a dynamic process of self-organization and adaptation within a particular setting. Central to this process is the interaction between the constraints associated with the performer, environment and task that provide the opportunity for individual transformation as a part of a group of collective learners (Newell 1986 as cited in Chow *et al.* 2007). The process of shaping the play is an example of how task constraints can be manipulated to provide challenging learning environments to facilitate the emergence of movement behaviours and decision-making skills. This process promotes learning in relevant contexts by connecting perceptual information and movement couplings, allowing time for the learner to become attuned to the key cues in specific play environments and to self-organize (Davids *et al.* 2008; Chow *et al.* 2007).

Focusing the practice is an important process used by teachers and coaches to *maximize students' understanding and improvement*. This process involves 'teaching *in* the game' to facilitate learning by re-emphasizing key concepts, cues or behaviour relating to fair play and resilience. The 'freeze re-play' is a critical method for focusing the play. This involves a thoughtful selection of key moments in a session, where the teacher uses a specific signal to freeze the play. Once the group has immediately stopped moving, the participants can be asked to reflect on the action replaying the scenario, and then through guided discovery consider key points for learning. Carefully handled, this strategy allows teachers and coaches to capture great teaching moments and use them to promote players' understanding of the game. It is also a very effective way of working with the chaotic scramble at the beginning of many games and of reducing the high error rate that is inevitable when beginners play. Time-outs can also be used as a focusing strategy, where teams are able to call a limited number of short (30 second) timeouts. This allows the opportunity to discuss what is happening, raise questions about the rules, or make necessary adjustments to their play.

Enhancing the play is an important process for engaging and maintaining learner commitment, and for maximizing enjoyment and improvement. Play Practice is a *pedagogy for engagement*, so teachers and coaches must learn to include a wide range of motivational tools to generate positive learning states. Play Practice outlines a range of authentic strategies that have been successfully used to enhance the level of commitment of even the most reluctant learners.

Some examples of these strategies include: ensuring fair and balanced game play by a continual rotation of opponents, a rebalancing of teams and controlling the playing time for games, particularly the use of 'random time'. Interest levels are maintained when participants are clear on what is expected of them, when they see the task as worthwhile, achievable and they understand the new learning will be applied in real game contexts. Varied and well-paced activities are key to sustained engagement, together with novel tasks and providing the opportunity for players to exert a degree of choice in the design of the learning environment. Other strategies such as counting down the time remaining, counting out loud the number of repetitions left or recording and emphasizing individual improvement, can influence individuals to sustain effort and persist. It is also possible to enhance the performance of a diversity of learners through personalizing practice. An example of differentiating learning, to include the more experienced players, is by giving them leadership roles such as 'playmaker', 'schemer' or 'quarterback'. Action fantasy games and exciting culminating events can be included into the experience as a key strategy for enhancement. These events provide purpose for participation and engage participants through the concept of 'cameo' where individuals taking on the identities of 'sporting greats' as they play in the 'World Cup', 'National Championships' or the 'playoffs'.

The process of *enhancing the play* is central to positioning Play Practice as a pedagogy for engagement and this is underpinned by a variety of theoretical perspectives. Play-based learning is embedded into the philosophy and the methods of Play Practice as learning situations are designed to harness the power of play to motivate, enthuse and generate feelings of enjoyment. Brown (2009) suggests that play energizes and enlivens human life. It stimulates creativity, generates new possibilities and kindles optimistic thinking. Learning through play promotes transformation, adaptability, the development of empathy and the capability to navigate social complexity. Shaping play is a key process for generating meaningful learning experiences to stimulate learner interest and promote positive and purposeful involvement. Challenges also engage learners' interest, promote task mastery, increase personal competence and build intrinsic motivation. As teachers and coaches applying the processes of shaping, focusing and enhancing the play, they enact play-based learning and embody a spirit of playfulness into their practice. The National Institute for Play (2009) suggests that play is a significant factor in promoting better educative, work, personal and relationship environments. In addition, they suggest that infusing play into education contributes to improved student engagement and optimized learning. Ryan, Williams, Patrick and Deci (2009) suggest that intrinsic motivation can be developed through the embodied enjoyment of movement, which can be facilitated by educators who design experiences that enable personal competence and confidence to emerge.

Play Practice adopts a learner-centred focus with an emphasis on relationships, student engagement, success and enjoyment as the foundation for building intrinsic motivation. Fair play, resilience and autonomy also feature as key factors to sustain the development of a positive, inclusive and success-orientated learning climate. Pink (2009) identified the significance of developing intrinsic motivation as a basis for learning. Ryan and colleagues (2009) support this and suggest intrinsic motivation is critical in developing lifelong activity habits. This form of motivation emerges as psychological needs for competence, autonomy and relatedness are fulfilled. The research further indicates that interest and engagement in physical activity are fostered by developing and demonstrating competence, by allowing choice and autonomy, by promoting connection and relationship and by maximizing enjoyment while minimizing anxiety (Ryan *et al.* 2009). The principles of Play Practice project this orientation by focusing on engaging students and sustaining intrinsic motivation through maximizing participation and developing competent, confident players. In addition, the specific process of enhancing the play is purposely directed to engaging the learner and inducing positive learning states.

Further support for the Play Practice model can be drawn from the contemporary field of positive psychology. Early work by Csikszentmihalyi (1990) on enjoyment and flow experiences suggests that novel, playful environments in which challenges are aligned to the performers' abilities generate a state of enjoyment, or flow, that provides a powerful internal motivator for human behaviour. This perspective is supported by Kretchmar (2005), who refers to experiences of delight to describe the joyful state generated when players move with this sense of flow. Both authors differentiate fun from enjoyment and align enjoyment with competence, fulfilment and achievement as the basis of intrinsic motivation. This aspect of engagement in games is also discussed by Light in Chapter 2. Play Practice advocates games and challenges that are shaped to match task and player ability. In so doing, and by applying the principles of alignment and differentiation, all participants are provided with opportunities to experience success and flow to sustain purposeful and engaged participation in physical activity. Seligman, Ernst, Gillhum, Reivich and Linkins (2009) suggest that learning experiences that develop capabilities of optimistic thinking, resilience, courage, compassion and meaningful engagement are valued in education for optimizing individual health and wellbeing. Resilience and fair play form the foundation of the model of skilled play and this enables many opportunities for students to develop these capabilities as they experience success and failure, cope with making mistakes, develop the courage to take risks and demonstrate increasing levels of personal and social responsibility. Play Practice also enables participants to find meaning and connection in small-sided teams and peer-supported activities that nurture a helping attitude and foster the development of compassion, empathy and tolerance.

The final step in the *process of teaching sport* is to provide an environment to allow *every child the opportunity* to participate in a programme of sports experiences. This allows them to adopt roles such as player, coach, manager, official, and arbitrator, and to take responsibility for their actions and the management of more complex group interactions. The key is to recognize practising as only a means to an end – the prime outcome is to enable all participants to become confident and competent players and to experience joyful participation in sports activity. This can be achieved through culminating events, intra-school games, inter-school or extended community competitions.

Conclusion

The foundations of Play Practice evolved in a pragmatic way, driven by the need to engage a diversity of learners and to find worthwhile alternatives to traditional methods. This innovative and authentic approach can be applied to a diversity of sports to introduce beginners to sport or to coach elite players. It is underpinned by theory, including learning as a complex, dynamic and adaptive process and a pedagogy of engagement.

A series of models are presented to guide professional practice in a highly complex field. The 'Ps of Pedagogy', model of 'skilled play' and the 'process' for implementing Play Practice provide an operational framework for improving practice. When these models are embedded into a meaningful structure of professional learning it is possible to develop self-determined, confident and competent professionals. Evidence from practice-based studies with pre-service teachers at the University of South Australia indicates the efficacy of this approach for developing capable, confident, creative and critically reflective practitioners.

Discussion questions

1. The elements of skilled play provide a framework for analyzing the activity and planning for learning. Identify the key definitions used in the model of skilled play and illustrate how they can be applied when analyzing an activity of your choice.
2. What is meant by the phrase 'what is tactically desirable must be technically possible?' and how might this impact on your teaching/coaching?
3. Why is it important to engage participants and to maintain positive learning states? Outline a variety of strategies that can be used to 'enhance the play' and justify why these methods foster student motivation.

References

Abernethy, B. (1986) 'Basic concepts of motor control: Psychological perspectives', in B. Abernathy, V. Kippers, L. Mackinnon, R. Neal and S. Hanrahan (eds) *Biophysical Foundations of Human Movement*, Melbourne: Macmillan, pp. 295–311.

Berliner, D. (1994) 'Expertise and the wonder of exemplary performances', in J. Mangieri and C. Collins-Block (eds) *Creating Powerful Thinking in Teachers and Students: Diverse Perspectives*, New York: Holt, Rinchart and Winston, pp. 1–42.

Berry, J., Abernethy, B. and Côté, J. (2008) 'The contribution of structured activity and deliberate play to the development of expert perceptual and decision making skill', *Journal of Sport and Exercise Psychology*, 30: 685–708.

Brown, S. (2009) *Play: How it Shapes the Brain, Opens the Imagination and Invigorates the Soul*, New York: Penguin Books.

Bunker, D. and Thorpe, R. (1983) 'A model for the teaching of games in secondary schools', *Bulletin of Physical Education*, 18(1): 1–4.

Butler, J. and Griffin, L. (2010) *More Teaching Games for Understanding: Move Globally*, Champaign, IL: Human Kinetics.

Chow, J., Davids, K., Button, C., Shuttleworth, R., Renshaw, I. and Araujo, D. (2007) 'The role of nonlinear pedagogy in physical education', *Review of Educational Research*, 77 (3): 251–278.

Clark, J. (1995) 'On becoming skillful: Patterns and constraints', *Research Quarterly for Exercise and Sport*, 66(3): 173–183.

Côté, J., Baker, J. and Abernethy, B. (2007) 'Practice and play in the development of sport expertise' in G. Tenenbaum and R.C. Eklund (eds) *Handbook of Sport Psychology* (third edition), Hoboken, NJ: Wiley, pp. 184–202.

Csikszentmihalyi, M. (1990) *Flow: The Psychology of Optimal Experience*, New York: Harper and Row.

Davids, K., Button, K. and Bennett, S. (2008) *Acquiring Movement Skill: A Constraint-led Perspective*, Champaign, IL: Human Kinetics.

Davis, B., Sumara, D. and Luce-Kapler, R. (2008) *Engaging Minds: Changing Teaching in Complex Times* (second edition), New York: Routledge.

Ericsson, K.A. (2006) 'The influence of experience and deliberate practice on the development of superior expert performance', in K.A. Ericsson, N. Charness,

P. Feltovich and R.R. Hoffman (eds) *Cambridge Handbook of Expertise and Expert Performance*, Cambridge: Cambridge University Press, pp. 685–706.

Hopper, T. (2009) 'Game-as-teacher in TGfU and video games: Enabling constraints in learning through game play', extended paper on keynote address, ACHPER 2009, Brisbane, Australia, 7–10 July.

Kretchmar, S. (2005) 'Teaching Games for Understanding and the delights of human activity', in L. Griffin and J. Butler (eds) *Teaching Games for Understanding: Theory, Research, and Practice*, Champaign, IL: Human Kinetics, pp. 199–212.

Launder, A. (1989) 'The *P*s of perfect pedagogy', *Sports Coach*, April–June: 21–23.

——(2001) *Play Practice: The Games Approach to Teaching and Coaching Sports*, Champaign, IL: Human Kinetics.

Launder, A. and Piltz, W. (in press) *Play Practice: Engaging and Developing Skilled Players* (second edition), Champaign, IL: Human Kinetics.

National Institute for Play (2009) www.nifplay.org/about_us (last accessed 12 June 2010).

Piltz, W. (2006) 'Influencing professional practice in games education through working models and principle based experiential learning', paper presented at the Asia-Pacific Conference on Teaching Sport and Physical Education for Understanding, Sydney, Australia, 14–15 December.

——(2008a) 'The advantages of sector games for promoting quality teaching and learning in batting and fielding games', paper presented at the Association Internationale des Ecoles Superieures d'Education Physique (AIESEP) World Congress, Sapporo, Japan, 21–24 January.

——(2008b) 'The influence of play practice principles and processes on pre-service teachers' conceptions and capabilities in games teaching', paper presented at the Association Internationale des Ecoles Superieures d'Education Physique (AIESEP) World Congress, Sapporo, Japan, 21–24 January.

Piltz, W. and Launder, A. (2012) 'An analysis of the nature of skilled play in games', paper presented at the 5th International TGfU Conference, Loughborough, UK, 14–16 July.

Pink, D. (2009) *Drive: The Surprising Truth About What Motivates Us*, New York: Riverhead Books.

Ryan, R., Williams, G., Patrick, H. and Deci, E. (2009) 'Self-determination theory and physical activity: The dynamics of motivation in development and wellness', *Hellenic Journal of Psychology*, 6: 107–124.

Seligman, M., Ernst, R., Gillhum, J., Reivich, K. and Linkins, M. (2009) 'Positive education: Positive psychology and classroom interventions', *Oxford Review of Education*, 25(5): 293–311.

Slade, D. (2010) *Transforming Play: Teaching Tactics and Game Sense*, Champaign, IL: Human Kinetics.

Syed, M. (2010) *Bounce: Mozart, Federer, Picasso, Beckham and the Science of Success*, New York: Harper Collins.

Part II

Research on the implementation of game-based approaches

6 Recent trends in research literature on game-based approaches to teaching and coaching games

Kendall Jarrett and Stephen Harvey

Introduction

As suggested by Curry and Light in Chapter 8, the expanding output of research on game-based approaches (GBAs) over the past decade has not been reflected in the expanding utilisation of GBAs in school-based physical education programmes and club-based sport coaching environments. Reasons for this lack of 'uptake' are varied and range from a lack of exposure to effective GBA professional development opportunities to the prolonged acceptance of a *performative* culture often embedded within physical education and youth sport programmes (Harvey and Jarrett in press; Dismore and Bailey 2010). The literature on games teaching published since Oslin and Mitchell's review of GBAs in 2006 continues to acknowledge the many benefits of using GBAs, but also acknowledges, and to a lesser extent addresses, the key challenges associated with the employment of learner-centred and GBA pedagogies. This chapter provides an overview of post-2005 research trends in the GBA literature to identify and discuss the prominent themes that arose from this meta-analysis.

Prominent research themes

The influence of context

The range of GBAs now available for practitioners to use in games teaching and coaching environments has developed considerably over the past three decades (see Chapter 2) but the literature suggests that selecting and implementing the appropriate pedagogical model/approach is strongly influenced by socio-cultural, institutional, political and other contexts. Selecting and effectively implementing a GBA requires a level of understanding of the main factors that influenced its conception, and which continue to influence it usage. In Chapter 8, Curry and Light present research conducted on the influence of school context, in one school, on health and physical education teachers' and school sports coaches' experiences of implementing TGfU. It provides institutional (local-level) insight into how a GBA was introduced in a school-wide community of practitioners, and teachers' personal experiences of it as

Table 6.1 Types of GBA, key text/article and country of conception

Type of GBA	Key text/article	Country of conception
Teaching games for understanding (TGfU)	Griffin and Butler (2005)	UK
The tactical games model (TGM)	Mitchell, Oslin and Griffin (2006)	USA
Play Practice (PP)	Launder (2001)	Australia
Game Sense (GS)	Light (2013a)	Australia
Tactical-decision learning model (TDLM)	Gréhaigne, Wallian, and Godbout, (2005)	France
Ball school (BS) model	Kröger and Roth (1999)	Germany
Games concept approach (GCA)	McNeill, Fry, Wright, Tan and Rossi (2008)	Singapore
Invasion games concept model (IGCM)	Tallir, Lenior, Valcke and Musch (2007)	Belgium

shaped by this context. This attention to context, and the social, cultural, institutional and political elements that contribute to shaping that context, are key factors in how/why many different types of GBA now exist (see Table 6.1).

Empirical research literature exploring teacher and coach perceptions of using/interpreting different GBAs provides its audience not only with an insight into the context of experience, but also with an understanding of the contextual differences that influence the development of each type of GBA. For example, Jarrett's (2011) report on the use of a Game Sense (GS) approach to engage undergraduate sports students on a taught university unit focused on games included comments from participants that highlighted a shift in expectations associated with a change of implementation of pedagogical approach. The use of GS (originally developed for sports coaches in Australia) in England was reported by participants as being 'different', 'more like club sport' and 'more engaging' in contrast to their British-based secondary school experiences of other game-centred approaches to learning (e.g. TGfU). Arguably, such comments highlight contextual factors that have shaped the development of each approach in each country of origin.

The prominence of contextual influence on the development of the games concept approach (GCA) in Singapore is also worth noting. In a study that explored the views of Singaporean teachers on a mandated change in curriculum pedagogy, Rossi, Fry, McNeill and Tan (2007) suggested that the regulative discourses framed by governmentality in Singapore meant that the implementation of a GBA was paradoxical in terms of the expectations of teachers in a climate of control. In addition, empirical and theoretical articles also emanating from Southeast Asia by Wang and Ha (2009) and King and Ho (2009) highlight perceived Eastern–Western social and cultural differences in teachers' 'value orientation' and 'management of discipline perceptions'. They further stress the different contextual influences on GBA and how context can influence its interpretation and implementation. These issues mentioned above are stark reminders of some of the challenges teachers face when implementing a GBA.

The influence of context on GBA teaching and learning experience, however, extends beyond just social and cultural agendas such as those highlighted in Light and Tan's (2006) study that identified different cultural meanings attached to sport and their effect on Australian and Singaporean generalist primary teachers' interpretations and understanding of TGfU and the games concept approach (GCA). In addition to Light and Curry's (Chapter 8) research into the influence of institutional context on TGfU implementation, Harvey, Cushion and Massa-Gonzalez (2010) suggested that the institutionalised context of a high school soccer coach's practice (e.g. a performative culture focused on winning) in the US made it difficult for him to develop his use of TGfU. Furthermore, participation cricket coaches trying to implement a TGfU approach in Roberts' (2011) study perceived the political context of their proposed intervention as challenging due to a perceived lack of resource support provided by the sport's national governing body.

Thus, contextual factors surrounding GBA implementation (for example, country of origin or institutional agenda) hold significance for teachers and coaches and the overall achievement of desired student learning outcomes. The initial and/or ongoing success of a selected GBA requires not only informed consideration of the context of implementation, but also consideration of contextual factors that were prominent in the conception of the approach.

Implementing a change in pedagogy

The challenges associated with implementing a change in pedagogy are exacerbated by what a review of post-2005 research suggests are typically short induction periods in teacher and coach GBA education programmes (see Harvey and Jarrett 2012 in press). Induction programmes offered to teachers at tertiary level are typically associated with a set unit of work, often confined to a limited period of time prior to a practicum experience. For example, research by McNeill, Fry, Wright, Tan and Rossi (2008) on the Singapore Government's mandated introduction of a games concept approach (GCA) to physical education teaching confirmed an induction period of only 18 hours prior to in-school delivery. Unsurprisingly, findings from the study suggested the need for greater emphasis on peer-teaching workshops and learning opportunities to better understand the games concept approach (GCA) in physical education teacher education (PETE) classes prior to practicum delivery. Similar findings are also reflected in studies by Wright, McNeill and Fry (2009), Wang and Ha (2009), Pearson and Webb (2010) and Pill (2011) and further support the need for more ecologically robust GBA induction and development opportunities (such as effective mentoring programmes as discussed in Wang and Ha 2012).

Feelings of insecurity and apprehension when undertaking a pedagogical change are prominent in GBA literature. In their study Casey and Dyson

(2009) suggest the need to provide school students with a short 'crash course in how to be taught this way' (p. 190) to help manage initial anxiety over a change in expectations and what can be a radically different experience for learners (Light 2013a). As noted by Nash (2009) a change in pedagogy may often be difficult to facilitate due to students' preconceived notions of traditional, formal curricula and the emphasis in certain learning environments on traditional technique-based instruction. Nevertheless, research has indicated a perceived improvement by pre-service physical education teachers in understanding GBA pedagogy when engaged in a supportive and active community of practice. The use of micro-teaching groups, peer observation and feedback expectations, access to online forums and the presence of 'community facilitators' to help 'maintain continued engagement' were all suggested by Nash (2009: 17) to help develop significant understanding of TGfU.

Furthermore, Light and Georgakis' (2007) study on pre-service primary school teachers clearly identified the potential for development in teaching confidence offered by exposure to GBAs. Their study suggested that utilisation of a GS pedagogy offered a useful means for developing generalist primary teachers' inclination and ability to teach physical education. Conclusions indicated that exposure to a GS approach when learning how to teach physical education provided pre-service generalist primary teachers with both a greater confidence to teach physical education and a greater appreciation of the value of sport and physical education provision in school. Positive perceptions of GBA induction and implementation have also been recorded in Southeast Asian contexts. Li and Cruz (2008) reported on pre-service teachers' perceptions that TGfU was a viable instruction model contributing to pupils' cognitive development and the provision of fun, whilst Wang and Ha (2009) confirmed in their study that 'the majority of pre-service teachers are likely to use TGfU in the future' (p. 407).

As the research above suggests, the opportunities and challenges associated with initiating and implementing a change in pedagogical practice are both context specific and subjective in nature. Evidence does however suggest that when pedagogical change expectations are set with appropriate support (e.g. active community of practice) in a realistic timeframe, greater appreciation and commitment to change can result.

Fidelity of approach

With the growing global appeal and use of GBAs, suggested by the ongoing international series of TGfU conferences and the expanding literature (Light 2013a), questions about fidelity of approach and the provision of ongoing GBA-related professional development opportunities have surfaced in the literature (Jarrett 2011; Harvey and Jarrett in press). Articulated verification of approaches/models used in GBA research has been limited, although a growing proportion of GBA-related research articles are now including comment on verification benchmarks used (e.g. Greco, Memmert and Morales 2010;

Harvey 2009; Harvey, Cushion, Wegis and Massa-Gonzalez 2010; Harvey, Cushion and Massa-Gonzalez 2010; Jarrett 2011; Memmert 2006, 2007). The articulation of verification procedures is important as it may help to provide practitioners with benchmark criteria to support their own implementation of GBA innovation. The research articles mentioned above have articulated the use of Metzler's 2000 and 2005 benchmarks and context-specific validation protocols to verify each GBA utilised.

While understanding that teachers and coaches can 'modify' their implementation of a GBA to suit their local context of implementation, Kirk (2011) suggests caution with the extent to which a teacher/coach can 'modify' an approach such as a GBA to its local context and still legitimately say that they are validly 'doing the approach'. An example of such modification and 'rebranding' of GBA implementation might be a teacher's/coach's simple decision to use of higher rates of questioning. What we must see from teachers and coaches is not only an espoused commitment to the particular GBA and the use of its terms, but also a practical understanding of it. As has happened with constructivist-informed teaching, teachers can pick up the language of constructivism but not practise it due to tension between its underpinning epistemology and the embedded beliefs of teachers (Light 2013a; Davis and Sumara 2003).

Developing skill

The development of learner/athlete skill outcomes has been synonymous with educational goals in physical education and sport coaching settings for generations. A focus on decontextualised skill training was a key feature of physical education and sport coaching programmes throughout the twentieth century (Kirk 2010) and arguably continues to dominate pedagogy used by physical education teachers and sports coaches today. According to Bunker and Thorpe (1986) such technique-focused programmes 'failed to take into consideration the contextual nature of games' (p. 6) and often led to an emphasis on declarative knowledge development rather than procedural knowledge development (Turner and Martinek 1999). As a fundamental principle of learning associated with the use of GBAs, skills developed in the context of game play offer the potential to expand learning opportunities beyond declarative, on-the-ball learning experiences (Light 2004; Harvey 2009), although the potential for GBAs to develop on-the-ball motor skills in game-play situations has been the focus of numerous research articles over the past two decades (for example, see Turner and Martinek 1999; Tallir *et al.* 2007; Gray, Sproule and Morgan 2009; Zhang *et al.* 2012). Arguably such research reflects the influence of the 'sports skill' approach (Kirk 2010). Literature highlighting the importance of off-the-ball movement and its relationship to skill development in and through games (see, for example, Gray and Sproule 2011) does suggest a growing appreciation of the fact that team games/sports have a higher percentage of game time when learners/athletes are engaged in off-the-ball movement. For example, Reilly and Thomas (1976) found that typically a player in soccer is in possession of the ball for less than 2 per cent of game time, suggesting that a learning approach forged from engagement in game play has significant appeal. Studies by Gray and Sproule (2011) and Harvey, Cushion, Wegis and Massa-Gonzalez (2010) provide evidence that employment of GBAs can improve participants' off-the-ball movement. The importance of developing this aspect of play was also highlighted by a coach in Light's (2004) study on sport coaches' experiences of using a GS approach.

> In a ninety minute game the ball is in play for say sixty minutes ... and each player averages at most three minutes touching the ball. So what are they doing for the rest of the game? They are running around making decisions.
>
> (participant comment in Light 2004: 120)

> Game Sense provides opportunities for enjoyment, for maximising activity, and creativity. They (players) develop an understanding of tactics of play whether they are on the ball or not.
>
> (participant comment in Light 2004: 120)

Assessment of performance

The importance of developing a player's off-the-ball movement and decision making has also been recognised in the development and validation of a number of performance assessment instruments. The Games Performance Assessment Instrument (GPAI; Mitchell, Oslin and Griffin 2006), Game Test Situations (GTS; Memmert and Roth 2003; Memmert 2006), Lee and Ward's (2009) 'supporting movement' coding instrument and the modified instrument used by Gray and Sproule (2011) can all be used to examine the contributions of off-the-ball play to both overall game performance *and* involvement. This recognition of the importance of off-the-ball movement and associated decision making should not be understated and reflects a growing acceptance in the literature that skill and tactical development is complex and relational. For example, MacPhail, Kirk and Griffin's (2008) replication of Rovegno, Nevett, Brock and Babiarz's (2001) study into 'throwing a catchable pass' emphasised the need to recognise the physical–perceptual and social–interactive elements of game play in the learning process. Thus, the need to assess knowledge-in-action as suggested by Light and Fawns (2003), or the body thinking, has justifiable importance and is central to *becoming* an intelligent games player.

Memmert (2006, 2007) and Greco *et al.*'s (2010) utilisation of Game Test Situations (GTS), which are assessment scenarios that utilise context-dependent, real-world settings that can provoke tactical solutions in ecologically valid situations, can also be adapted to use as a school physical education or sports club-appropriate assessment tool. The use of the Games Performance Evaluation Tool (G-PET) – a tool developed by Gutierrez Diaz del

Campo, Villora, Lopez and Mitchell (2011) from initial work by Nevett, Rovegno, Babiarz and McCaughtry (2001) – which allows for the examination of on- and off-the-ball technical and tactical skills as well as 'tactical context adaptation', might also be an effective tool for assessment in various learning environments.

Developing tactical awareness/cognition

A focus on the potential of GBAs to facilitate tactical transfer between games of similar classification and from practice to match scenarios is a feature of numerous post-2005 GBA studies (see Memmert and Harvey 2010; Memmert and Roth 2007; Memmert, 2006; Lee and Ward 2009; Hastie and Curtner-Smith 2006 and Harvey 2009). Such research follows on from pre-2005 studies by Mitchell and Oslin (1999), Jones and Farrow (1999) and Contreras Jordan, Garcia Lopez and Ruiz Perez (2003), which highlighted the potential for transfer between games in the same category. Memmert and Harvey's (2010) study on the identification and validation of non-specific tactical tasks in invasion games supported previous TGfU theorists' proposals about the use of GBAs to facilitate tactical transfer between different invasion games within the same category. Here the authors studied the transfer of appropriate tactical responses from small-sided, four-against-four practice scenarios to game play in soccer utilising Launder's (2001) Play Practice approach. Analysis of the data demonstrated that the intervention proved effective for 'more able' participants with regards to the percentage of appropriate tactical responses recorded during game play; a trend also observed in Memmert's 2006 study of creative thinking development between gifted and non-gifted children completing a sport enrichment programme.

Furthermore, a study by Lee and Ward (2009) showed that tactics associated with 'supportive behaviour' in a 20-lesson unit of tag rugby were able to be transferred from four-against-four instructional games to four-against-four match-play games. Such findings continue to validate the use of GBAs to develop game-play cognition, especially within both school-based curricula where the multi-sport approach to teaching often prevails as well as single sport coaching contexts where transfer of tactical development from practice to match scenarios is emphasised. It is also important to recognise, though, comments made by Harvey (2009), which highlight the potential for the negative transfer of tactical awareness and decision making from modified/conditioned games to match-play situations when the coach did not 'get the game right'.

The main focus of GBA implementation is an emphasis on game players' understanding of 'what' and 'why' to do something before a focus on 'how to do it' (Bunker and Thorpe 1986; Memmert 2010). The research discussed above supports the potential for learning to be transferred from one context to another (e.g. practice to match scenarios) and in doing so continues to validate GBA as a means of improving game-play performance.

Developing tactical intelligence/creativity

Memmert and Roth (2007) argue that 'the teaching of ball games and the measurement of its success should focus on relevant competencies that cannot much be improved upon in later training phases' (p. 1423). For games teachers and coaches this concerns the development of tactical creativity. In response, studies by Memmert (2006, 2007) and colleagues (Memmert and Roth 2007; Memmert and Harvey 2010; Greco *et al.* 2010) have focused on the assessment of athletes' tactical creativity where an emphasis is placed on attaining measures of originality (i.e. the unusualness of ideas) and flexibility (i.e. the diversity of tactical solutions offered). A better understanding and use of these constructs (typically measured in the research by 'concept-orientated expert ratings') might arguably help dissect the often complex and varied interpretations of appropriate tactical awareness progressions and help teachers and coaches facilitate achievement of one of the primary learning outcomes associated with GBA use.

The links within the research literature between the use of GBAs and the development of creative behaviour though remain prominent. For example, Memmert's (2007) study into the development of tactical creativity via an attention-broadening training programme (facilitated through the use of non-specific teaching methodologies such as those inherent with Ball School – see Rabb 2007; Memmert and Roth 2007) focused on the role of the teacher/coach and the use (or absence) of explicit tactical instruction. Results indicated that over a six-month period the attention-broadening training group improved its creative performance considerably more than the attention-narrowing training group.

Such results not only bring into focus the potential of a non-specific training programme when trying to develop players' tactical creativity, but also the quantity of instruction given to players and its impact on players' breadth of attention (Memmert 2010). This diversion or narrowing of attention is often referred to as inattentional blindness and is a phenomenon caused when a teacher/coach gives tactical instructions that narrow a player's attention to certain factors (Most, Scholl, Clifford and Simons 2005; Memmert 2006). Thus, the research suggests that the use of GBAs such as ball school and TGfU can provide greater opportunity to develop (and keep) a wide visual attention, and if a player has a wide visual attention then arguably they can be more creative (Memmert 2010).

Developing students'/athletes' higher order thinking

The promotion of higher order thinking has been both a catalyst and a goal of GBA use since a shift in pedagogical approach to games teaching and coaching arguably began in the mid-1980s. Even prior to the publication of Bunker and Thorpe's development of a 'model for the teaching of games' in 1982 (Bunker and Thorpe 1982), the work of Mahlo (1974) and Deleplace (1966) suggested a growing interest in the role of cognition within the contextualised learning of motor skills. Asking questions that (1) generate dialogue and learning and (2) provide opportunities for formulating, testing and evaluating solutions, as well as facilitate a 'debate of ideas', are now recognised as stalwarts of effective GBA implementation and offer a roadmap to engaging students/athletes in higher order thinking (Gréhaigne, Richard and Griffin 2005; Light 2013a). Yet the literature still reports on problems arising from both the effectiveness of questioning (McNeill *et al.* 2008; Harvey, Cushion and Massa-Gonzalez 2010; Evans and Light 2008; Roberts 2011; Jarrett 2011) and pedagogical content knowledge limitations (e.g. Wright *et al.* 2009; McNeill *et al.* 2008). The existence of such issues could be considered to be indirectly attributable to many teachers' and coaches' conceptual misunderstanding of GBAs and subsequent difficulty with GBA implementation. Typically, we still see teaching and coaching practice that, although planned as student centred, inherently lacks effective questioning (arguably predominantly divergent) or the facilitation of opportunities for reflection/discussion (Davis and Sumara 2003).

As Light (2013b and in Chapter 2) alludes to in his developing body of work that conceptualises GBAs as 'Positive Pedagogy', questioning is the central mechanism employed for promoting student-centred learning and a stimulant for dialogue, reflection and the conscious processing of ideas. A recent study by Vande Broek, Boen, Claessens, Feys and Ceux (2011) comparing instructional approaches to enhance tactical knowledge in volleyball found that the 'student-centered with tactical questioning' group significantly improved their tactical awareness test results when compared with the two other instructional groups (that being teacher centred and student centred without questioning). These findings highlight the importance of effective questioning within a student-centred approach to enhance the tactical decision-making process. Appropriate support and education of teachers and coaches is therefore needed in helping them develop a questioning approach, which is seen as central to effective games-based teaching/coaching.

It is also important to comment on practitioner perceptions of GBA use and related improvements in cognition, or higher order thinking, during game play. In Spain, Díaz-Cueto, Hernández-Álvarez and Castejón (2010) reported that in-service teachers implementing a 14-lesson TGfU unit of either basketball or handball noted the positive changes in pupils' decision making and tactical performance, and, in England, Jarrett's (2011) study on perceptions of a change to Game Sense pedagogy identified a range of cognitive learning opportunities provided to participants through the use of Game Sense.

Student motivation

As Mandigo, Holt, Anderson and Sheppard (2008) state, 'one way to improve children's engagement in PE is to increase their intrinsic motivation' (p. 408). Results from their study into children's motivational experiences following

TGfU-autonomy supportive games lessons found high levels of motivation in pupils in Grades 4–7. Girls reported higher levels of enjoyment, perceived autonomy support and optimal challenge whereas boys reported higher perceived competence levels. Similar results were found by Jones, Marshall and Peters (2010) in their study into the intrinsic benefits of TGfU reported by nine to 13 year olds after a unit of work. Gray *et al.*'s (2009) study into the motivational climate exhibited by students when taught team invasion games using a GBA further reflected a positive motivational response from students, and McNeill, Fry and Hairil's (2011) study into the use of the games concept approach (GCA) to generate motivational experiences for children in elementary school physical education found results that supported the use of a GCA to motivate participation. And although empirical research into motivational climate generated by use of GBAs in club/elite sport settings is limited, Evans and Light (2008) highlighted in their study on rugby coaches' implementation of Game Sense pedagogy that players had experienced greater motivation when engaged in autonomy supportive coaching environments. Evans and Light (2008) also commented on how GBAs had the potential to develop positive coach/player relationships based on a more equal distribution of power.

Developing positive affective response/engagement

Research and commentary on the development of learning in the affective domain has continued to be recognised in GBA literature (e.g. Allison and Thorpe 1997; McKeen, Webb and Pearson 2006; Jones *et al.* 2010; Jones and Cope 2010; Curry 2012; Stoltz and Pill 2012). The area of teacher and learner perceptions of GBAs has received particular empirical attention (e.g. Rossi *et al.* 2007; Light and Evans 2010). As Light (2010) suggests, the nature of affective experience is an important dimension of sport participation. However, research into personal and social development as well as an exploration of the cross-domain potential of GBA implementation (e.g. relationship between psychomotor, cognitive and affective domains of learning) is still limited. Harvey and Jarrett (in press) note the holistic view of learning within games still lacks prominence in GBA literature, although recent texts by Light (2013a) and Harvey and Light (2013) begin to expand commentary on the potential for GBA use to develop personal, social and ethical dimensions of learning.

Conclusion

This chapter identifies recent trends in GBA literature that continue to inform our practices as physical education teachers and sports coaches. The influence of context on the conception of different types of GBA was recognised (e.g. the games concept approach in Singapore by Rossi *et al.* 2007) as well as the influence of context on aspects of implementation (e.g. Roberts 2011). Practitioner anxiety (see Casey and Dyson, 2009) and the limited length of induction programmes were highlighted as a challenge for physical education teachers and coaches when trying to implement a change in pedagogy (e.g. McNeill *et al.* 2008), although research from Light and Georgakis (2007) reported on the potential for development in teaching confidence offered by exposure to GBAs. Questions about fidelity of approach and the provision of ongoing GBA-related professional development opportunities were discussed (see Harvey and Jarrett in press) along with opportunities for skill development offered within contextualised game play synonymous with GBAs (e.g. Harvey, et al. 2010). A range of performance assessment options utilised in GBA research were presented (e.g. Lee and Ward 2009; Memmert 2007) and research exploring the impact of GBAs on the development of tactical awareness and creativity was identified (e.g. Memmert and Harvey 2010). The potential for GBAs to develop both pupils'/athletes' higher order thinking skills (e.g. Light 2013a) and motivation (Jones *et al.* 2010) was recognised as were links made between GBAs and the potential for development of learning in the affective domain (e.g. Curry 2012).

What does the future hold?

The future of GBA implementation in teaching and coaching environments begins with reflection on current practice. Working with pupils and athletes in dynamic environments to enhance the achievement of desired learning outcomes requires an informed understanding of the empirical research and theoretical commentary associated with GBA implementation and pedagogical change. This chapter provides an overview of recent research trends in GBA literature to help games practitioners reflect on the various benefits and challenges associated with GBA implementation and to inform future use. Empirical developments in pedagogical function should provide practitioners with dialogue opportunities to address implementation and support issues. This is especially important in light of a growing awareness of performative climates in our physical education and sport team environments that are dominated by the need to measure success only via results. Further GBA research is needed though, especially in the areas of context-appropriate performance assessment, implications for GBA implementation in coaching contexts, longitudinal research designs and the breadth of research methodologies used to generate information about subjective experiences of learning with GBA.

Discussion questions

1. The potential for GBA use to develop pupils' cross-domain learning is synonymous with practitioners' reasoning for implementation. What are the key aspects of GBA implementation that promote holistic learning?

2. What does the literature suggest about how teachers can ensure learning is maximised when using GBAs?
3. Outline one or two key areas of GBA research identified in the chapter that need to be conducted. With a colleague discuss possible research designs for each of the key areas identified that expand the breadth of research methodologies currently associated with GBA research.

References

Allison, S. and Thorpe, R. (1997) 'A comparison of the effectiveness of two approaches to teaching games within physical education, a skills approach versus a games for understanding approach', *The British Journal of Education*, 28(3): 9–13.

Bunker, D. and Thorpe, R. (1982) 'A model for the teaching of games in secondary school', *Bulletin of Physical Education*, 18: 5–8.

Bunker, D. and Thorpe, R. (1986) 'The curriculum model', in R. Thorpe, D. Bunker and L. Almond (ed.) *Rethinking Games Teaching*, Loughborough: University of Technology.

Casey, A. and Dyson, B. (2009) 'The implementation of models-based practice in physical education through action research', *European Physical Education Review*, 15(2): 175–199.

Contreras Jordan, O.R., Garcia Lopez, L.M. and Ruiz Perez, L.M. (2003) 'Transfer of procedural knowledge from invasion games to hockey' (abstract), paper presented at the 2nd International Conference: Teaching Sport and Physical Education for Understanding, 11–14 December, the University of Melbourne, Australia.

Curry, C. (2012) 'Why Public Primary Schools need specialist PE teachers', *ACHPER Healthy and Active Magazine*, 19(2): 17–19.

Davis, B. and Sumara, D. (2003) 'Why aren't they getting this? Working through the regressive myths of constructivist pedagogy', *Teaching Education*, 14: 123–140.

Deleplace, R. (1966) *Le Rugby*, Paris: Colin-Bourrelier.

Díaz-Cueto, M., Hernández-Álvarez, J. and Castejón, F. (2010) 'Teaching Games for Understanding to in-service physical education teachers: Rewards and barriers regarding the changing model of teaching sport', *Journal of Teaching in Physical Education*, 29: 378–398.

Dismore, H. and Bailey, R. (2010) '"It's been a bit of a rocky start": attitudes toward physical education following transition', *Physical Education and Sport Pedagogy*, 15 (2): 175–191.

Evans, J. and Light, R. (2008) 'Coach development through collaborative action research: A rugby coach's implementation of Game Sense', *Asian Journal of Exercise and Sports Science*, 5(1): 31–37.

Gray, S. and Sproule, J. (2011) 'Developing pupils' performance in team invasion games', *Physical Education and Sport Pedagogy*, 16(1): 15–32.

Gray, S., Sproule, J. and Morgan, K. (2009) 'Teaching team invasion games and motivational climate', *European Physical Education Review*, 15(1): 65–89.

Greco, P., Memmert, D. and Morales, J.C.P. (2010) 'The effect of deliberate play on tactical performance in basketball', *Perceptual and Motor Skills*, 110: 849–856.

Gréhaigne, J.-F., Richard, J.-F. and Griffin, L. (2005) *Teaching and Learning Team Sports and Games*, New York: Routledge Falmer.

Gréhaigne, J.-F., Wallian, N. and Godbout, P. (2005) 'Tactical-decision learning model and students' practices', *Quest*, 47, 490–505.

Griffin, L. and Butler, J. (eds) (2005) *Teaching Games for Understanding: Theory, Research and Practice*, Champaign, IL: Human Kinetics.

Gutierrez Diaz del Campo, D., Villora, S.G., Lopez, L.M.G. and Mitchell, S. (2011) 'Differences in decision-making development between expert and novice invasion game players', *Perceptual and Motor Skills*, 112(3): 871–888.

Harvey, S. (2009) 'A study of interscholastic soccer players perceptions of learning with Game Sense', *Asian Journal of Exercise and Sports Science*, 6(1): 1–10.

Harvey, S. and Jarrett, K. (in press) 'A review of the game-centred approaches to teaching and coaching literature since 2006', *Physical Education and Sport Pedagogy.*

Harvey, S. and Light, R. (eds) (2013) *Ethics in Youth Sport: Policy and Pedagogical Applications*, London and New York: Routledge.

Harvey, S., Cushion, C. and Massa-Gonzalez, A. (2010) 'Learning a new method: Teaching Games for Understanding in the coaches' eyes', *Physical Education and Sport Pedagogy*, 15(4): 361–382.

Harvey, S., Cushion, C., Wegis, H. and Massa-Gonzalez, A. (2010) 'Teaching games for understanding in American high-school soccer: a quantitative data analysis using the game performance assessment instrument', *Physical Education and Sport Pedagogy*, 15(1): 29–54.

Hastie, P. and Curtner-Smith, M. (2006) 'Influence of a hybrid Sport Education—Teaching Games for Understanding unit on one teacher and his students', *Physical Education and Sport Pedagogy*, 11(1): 1–27.

Jarrett, K. (2011) 'Undergraduate sport students' perceptions of a change to Game Sense pedagogy', *Asian Journal of Exercise & Sport Science*, 4(1): 1–17.

Jones, C. and Farrow, D. (1999) 'The transfer of strategic knowledge: A test of the games classification curriculum model', *Bulletin of Physical Education*, 9: 41–45.

Jones, R. and Cope, E. (2010) 'Thinking (and feeling) outside the box: Affect and the teaching of games', *Physical Education Matters*, 5(2): 16–19.

Jones, R., Marshall, S. and Peters, D. (2010) 'Can we play a game now? The intrinsic benefits of TGfU', *European Journal of Physical and Health Education*, 4(2): 57–63.

King, W. and Ho, Y. (2009) 'Western philosophy and Eastern practice in physical education – A study of the games teaching approach in Sydney and Hong Kong', *International Journal of Physical Education*, 46(3): 28–38.

Kirk, D. (2010) *Physical Education Futures*, London: Routledge.

——(2011) 'The normalization of innovation, models-based practice, and sustained curriculum renewal in PE', presentation at the AIESEP Conference, 23 June, Limerick, Ireland.

Kröger, C. and Roth, K. (1999) *Ballschule*, Frankfurt, Germany: Hoffman.

Launder, A. (2001) *Play Practice: The Games Approach to Teaching and Coaching Sports*, Champaign, IL: Human Kinetics.

Lee, M-A. and Ward, P. (2009) 'Generalization of tactics in tag rugby from practice to games in middle school physical education', *Physical Education and Sport Pedagogy*, 14(2): 189–207.

Li, C. and Cruz, A. (2008) 'Pre-service PE teachers' occupational socialization experiences of teaching games for understanding', *New Horizons in Education*, 56(3): 20–30.

Light, R. (2004) 'Coaches' experiences of games sense: opportunities and challenges', *Physical Education & Sport Pedagogy*, 9(2): 115–131.

——(2010) 'A cross-cultural study on meaning and the nature of children's experiences in Australian and French swimming clubs', *Asia Pacific Journal of Health, Sport and Physical Education*, 1(3): 37–43.

——(2013a) *Game Sense: Pedagogy for Performance, Participation and Enjoyment*, London: Routledge.

——(2013b) 'O Game Sense como pedagogia positiva para treinar o desporto juvenil [Game Sense as positive pedagogy for coaching youth sport]', in C. Congalves (ed.) *Educação Pelo Desporto e Associativismo Desportiva* [*Youth Sport: Between Education and Performance*], Instituto do Desporto de Portugal/IDP (national institute of sports): Lisbon, Portugal, pp. 111–131.

Light, R. and Evans, J. (2010) 'The impact of Game Sense pedagogy on Australian rugby coaches' practice: a question of pedagogy', *Physical Education and Sport Pedagogy*, 15(2): 103–115.

Light, R. and Fawns, R. (2003) 'Knowing the game: Integrating speech and action in games teaching through TGfU', *Quest*, 55: 161–175.

Light, R. and Georgakis, S. (2007) 'The effect of Game Sense pedagogy on primary school pre-service teachers' attitudes to teaching physical education', *ACHPER Healthy Lifestyles Journal*, 54(1): 24–28.

Light, R. and Tan, S. (2006) 'Culture, embodied experience and teachers' development of TGfU in Australia and Singapore', *European Physical Education Review*, 12(1): 99–117.

MacPhail, A., Kirk, D. and Griffin, L. (2008) 'Throwing and catching as relational skills in game play: Situated learning in a modified game unit', *Journal of Teaching in Physical Education*, 27:100–115.

Mahlo, F. (1974) *Acte Tactique en Jeu*, Paris: Vigot.

Mandigo, J., Holt, H., Anderson, A. and Sheppard, J. (2008) 'Children's motivational experiences following autonomy-supportive games lessons', *European Physical Education Review*, 14(3): 407–425.

McKeen, K., Webb, P. and Pearson, P. (2006) 'Promoting physical activity through teaching games for understanding in undergraduate teacher education', in *Proceedings of AIESEP, 2005 World Congress, 17–20 November*, Lisbon: Universidade Técnica de Lisboa, pp. 251–258.

McNeill, M., Fry, J. and Md Hairil, J. B. (2011) 'Motivational climate in Games Concept lessons', *ICHPER–SD Journal of Research in Health, Physical Education, Recreation, Sport & Dance*, 6(1): 34–39.

McNeill, M., Fry, J. M., Wright, S., Tan, C. and Rossi, T. (2008) 'Structuring time and questioning to achieve tactical awareness in games lessons', *Physical Education and Sport Pedagogy*, 13(3): 231–249.

Memmert, D. (2006) 'Developing creative thinking in a gifted sport enrichment program and the crucial role of attention processes', *High Ability Studies*, 17: 101–115.

——(2007) 'Can creativity be improved by an attention-broadening training program? – An exploratory study focusing on team sports', *Creativity Research Journal*, 19: 281–291.

——(2010) 'Development of creativity in the scope of the TGfU approach', in J. Butler and L. Griffin (eds) *More Teaching Games for Understanding*, Champaign, IL: Human Kinetics, pp. 231–244.

Memmert, D. and Harvey, S. (2010) 'Identification of non-specific tactical tasks in invasion games', *Physical Education and Sport Pedagogy*, 15(3): 287–385.

Memmert, D. and Roth, K. (2003) 'Individualtaktische Leistungsdiagnostik im Sportspiel' [Diagnostics of individual tactical performance in sports games], *Spektrum der Sportwissenschaft* [Spectrum of sport science], 15: 44–70.

——(2007) 'The effects of non-specific and specific concepts on tactical creativity in team ball sports', *Journal of Sports Sciences*, 25(12): 1423–1432.

Metzler, M. (2000) *Instructional Models for Physical Education*, Needham Heights, MA: Allyn & Bacon.

——(2005) *Instructional Models for Physical Education*, Scottsdale, AZ: Holcomb Hathway

Mitchell, S. A. and Oslin, J. L. (1999) 'An investigation of tactical transfer in net games', *European Journal of Physical Education*, 4: 162–172.

Mitchell, S., Oslin, J. and Griffin, L. (2006) *Teaching Sport Concepts and Skills: A Tactical Games Approach* (second edition), Champaign, IL: Human Kinetics.

Most, S., Scholl, B., Clifford, E. and Simons, D. (2005) 'What you see is what you set: Sustained inattentional blindness and the capture of awareness', *Psychological Review*, 112: 217–242.

Nash, M. (2009) 'Using the idea of "communities of practice" and TGfU to develop physical education pedagogy among primary generalist pre-service teachers', *Asian Journal of Exercise and Sports Science*, 6(1): 15–21.

Nevett, M., Rovegno, I., Babiarz, M. and McCaughtry, N. (2001) 'Changes in basic tactics and motor skills in an invasion-type game after a 12-lesson unit of instruction', *Journal of Teaching in Physical Education*, 20(4): 352–369.

Pearson, P. and Webb, P. (2010) 'The integration of TGfU into the secondary school physical education curriculum – how successful has it been?', in A. Rendimiento, (ed.) *Proceedings of the AIESEP Conference*, 26–29 October, La Coruña, Portugal, pp. 1004–1015.

Pill, S. (2011) 'Teacher engagement with teaching games for understanding – game sense in physical education', *Journal of Physical Education and Sport*, 11(2): 115–123.

Rabb, M. (2007) 'Think SMART, not hard – A review of teaching decision making in sport from an ecological rationality perspective', *Physical Education & Sport Pedagogy*, 12(1): 1–22.

Reilly, T. and Thomas, V. (1976) 'A motion analysis of work-rate in different positional roles in professional football match-play', *Journal of Human Movement Studies*, 2: 87–97.

Roberts, S. (2011) 'Teaching Games for Understanding: the difficulties and challenges experienced by participation cricket coaches', *Physical Education & Sport Pedagogy*, 16(1): 33–48.

Rossi, T., Fry, J., McNeill, M. and Tan, C. (2007) 'The Games Concept Approach (GCA) as a mandated practice: views of Singaporean teachers', *Sport, Education & Society*, 12(1): 93–111.

Rovegno, I., Nevett, M., Brock, S. and Babiarz, M. (2001) 'Teaching and learning basic invasion-game tactics in 4th grade: A descriptive study from situated and constraints theoretical perspectives', *Journal of Teaching in Physical Education,* 20(4): 370–388.

Stoltz, S. and Pill, S. (2012) 'Making sense of Game Sense', *ACHPER Active and Healthy Magazine*, 19(1): 5–8.

Tallir, I., Lenoir, M., Valcke, M. and Musch, E. (2007) 'Do alternative instructional approaches result in different game performance learning outcomes? Authentic assessment in varying conditions', *International Journal of Sport Psychology*, 38(3): 263–282.

Turner, A. and Martinek, T. (1999) 'An investigation into teaching games for under-standing: Effects on skill, knowledge, and game play', *Research Quarterly for Exercise and Sport*, 70(3): 286–296.

Wang, C. and Ha, A. (2009) 'Pre-service teachers' perception of Teaching Games for Understanding: A Hong Kong perspective', *European Physical Education Review*, 15(3): 407–429.

——(2012) 'Mentoring in TGfU teaching: Mutual engagement of pre-service teachers, cooperating teachers and university supervisors', *European Physical Education Review*, 18(1): 47–61.

Wright, S., McNeill, M. and Fry, J. (2009) 'The tactical approach to teaching games from teaching, learning and mentoring perspectives', *Sport, Education & Society*, 14(2): 223–244.

Vande Broek, G., Boen, F., Claessens, M., Feys, J. and Ceux, T. (2011) 'Comparison of three instructional approaches to enhance tactical knowledge in volleyball among university students', *Journal of Teaching in Physical Education*, 30: 375–392.

Zhang, P., Ward, P., Li, W., Sutherland, S. and Goodway, J. (2012) 'Effects of Play Practice on teaching table tennis skills', *Journal of Teaching in Physical Education*, 31: 71–85.

7 'Girls get going'

Using Game Sense to promote sport participation amongst adolescent girls in rural and regional contexts

Amanda Mooney and Meghan Casey

Introduction

Albert Einstein once defined the term 'insanity' as doing the same thing over and over again and expecting a different outcome. Whilst we are not advocating that attempts to address issues surrounding girls' physical activity (PA) participation are in vain or that all attempts have been similar in nature, we do acknowledge that these concerns, and research conceived to address these issues, are not particularly new. In fact, many authors have discussed the reported decline in PA participation by adolescent girls (and the reasons for this) both within Australian contexts (Australian Bureau of Statistics 2011; Garrett 2004; Slater and Tiggemann 2010; Wright, Macdonald and Groom 2003) and internationally (Flintoff and Scraton 2001; O'Donovan and Kirk 2008). More recently, similar trends have been highlighted in research conducted in Australian rural and regional contexts (Barnett *et al.* 2002; Casey, Eime, Payne and Harvey 2009).

As such, a growing number of studies have sought to reverse this trend with interventions aimed at both school and community settings, yet, only modest improvements in PA participation have been noted (see, for example, Sallis *et al.* 1997; Webber *et al.* 2008). As others have argued, these outcomes are not particularly surprising given relatively little work has addressed issues surrounding transitions between school and community sporting clubs (Eime and Payne 2009) or the localized social and cultural discourses that are active in shaping adolescent girls' physically active identities (Garrett 2004; Mooney, Casey and Smyth 2012). In response, the 'Girls get going' or 'Triple G' programme reported on in this chapter was designed to consider many of these issues as they apply to adolescent girls who live in rural and regional areas in Victoria, Australia. More specifically, it attempted to achieve this through fostering industry linkages with Tennis Victoria, Football Federation Victoria (soccer) and the YMCA as community leisure providers. In particular, an explicit intent of this programme was the promotion of PA and wellbeing amongst rural- and regional-living adolescent girls (see Casey *et al.* in press).

A key feature of this programme was the collaborative development of the physical education (PE) curriculum that drew on 'Game Sense' pedagogy for the delivery of a six-week unit in tennis and soccer that was linked with a community sports-club transition programme. Here, after Light (2013), we intentionally use capital letters to distinguish between 'Game Sense' as pedagogy and the broader acceptance of 'game sense' as a practical understanding (or sense) of the game. Further, we recognize Game Sense pedagogy as one of many 'game-based approaches' (GBA) that could be helpful in the teaching of sports and team games and found that the tennis and football coaches involved in our study regularly used this term to describe recent innovations in their coaching practice. The collaboration between community-based sports coaches, PE teachers, academics and girls (aged 14–16) was considered to be a rather unique (and perhaps challenging) approach, which will be discussed further herein. Additionally, the actual implementation of the programme sought to draw on the expertise of both community-based sports coaches (in tennis and soccer) and PE teachers through a cooperative delivery model during timetabled PE lessons in eight rural or regional school sites (across six communities) in Victoria.

In previous attempts to foster interest in these sports, state sporting organizations (SSOs) have typically offered 'come and try' days or 'introductory' sessions within their sporting clubs; or alternatively they have provided school-based activity sessions usually delivered by sports coaches or community club representatives. As Casey and colleagues (in press: 2) outline, based on work by Eime and Payne (2009) in the state of Victoria, almost 90 per cent of SSOs had used the school setting for the delivery of sports programmes aimed at exposing and attracting children and youth to their sport. Yet, many of these school-based programmes failed to provide transition opportunities or links between what occurred in the school setting and the opportunities that existed for participation in community sporting clubs, and this, Eime and Payne (2009) argue, is important if the intended objective of promoting community-based sports participation is to be realized.

In the school setting these sessions are typically delivered through the PE or sport education curriculum yet relatively little empirical work has considered the ways in which PE teachers and sports coaches are 'positioned' within, and by, these approaches. Given that teachers and coaches have significant influence over the ways in which adolescent girls receive and respond to school-based PA sessions (Humbert 2006; Luke and Sinclair 1991) we argue that the positioning of teachers and coaches is a key aspect of the provision of such sessions. This is especially so when consideration is given to how school-based PA sites (through PE or sport education) are charged with the responsibility of developing competence and confidence in students to pursue an active lifestyle in adulthood (Capel, Hayes, Katene and Velija 2009).

The purpose of this chapter is therefore to offer a reflexive account of this collaborative approach to programme development by drawing on the expertise of the various stakeholders (sports coaches, academics, teachers and students). We begin by examining some of the pedagogic assumptions that informed the adoption of Game Sense pedagogy in the development of this curriculum with a particular focus on its potential for girls' PE and continue with a brief overview of the project methodology. We then discuss some emerging trends from process evaluation data and consider these in light of their implications for practice. In much of our analyses of interviews with tennis and football (soccer) coaches, PE teachers and female students as programme participants from each of the school/community settings, we draw on Foucauldian poststructuralist approaches to explore the ways in which dominant discourse power relations shaped approaches to, and experiences of, the Triple G programme.

Girls, physical activity and sport participation in rural and regional contexts – potential for 'Game Sense' approaches?

In earlier papers we have argued that opportunities for rural- and regional-living adolescent girls to be physically active usually exist in the form of school-based PE and sport, organized community sport and unstructured PA or leisure (Casey *et al.* 2009; Mooney *et al.* 2012). As such, we believe that any intervention designed to enhance PA participation and wellbeing more broadly needs to provide connections between each of these settings. Twenty years ago Tinning and Fitzclarence (1992) acknowledged this in their argument that there was a crisis in Australian secondary school PE. This crisis was 'evident in, among other things, the fact that school physical education is irrelevant or boring for many adolescents. The curriculum does not excite or stimulate adolescents who outside of school live in … a postmodern youth culture' (p. 287). Yet, ironically, Tinning and Fitzclarence pointed out that many youth in their study considered PA as important to them outside of the school context. In essence, they argued that a significant disjuncture existed between what PE offered and the types of physical activities popularized by youth culture. Further, they argued that PE teachers had perhaps misunderstood the perceived apathy of their students. In recent work that seeks to continue this dialogue, Gard and colleagues reflect on how, 'it wasn't that young people were lazy; it was that teachers failed to appreciate the cultural shifts that were occurring outside their classrooms' (Gard, Hickey-Moodey and Enright 2012: 3). Both of these contributions seem to speak to the influence of institutional and cultural discourses that young people draw on in their (re)construction of particular identities and social practices connected with sport, PE and wider PA participation (Mooney *et al.* 2012).

A rich collection of work now exists to examine the influence of socio-cultural discourses on adolescent girls' PA participation. For example, in her study of Canadian secondary schools, Olafson (2002) identified PE as a site of resistance for adolescent girls. In particular she cites a curriculum (activities and their instruction) based upon male-defined standards of power and strength and a school culture that emphasized dominant constructions of femininity as significant factors shaping adolescent girls' participation levels. Similarly, Azzarito (2009) in her study of two public high schools in the United States reports on a desire to conform to dominant identity positions, the 'cheerleader' and the 'slender girl', as significant in shaping participation patterns. In her work with Australian young women, Garrett (2004) discusses how, for her participants, physical education experiences usually centre on competition, individualism and a reliance on games and team sport in which 'more often than not boys were in control of the games and ... excelled ... perpetuating hierarchal arrangements around gender in the wider society' (p. 228).

Collectively, these contributions point to the ways in which dominant discourses around femininity (and gender more broadly), operate in PE settings to limit the ways in which adolescent girls can think of themselves as physically active (Mooney *et al*. 2012). And while the contributions identified above have been limited to the influence of gendered discourses, this is not to suggest that these are the only influential discourses to shape adolescent girls' notions of physical activity. Rather (given the scope of this paper) it is to demonstrate the discursive effects that dominant, taken-for-granted assumptions can have on identity formation – in this case a 'physically active' identity.

Elsewhere we have argued that sport is a culturally valorized institution in rural and regional areas and that for many adolescents participation in or (self) exclusion from popular sporting clubs – such as the football–netball club – appears to influence how adolescent girls view themselves in terms of a physically active identity (Mooney *et al*. 2012). For many of our participants, discussions around how these constructions were shaped nearly always commenced with the girls commenting on the nature of the sport or leisure pursuits they were engaged with. Perhaps most alarmingly, given the privileged position that traditional (gendered) sporting activities have in the school PE curriculum, it appears that many adolescent girls arrive at the PE classroom with strongly entrenched ideas about their own physical ability with respect to different activities – and this appears to shape their attitudes towards, and participation in, PE and sport classes. For example, given small (and often declining) population numbers in many of these rural/regional community settings, girls often spoke of a heightened sense of surveillance and visibility that was difficult to escape in the community, and which followed them into the school setting. As a result the boundaries that may be able to be drawn around different 'physically active' identities in various contexts become somewhat blurred in these rural and small regional communities. In short, the same 'physically active' girls seem to dominate participation in community sports clubs and school-based PE and sport, and those who do not consider themselves as 'sporty' tend to participate in unstructured PA or less 'popular' activities or failed to participate in any form of regular PA at all – and everyone knew about it!

So, returning to the focus of this chapter, we believed that this curriculum intervention needed to 'look' quite different to previous school-based versions of tennis, football (soccer) and lifestyle PA to address girls' preconceived notions of their own competence in these activities. As Kirk (2010) argues, students have regularly told researchers of their dissatisfaction with (or the design flaws of) dominant forms of physical education. In particular, traditional 'command-orientated' and 'teacher/coach directed' pedagogies, often connected with competitive team sports, tend to exacerbate 'masculine' approaches to pedagogy (Light and Kentel 2010) and it is possible that this could act to further alienate adolescent girls from PE engagement. As Gard *et al.* (2012: 10) comment:

> These design flaws are so serious that they cause some young people to fake a variety of illnesses and injuries in order to avoid physical education, and others to avoid out-of-school physical activity because of negative experiences of being physically active they have had in school. It is one thing to listen to student voices but quite another to decipher their implications for practice.

In attempting to address this challenge, and led by the (perceived) innovations in sports coaching in soccer and tennis, we were drawn to the possibilities that a Game Sense approach might offer in this context. Light (2013) suggests that relatively little attention has been 'paid to the larger cultural and social contexts or fields within which learning environments are constructed' (p. 9) in the teaching games for understanding (TGfU) literature, and contends that Game Sense pedagogy offers potential for this. Originating from the work of Bunker and Thorpe (1982), Game Sense as an Australian iteration of TGfU is grounded in a constructivist approach to learning (Light 2013). As Light (2013: 25) argues, these variations 'sit upon the same philosophical, ontological and epistemological assumptions' as approaches such as 'situated learning theory' (Lave and Wenger 1991) amongst others. In essence, what these approaches to learning espouse is that learning is an *active process* of knowledge construction (Rovegno and Dolly 2006) and that social interactions provide the contexts for this learning. Further, Light (2013) points out that this approach can empower teachers and coaches in their practice. He contends that through a Game Sense approach, teachers and coaches can 'understand learning and learners, maximize learning opportunities for them and critically reflect upon their own practice in an ongoing process of developing and refining their teaching and coaching' (p. 26). In describing this pedagogical approach, Light (2013: 48) argues that:

> At its most basic level taking a Game Sense approach involves designing a game or sequence of games to achieve particular outcomes, asking questions to stimulate thinking and reflection, and ensuring that there are opportunities for group discussion, collaboration and the formulation of ideas/solutions that are tested and evaluated.

The remainder of this chapter seeks to provide a reflexive account of the trials, tribulations and key learning from this collaborative approach to the design and implementation of the school-based curriculum component of a larger intervention for the sports of tennis and football (soccer).

The study

This chapter reports on data collected as part of the process evaluation of a much larger longitudinal mixed-methodology study, designed to promote PA and wellbeing amongst rural and regional living adolescent girls (for further detail see Casey *et al.* in press). The curriculum component of this intervention was designed collaboratively between community sports coaches and PE academics after a six-month ethnographic fieldwork phase in seven secondary schools (from six communities) across the state of Victoria, Australia. Although our approach to this preliminary work was not to conduct 'ethnographies' per se, we employed ethnographic approaches that included classroom observations of girls in PA contexts, and semi-structured group and individual conversations with both teachers (n = 25) and girls aged approximately 15 to 16 years (n = 138) to enhance our understanding of the contextual factors that shaped girls' participation in PA. We considered this an important undertaking prior to the development of a curriculum intervention, for as Gard and colleagues (2012: 8) suggest: 'curriculum policy and pedagogical practices, need to be more attuned to youth voices'.

The key findings from this ethnographic work were discussed collaboratively with sports coaches and used to inform the development of a teaching resource manual (Mooney, Casey, Payne and Telford 2011) and programme for implementation. This manual was used in professional development sessions conducted collaboratively by PE academics and tennis and football sports coaches that sought to familiarize teachers with the intentions of the programme and the Game Sense pedagogy that underpinned the lessons. Following these sessions the programme was implemented during the 2011 school year. A detailed process evaluation was then conducted to explore how the programme was received by adolescent girls and to determine if any improvements in PA participation could be attributed to programme involvement.

Participants

As part of the process evaluation, 29 PE teachers from seven intervention schools participated in focus group discussions that sought to understand their experience of implementing the programme. Further, community football (soccer) coaches (n = seven) and tennis coaches (n = six) who were involved in the cooperative delivery of the Triple G school football and tennis programme were interviewed about their experiences in the school setting. Finally, a total of 125 female students from seven secondary schools participated in 22 focus group discussions with approximately eight to ten students in each (Year 7 n = 52; Year 8 n = 39; Year 9 n = 34). These discussions focused on the girls' experiences of the programme during the 2011 school year. The data was transcribed verbatim and pseudonyms assigned to protect the anonymity of participants before being collaboratively coded into emergent themes using a constant comparative method (Patton 2002). Given this large data set, and the scope of this paper, data predominantly collected from the teachers and sports coaches are discussed herein.

Data analysis

Drawing on poststructuralist perspectives and the work of Foucault (1972, 1977, 1983) in particular, analyses were concerned with the workings of discourse and power to examine the conditions under which some statements were made, and others not, about participants' experiences in the Triple G programme. Further, this lens allowed us to consider how the workings of discourse and power in context influenced the 'positioning' of both teachers and coaches in the Triple G lessons. As Wright (2006) argues, analysis of discourse can reveal workings of power that act to normalize certain behaviours, practices or ways of being. Specifically this analysis sought to understand and trouble some of the taken-for-granted assumptions that appeared to underpin sports coaches and PE teachers' approaches to Game Sense pedagogy throughout the Triple G programme, and to consider the factors that shaped adolescent girls' experiences with, and responses to, this curriculum.

Learning from the field

Shared understandings? – acknowledging the limitations of terminology in collaborations

In the introductory section of this chapter we mentioned three points to which we will now return. First, that we had perhaps assumed key stakeholders, particularly coaches and teachers, would have shared understandings of terminology such as Game Sense (given their familiar use of the term) and that we had possibly underestimated the implications of diverse perspectives in the collaborative curriculum writing process. Second, we mentioned that we intended to provide a reflexive account of this process and third, that we were interested in the ways in which teachers and coaches were 'positioned' through a cooperative delivery model. In considering the notion of 'reflexivity', Webster (2008: 65) suggests that this term has been 'relied upon as a kind of talisman' in social science research to convey a sense of 'truthfulness'. Yet as Webster points out, consensus about what this actually means is far from ubiquitous. He states: '[T]he term "reflexivity" remains poorly defined. No one *really* knows what reflexivity means in the work of others, even if they claim to know what it means within their own' (Webster 2008: 65). In this paper we adopt the term 'reflexivity' to acknowledge that it is not always possible to separate the relationship between the researcher and the research and to foreground the importance of a central and visible position of the researcher in this process. Further, after Mordal-Moen and Green (2012), we consider the potential of reflexivity, employed in its strongest sense, as a process that necessitates continual reviewing and reconstructing taken-for-granted assumptions about PE, sport, pedagogy and education itself.

In this sense, we return to our first point about the importance of shared understandings in a collaborative curriculum writing exercise. Despite literature that demonstrates differing philosophical orientations that underpin the approaches of teachers and coaches to pedagogy (Green 2002; Light 2013; Tinning 2010) we perhaps underestimated a presumed starting point in understanding the term 'Game Sense'. In conversations with coaches this language was regularly drawn on, which we assumed was the result of discourses operating in coaching circles to position 'Game Sense' as 'the' new innovation in coaching pedagogy. Tom, a football coach, explains:

> Everything is Game Sense now, before it was all drills – one person stands here and another there and you pass to each other, backwards and forwards ... You don't do that in a game so spending lots of time training to pass like that, if you played soccer like that the ball doesn't go anywhere. So you spend so much time in a session doing that but we never do it in a game, there are no decisions being made and gee I'm really good at passing straight back, wow, no good. The other one is running through cones, well there are no cones on a soccer pitch ... so why are we doing it now? In a game of football, it's not I'm going to run here, there, and that, it's free, it's decisions that are made instantly. In Game Sense you're developing your technical skills in a game environment but you are also making tactical decisions, doing decision making which are game-based decisions.

Similarly, Rob discusses this in the context of tennis.

> I told the coaches, no trolleys today guys. It was like, what? I said no you're not allowed to take your trolley out, all I want you to do is take a bucket of balls out for your court, the kids have to do it all themselves, give them a task and away you go. They came back to me and said they had so much fun with it ... You need a more indirect way as opposed to the coach going out with a direct approach, they have to learn to understand if the ball comes on this side you hit a forehand with straight strings to get it back into play rather than worrying about if it is the right technique first up ... If you've got girls from say 12 to 15 years do some instruction but at the end of the day make it so they are actually playing something that's interesting ... they get thrown to the wolves a bit with the old style so you've got to implement a different strategy.
>
> (Rob, tennis)

In the above accounts there is evidence to suggest a commitment to a pedagogical approach that seeks to develop the learners' understanding of performing skills in context and some consideration of the tactics and strategies that enhance game participation. Yet, as we worked with more coaches, it became apparent that there were varied degrees to which they subscribed to the pedagogic intentions of a Game Sense approach as illustrated in the comments below.

> Ok, first we have to look at a Game Sense program. Not so much 'coaching' but they are playing modified games and they are doing modified drills to improve their games and have an understanding of that and then they will see improvement in their skill level. Improvement in their skill level will come the longer they are there because they are starting to learn to play competition and learn defeat as well as what it is like to win. The good old days there was a lot of line ups and harder drills, I guess, hit a couple of shots and go to the back of the line ... those days are gone which is good because it is a lot more about rallying, *backwards and forwards ... then you get technique.*
>
> (Ben, tennis)

> In community coaching we don't want a coach who stops the game every three minutes and tells off the players, so just be more of a facilitator and make activities a bit more fun for players, modify within that game structure what perhaps you want to get out of it ... just put them in a position and the players don't even know what impact it is having on them to learn, there is a big focus on observing what's going on and then making the necessary changes to get what you want. In the younger age group it is probably just on skill, passing and receiving ... when you receive the ball, what happens is your first touch is really important because that determines what happens next ... that's a skill.
>
> (Nicko, football)

> In Game Sense, competition comes in much quicker or recording their own scores or whatever because I've always had kids who look at their score and think how could I do that better ... You start off with the more fun type games which entertain them while they are doing their fitness work.
>
> (Dean, football)

Inherent in each of the above accounts are the lingering effects of 'performance' discourses (Tinning 2010) in which biophysical interests in skill, technique and fitness are privileged. Rather than a commitment to the 'problematization' of performance in context, which Game Sense approaches encourage, there appears to be a more general commitment to 'playing games' without an obvious pedagogical intent to underpin it. In Ben's account we see a rather unproblematic assumption that through playing games technique will inevitably improve and participants will learn more about how to 'compete'. Our concern is an apparent lack of questioning about whether competition is important or necessary at all in a programme that seeks to improve participation and wellbeing. On reflection, it was tensions such as these that required ongoing negotiations during the collaborative curriculum writing process to ensure that the end product reflected the aims of the programme intervention.

Possibilities, potential and pitfalls – the implementation of a 'Games Sense' approach

Throughout the preparatory phases for programme implementation we further assumed that in drawing on coaches' expertise in relation to their sport, these ideas could be easily translated into a school context. Just as diversity existed amongst the ways in which coaches understood Game Sense pedagogy, variations in teachers' understanding and confidence to implement this approach was also observed, a point that has been reflected in other research findings (Light and Georgakis 2005). The development and implementation of a one-day professional development workshop that was co-delivered by PE academics and sports coaches was offered to teachers from the intervention schools. Through analyses of process evaluation data there was evidence to suggest that the provision of teaching resources and professional development sessions introduced teachers to alternative ways to deliver the PE curriculum. For example, one teacher described how tennis was previously neglected in the curriculum at their school because they did not feel particularly confident in teaching it. After being involved in the Triple G programme they considered that their previous attempts had been rather instructionally orientated and, through their involvement in this programme, they had developed more student-orientated approaches to teaching tennis. On reflection, however, whilst many teachers indicated they felt the professional development sessions were a useful exercise, we questioned this as an effective strategy to implement sustained change in schools, as have others (for example, Armour and Yelling 2004). Perhaps one of the unintended outcomes of this approach was the hierarchical 'positioning' that resulted between some sports coaches and teachers that was perpetuated in the school setting as illustrated in the comments below.

> I would go through the manual and read up on the drills, sometimes I didn't have the time to do all three or four but I would do a couple of them and then get into the game bit, with tennis I just left it for Rob because he was the expert. I don't really know whether they were fol- lowed enough ... We absolutely rely on that professional to come in and I would learn from them, that is how I treated it.
>
> (teacher, Henty)

> Well Mitt, the tennis guy, there was no game sense, he was purely instructional ... whatever he came up with at the time, hadn't even looked at the manual, he just taught the girls like he teaches down at the tennis courts which was disappointing because he is supposed to be the expert here.
>
> (teacher, Lennonville)

I think the activities assumed the skill level would be better. So okay, it was all on this Game Sense stuff but if you couldn't kick accurately to this person or it's gone out of bounds ... I mean there are some kids that had no hope of even getting it in a smaller box for tennis when they were standing at the net ... if the coach can't get them to do this, I've got no hope in my other classes ...

(teacher, Marysville)

We are cognizant that there was always going to be variation in the degree to which the programme was implemented and of the possibilities for coaches and teachers to assume the roles of co-learners through this mode of cooperative lesson delivery. Perhaps a key learning here is that the provision of opportunities to critically reflect and debrief after each session to promote co-learning would enhance the design of future programmes. As Light (2013: 38) argues, although there is some commonality between games teaching in sport and in PE contexts, 'there are also very significant differences in aims, methods, cultures and measures of success'.

Conclusion: pedagogical possibilities for enhancing girls' physical activity

With an already extensive research field committed to understanding the factors that impact on adolescent girls' physical activity participation, this programme sought to develop and implement pedagogic approaches that were sensitive to the barriers commonly identified by adolescent girls from rural and regional living contexts. Although we believe Game Sense, as an underpinning pedagogy, has the potential to disrupt and challenge some of the deeply entrenched ideas many girls embodied about their own physical competence in particular activities, the actual success of this strategy was highly contingent upon those responsible for delivering it. In particular we considered the use of cognitive problematizing in tactics and strategies (and subsequent questioning) a good starting point for addressing concerns around a perceived focus on skill and physical performance. Further, the provision of 'scaffolded' learning activities in the form of minor games that sought to develop understanding progressively was, amongst other things, an attempt to reduce the amount of student peer surveillance that typified other PE lessons. Above all, we consider these sessions, offering a pedagogical approach that promotes learning as highly contextual and situated in students' experiences with others, have the potential to address many of the issues girls raised about their learning environment.

As Light (2013: 8) argues: '[T]eaching and coaching must always involve learning for the teachers and coaches as well as their student/players'. In this chapter we have argued that, for student learning to be enhanced, teacher and coach 'learning' about the ways in which dominant discourses can perpetuate taken-for-granted notions of pedagogy (and Game Sense pedagogy in particular) is paramount. As Azzarito (2009: 36) argues: 'Physical education practices themselves are neither liberating nor oppressive. Rather, it is the individual's awareness of their agency in negotiating dominant discourses that makes transformation possible'. On the basis of evidence presented here, there was far from universal understanding and commitment to the intentions of a Game Sense approach and the strategies that were drawn on to promote this, such as the professional development workshop and cooperative delivery model. In fact it appears that these strategies have made only modest gains towards achievement of this understanding and commitment. Further, whilst these strategies had the potential to empower teachers and coaches as Light (2013) suggests, we are cognizant that a greater awareness of the unintended outcomes, for example, the hierarchical 'positioning' of coach as expert in cooperative teaching models, is needed. Whilst awareness alone does not always lead to pedagogic translation, problematizing the implications of these unintended outcomes opens up possibilities for addressing their dangerous manifestations. As Foucault (1983: 231–232) says of problematizing: 'My point is not that everything is bad, but that everything is dangerous, which is not exactly the same as bad. If everything is dangerous, then we always have something to do'.

Considering Foucault's point in connection with the evidence presented here, it appears that there is still much work to do in school PA sites if the potential of Game Sense (and broader game-based approaches) for enhancing girls' PA is to be realized. In particular, ongoing professional learning opportunities (as opposed to one-day decontextualized sessions) that focus on developing sensitivities to the ways in which different discourses and experiences shape perceptions about PE pedagogy are needed for teachers and coaches to identify, first, the limitations of dominant and pervasive practices, and, second, the potential of other approaches. Such awareness may provide teachers and coaches with opportunities to 'position' themselves differently within the classroom as 'facilitators' of student learning through the provision of contextually relevant learning opportunities for adolescent girls.

Discussion questions

1. The authors suggest that Game Sense may provide ways to address some of the barriers to physical activity and sports participation commonly reported by adolescent girls in rural and regional living areas. Drawing on your understandings of Game Sense pedagogy, discuss the ways in which this may be achieved.
2. The authors consider Game Sense as a more readily adopted pedagogical approach in coaching settings than PE contexts. Suggest reasons why you think particular game-based approaches (such as Game Sense) might be more readily adopted in one context rather than another.

3. In which ways do you think a cooperative teaching model (between PE teachers and community sporting coaches) may influence the 'position' adopted by each in the classroom setting? How might this influence the ways students receive, and respond to, the lesson?

References

Armour, K. and Yelling, M. (2004) 'Continuing professional development for experienced physical education teachers: Towards effective provision', *Sport, Education and Society*, 9(1): 95–114.

Australian Bureau of Statistics (2011) *Sports and Physical Recreation: A Statistical Overview, Australia 2011*, Canberra: Australian Bureau of Statistics.

Azzarito, L. (2009) 'The panopticon of physical education: Pretty, active, and ideally white', *Physical Education & Sport Pedagogy*, 14(1): 19–40.

Barnett, L., van Beurden, E., Zask, A., Brooks, L. and Dietrich, U. (2002) 'How active are rural children in Australian physical education?', *Journal of Science and Medicine in Sport*, 5(3): 253–265.

Bunker, D. and Thorpe, R. (1982) 'A model for the teaching of games in secondary schools', *Bulletin of Physical Education*, 18(1): 5–8.

Capel, S., Hayes, S., Katene, W. and Velija, P. (2009) 'The development of knowledge for teaching physical education in secondary schools over the course of a PGCE year', *European Journal of Teacher Education*, 32(1): 51–62.

Casey, M., Eime, R., Payne, W. and Harvey, J. (2009) 'Using a socioecological approach to examine participation in sport and physical activity for rural adolescent girls', *Qualitative Health Research*, 19(7): 881–893.

Casey, M., Mooney, A., Eime, R., Harvey, J., Smyth, J., Telford, A. and Payne, W. (in press) 'Linking Physical Education with community sport and recreation: A program for adolescent girls', *Health Promotion Practice*.

Eime, R. and Payne, W. (2009) 'Linking participants in school-based sport programs to community clubs', *Journal of Science and Medicine in Sport*, 12(2): 293–299.

Flintoff, A. and Scraton, S. (2001) 'Stepping in active leisure? Young women's perceptions of active lifestyles and their experiences of school physical education', *Sport, Education & Society*, 6(1): 5–21.

Foucault, M. (1972) *The Archaeology of Knowledge*, London: Tavistock Publications.

——(1977) *Discipline and Punish: The Birth of the Prison*, A. Sheridan (trans.), New York: Pantheon.

——(1983) 'The subject and power', in H. Dreyfus and P. Rabinow (eds), *Michel Foucault: Beyond Structuralism and Hermeneutics* (second edition), Chicago, IL: University of Chicago Press, pp. 231–232.

Gard, M., Hickey-Moodey, A. and Enright, E. (2012) 'Youth culture, physical education and the question of relevance: after 20 years, a reply to Tinning and Fitzclarence', *Sport, Education & Society*, 1–18: 97–114.

Garrett, R. (2004) 'Negotiating a physical identity: girls, bodies and physical education', *Sport, Education & Society*, 9(2): 223–237.

Green, K. (2002) 'Physical Education teachers in their figurations: A sociological analysis of everyday "philosophies"', *Sport, Education & Society*, 7(1): 65–83.

Humbert, L. (2006) '"Listening for a change": Understanding the experiences of students in physical education', in E. Singleton and A. Varpalotai (eds), *Stones in the Sneaker: Active Theory for Secondary School Physical and Health Educators*, London, ON: the Althouse Press.

Kirk, D. (2010) *Physical Education Futures*, Abingdon: Routledge.

Lave, J. and Wenger, E. (1991) *Situated Learning: Legitimate Peripheral Participation*, Cambridge: Cambridge University Press.

Light, R. (2013) *Game Sense: Pedagogy for Performance, Participation and Enjoyment*, London and New York: Routledge.

Light, R. and Georgakis, S. (2005) 'Integrating theory and practice in teacher education: The impact of a Game Sense unit on female pre-service primary teachers' attitudes towards teaching physical education', *Journal of Physical Education New Zealand*, 38: 67–80.

Light, R. and Kentel, J. (2010) 'Soft pedagogy for a hard sport: Disrupting hegemonic masculinity in high school rugby through feminist-informed pedagogy', in M. Kehler and M. Atkinson (eds), *Boys' Bodies: Speaking the Unspoken*, New York: Peter Lang Publishing, Inc., pp. 133–154.

Luke, M. and Sinclair, G. (1991) 'Gender differences in adolescents' attitudes towards school physical education', *Journal of Teaching in Physical Education*, 11: 31–46.

Mooney, A., Casey, M. and Smyth, J. (2012) '"You're no-one if you're not a netball girl": rural and regional adolescent girls' negotiation of physically active identities', *Annals of Leisure Research*, 15(1): 19–37.

Mooney, A., Casey, M., Payne, W. and Telford, A. (2011) *Triple G: Girls Get Going in Tennis, in Football and at the YMCA Teaching Resource Manual*, Ballarat. University of Ballarat.

Mordal-Moen, K. and Green, K. (2012) 'Neither shaking nor stirring: A case study of reflexivity in Norwegian physical education teacher education', *Sport, Education and Society* , DOI:10.1080/13573322.2012.670114.

O'Donovan, T. and Kirk, D. (2008) 'Reconceptualizing student motivation in physical education: An examination of what resources are valued by pre-adolescent girls in contemporary society', *European Physical Education Review*, 14(1): 71–91.

Olafson, L. (2002) '"I hate phys. ed': Adolescent girls talk about physical education', *Physical Educator*, 59(2): 67–74.

Patton, M. (2002) *Qualitative Research and Evaluation Methods* (third edition), Thousand Oaks, CA: Sage Publications.

Rovegno, I. and Dolly, J. (2006) 'Constructivist perspectives on learning', in D. Kirk, D. Macdonald and M. O'Sullivan (eds), *The Handbook of Physical Education*, London: Sage Publications Ltd.

Sallis, J. F., McKenzie, T. L., Alcaraz, J. E., Kolody, B., Faucette, N. and Hovell, M. (1997) 'The effects of a 2-year physical education program (SPARK) on physical activity and fitness in elementary school students. Sports, Play and Active Recreation for Kids', *American Journal of Public Health*, 87(8): 1328–1334.

Slater, A. and Tiggemann, M. (2010) '"Uncool to do sport": A focus group study of adolescent girls' reasons for withdrawing from physical activity', *Psychology of Sport and Exercise*, 11(6): 619–626.

Tinning, R. (2010) *Pedagogy and Human Movement: Theory, Practice, Research*, London: Routledge.

Tinning, R. and Fitzclarence, L. (1992) 'Postmodern youth culture and the crisis in Australian secondary school physical education', *Quest*, 44(3): 287–303.

Webber, L. S., Catellier, D. J., Lytle, L. A., Murray, D. M., Pratt, C. A., Young, D. R., Elder, J. P., Lohman, T. G., Stevens, J., Stevens, J. B. and Pate, R. R. (2008) 'Promoting physical activity in middle school girls: Trial of Activity for Adolescent Girls', *American Journal of Preventive Medicine*, 34(3): 173–184.

Webster, J. (2008) 'Establishing the "truth" of the matter: Confessional reflexivity as introspection and avowal', *Psychology and Society*, 1(1): 65–76.

Wright, J. (2006) 'Physical education research from postmodern, poststructural and postcolonial perspectives', in D. Kirk, D. Macdonald and M. O'Sullivan (eds), *The Handbook of Physical Education*, London: Sage Publications Ltd.

Wright, J., Macdonald, D. and Groom, L. (2003) 'Physical activity and young people: Beyond participation', *Sport, Education and Society*, 8(1): 17–33.

8 The influence of school context on the implementation of TGfU across a secondary school physical education department

Christina Curry and Richard L. Light

Introduction

Over the past decade Teaching Games for Understanding (TGfU) has enjoyed a sustained revival of interest from researchers and practitioners across the globe that is strong enough to be described as a 'movement' (see, for example, Light 2005). Along with other game-based approaches (GBA) it has come to form one of the more prominent areas of research interest in physical education with a well-attended series of international conferences on TGfU established from 2001, and with the most recent one held in TGfU's 'birthplace' at Loughborough University in the UK in July 2012. Research consistently confirms the effectiveness of this approach to teaching in terms of developing better games players, generating positive affective experiences of learning and promoting a range of positive social, moral and personal learning (see, for example, Butler and Griffin 2010; Holt, Ward and Wallhead 2007; Light 2013 and Chapter 6 by Jarrett and Harvey). Despite these positive developments, the uptake of TGfU and other game-based approaches (GBA) by physical education teachers across the globe remains limited. Even in Singapore, where a variation of TGfU, the games concept approach (GCA), was mandated by the Ministry of Education, a sustained body of research conducted over the past decade suggests that it is yet to make a significant impact upon practice (see Chapter 3 by Fry and McNeill).

There has been a number of studies on teacher and pre-service teacher responses and implementation of game-based approaches conducted across a range of countries that have identified the ways in which deeply embedded beliefs about teaching and learning can conflict with games-based pedagogy (see, for example, Butler 1996; Light 2002; Light and Tan 2006 and Chapter 6 by Jarrett and Harvey). A few have also highlighted how the cultural, social and institutional contexts within which pre-service and early service teachers attempt to implement GBA critically shape their experiences and interpretation of this pedagogy (see, for example, Light and Butler 2005; Light and Tan 2006). While this research identifies some common challenges that might explain implementation challenges, there have been few, if any, longitudinal studies on the implementation of game-based teaching that have inquired into the ways in which socio-cultural and/or institutional contexts influence the implementation of TGfU and other GBA. This chapter redresses this oversight in the literature by drawing on a two-year study that looked into the implementation of TGfU across a large HPE (health and physical education) department in an Australian, elite, independent secondary school to focus on how the specific context of the school shaped teachers' experiences of it.

The school

Established late in the nineteenth century, Vastground (a pseudonym) is an elite, independent school in a major city in Australia serving the privileged sections of society that Connell (1996) refers to as the ruling classes. It boasts excellent educational and sporting facilities, highly qualified staff and excellent results in the state-wide, year-12 exit exams. Competitive sport is immensely important in the school with results in major sports acting as markers of educational status and of the values of the class of clients attracted to these schools (Light and Kirk 2001: Sherrington 1983). Sport provides an explicit and dramatic indicator of how different schools compare to each other within the elite independent groupings, with large financial resources poured into achieving the best possible results in high status sports such as rugby and rowing.

The TGfU project

The study examined physical education teachers' experiences of the implementation of a department-wide change to teaching games from a 'sport skills' (Kirk 2010) approach to a TGfU approach initiated by the new head of the HPE department, Mark (a pseudonym). It focuses on how this implementation was influenced by contextual factors in the school such as the powerful influence of interschool sport and the introduction of an online course in teaching for understanding (TfU). Due to the significance of the ways in which Mark managed this considerable change, we also provide a very brief overview of his management of this change. Although he had a minimal understanding of TGfU he saw it as being an ideal mechanism for challenging the dominance of sport in the school and for distinguishing physical education from it. He had read about TGfU and after attending a conference on it in 2006 he embarked upon making a major pedagogical and cultural change in the HPE department.

His early attempts at managing change were severely impeded by his lack of depth of understanding of TGfU and a management approach that lacked consultation, communication and collaboration. This created far more tension with sport in the school than there needed to have been and made us, as researchers, doubt in the early stages of the implementation that he could succeed. However, after almost a year of relentless challenges for Mark things began to change as he and his staff began to understand TGfU and to see the increasingly positive student responses to it.

Method

Participants and site

The study examined the implementation of TGfU across an entire department of 16 staff that grew to 18 but focused on eight key informants. All 16 HPE staff, aged between 27–60, were invited to complete a questionnaire following an introductory workshop and were given the option to express their interest in continuing to participate in interviews and observations. Eight teachers agreed, which we considered to be a viable number as they represented half the PE staff population. The names used in this chapter for the participants and the school are pseudonyms used to protect their anonymity. The school at which the study was conducted is an elite, independent secondary school in a major Australian city.

The head of the HPE department, Mark (a pseudonym), initiated the intervention and began by having academics working in games teaching pedagogy, including the first author, conduct several seminars in the school during the first month. He then provided some readings for staff and asked them to search for and read relevant publications. His understanding of TGfU was limited and this created some problems with the intervention. This was particularly evident when he insisted that the swimming and athletics coaches use games in their coaching. The management process lacked cohesion, particularly in the first year, but as the teachers worked through the challenges that arose through discussion and collaboration the process moved more smoothly.

Data generation and analysis

The study was conducted using a grounded theory approach in which data were generated through noted observations of all staff in the HPE department and semi-structured interviews with eight key informants (teachers), including the head teacher and an interview with the headmaster. Three rounds of in-depth, one-on-one interviews with the key informants were conducted over a two-year period following a grounded theory approach (Glaser 1978). This involved the generation of data from one round of interviews, informed by observations and field notes from which themes and ideas emerged and were tested in the following rounds. This constant comparative process of analysis led to the development of theory grounded in the data that was then connected to the formal theory of social constructivism. This involved drawing on social constructivism to provide understanding of how the key informants interpreted and implemented the TGfU approach. This was achieved by looking at the teachers as learners who drew on prior knowledge and experiences to interpret, make sense of, and use the TGfU approach.

The connection of the grounded theory to the formal theory of social constructivism in the later stages of the study allowed us to see the teachers' experiences of developing a TGfU approach as a process of learning. This theoretical perspective led us to consider how the teachers' pre-existing knowledge and sets of dispositions influenced their interpretation of the learning experiences managed by the head teacher and how they made sense of them to construct and enact their own understandings. This also allowed for consideration of how the specific nature of the 'learning' context shaped their eventual interpretation and practice of TGfU.

Results

The following section identifies the main contextual factors that influenced the teachers' implementation of TGfU. Presented in order of importance they are: (1) the place of sport in the school, (2) the role of physical education in the school, (3) the implementation of an online course in teaching for understanding (TfU-Cohen, McLaughlin and Talbert 1993), (4) the gender of teachers and (5) the pressures of teaching.

The power and influence of sport

> The wellbeing of the school is found on the field.
>
> (Daniela, interview 2, August 2009)

This quote from Daniela captures the importance placed on sport as a central practice at the school and accepted all the teachers in this study. It is confirmed by the school website, which explains how '[a]ll students are required to play competitive sport; selection in a school team is a matter of pride. As a result, sport takes priority over other activities. Participation in sports is compulsory' (school website, 2012). Students are usually required to train twice a week in any sport team (either before or after school) and must commit to competing on Saturdays with PE staff required to give up their Saturdays for school sport.

All the teachers in this study consistently commented upon how the headmaster emphasised the importance of performance in interschool sport, suggesting that he valued it far more than PE:

> I think, to be quite frank, he (Headmaster) is a traditionalist. Rugby in his eyes is the most important sport. That is where the tradition is, that is what your school is all about, its rugby. I don't think he personally believes in the value of our (PE) programme.
>
> (Rosie, interview 1, August 2008)

Interschool sport held a far more important position than physical education did, which is something that disappointed and frustrated the physical education staff:

> I mean, even our head of sport who is no longer, said once in a meeting, 'that I think it's a crying shame that if they (the students) are going to come out of year 10 and not be able to play a straight batted shot in cricket'.

As if that is the hallmark of a successful PE programme! So yeah, I think some of them are very stubborn and aren't willing to see it for what it is.

(Tayla, interview 2, August 2008)

From the participants' perspectives there was significant tension between physical education and sport that created problems for the introduction of TGfU. This tension was exacerbated by the head teacher's way of implementing it and particularly by his misinterpretation of it at the beginning of the process. Owing to his misinterpretation of TGfU in the early stages of the implementation, Mark alienated the school sports department, many of the coaches and, at one stage, the headmaster, who saw it as something of a threat to success in interschool sport. This created a major problem for the head teacher of HPE, Mark, and his staff when the headmaster was convinced by a small number of coaches who were bitterly opposed to TGfU that it had caused a drop in interschool sport results across all sports. The sporting results improved again the following year with some of the HPE staff suggesting that it was just a bad year with less talented athletes. By this time Mark had a far better understanding of TGfU, the PE staff had progressed well with their TGfU teaching and the coaches who were so vocal in their opposition to TGfU had left the school. All these developments relieved the pressure on the HPE programme, created by Mark's misinterpretation of TGfU and his lack of consultation with his staff.

The role of HPE at the school

All teachers in the study saw the traditional role of the HPE department in the school as involving serving the needs of sport as a particular challenge during the early stages of the TGfU implementation process:

Well, we experienced some difficulty very early on in the implementation of this programme. There was this perceived idea that there were two major driving forces for our programme. One was teaching HPE and using things like TGfU to support that, and the second was the supporting of the sports programme. We've got a very large co-curricular programme, very competitive right across all the sports we play and there was a pressure that was felt upon some of us, if not all of us, between these competing demands between preparing kids for competitive sport and trying to develop wider, broader understanding amongst the students in HPE.

(Leo, interview 1, August 2008)

The HPE teachers were unhappy with the dominance of sport in the school that created tension between HPE staff and coaches at the beginning of the implementation: 'So, just the whole sport versus HPE sort of debate and, yeah, the whole games for understanding versus sport skills and the philosophical differences and the agendas, I suppose of staff' (John, interview 1, August

2008). Prior to the TGfU implementation the physical education curriculum had been delivered with a focus on sport skill development and on supporting the school sport programme. It had been introduced fleetingly by a previous HOD but had not been sustained.

Despite their involvement in coaching sport teams, all the HPE teachers in the study identified themselves most strongly as teachers:

> There are two philosophies in our department. One is the being employed for sport basis and the other is the physical educator and I believe I am a physical educator … My role; my primary role is to be an HPE teacher. My second role is to be a tutor and my third role is to sport.
>
> (Rosie, interview 1, August 2008)

The tensions between the traditional role of physical education as serving sport and the new role that the introduction of TGfU was used to forge led to some very heated disagreements and arguments between HPE and coaching staff but dissipated over time as the implementation of TGfU progressed. It was also critically assisted by the departure of a few of the most vocal and determined coaching staff who opposed it, as Rosie suggested toward the end of the study:

> The number one issue at that time was the dynamic of the staff, but over the last couple of years new staff members have been employed who were willing to adopt it and so then you change that balance of power I suppose in terms of, yeah, not intimidation but influence.
>
> (Rosie, interview 3, August 2010)

During the second year of the implementation all teachers felt that HPE and sport were significantly separated. Max believed the main reason for this was because, by this time, they had been able to see the advantages of TGfU:

> For instance, an area like invasion games, you're not always going to be looking at the traditional sports to learn the lessons that want to be learnt there, so that means you're not going down the path of always doing traditional sports and physical education classes, you're doing other activities which are going to obviously help the students' understanding of playing those types of games, but it's not as specifically structured as it may have been in the past. And that's a huge benefit to many of the kids that don't play a particular traditional sport.
>
> (Max, interview 3, August 2010)

The teaching for understanding initiative

Prior to Mark deciding to implement a TGfU approach the school executive had been considering adopting the teaching for understanding (TfU) framework across the school. During the first few months of the implementation of

TGfU, TfU was introduced across the whole school. This included an expectation that all staff would enrol in a TfU online course offered by Harvard University and this significantly facilitated the implementation of TGfU due to the positive response to Mark's proposal by the executive and support for the approach by all the school staff and the headmaster: 'It had that really big push from the executive to meet the cutting edge of technology, to be going in the same direction, so I think there has been a big push from that' (Rosie, interview 1, August 2008). According to the teachers in the study, the introduction of TfU helped because it encouraged staff to see it as maintaining and boosting the school's academic status and being innovative and active in seeking to improve teaching and student achievement.

The TfU framework is a tool for designing, conducting and reflecting on classroom practices that promote student understanding and teachers as guides, coaches or facilitators to student learning (Cohen *et al.* 1993). It is the result of a five-year research project involving teachers in over 60 schools and systems that led to the development of a research-based and classroom-tested approach to teaching for understanding within a framework consisting of:

1. Generative topics.
2. Understanding goals.
3. Performances of understanding.
4. Ongoing assessment.

Mark and the HPE department were able to align TGfU with the school TfU approach as Mark suggested: 'I think from the school's perspective they value it and think it's important and they can see the relationship with teaching for understanding' (interview 3, August 2010). Most teachers in this study commented positively on the influence of TfU on the implementation of TGfU due to the way that it helped having it accepted and supported by the school and in helping them better understand TGfU: '[I]t fits into the whole school ethos and it's being supported from above' (Cathryn, interview 2, August 2009).

Initial strong support from the headmaster for TGfU due to its alignment with TfU made the HPE staff feel more comfortable with the change and encouraged them to feel that what they would be doing in the HPE programme would be best practice that provided quality education: '[T]he school stays well informed with trends in teaching and learning so they would have done their research' (Tayla, interview 2, August 2008). Some of the HPE teachers felt that the TfU initiative validated what they were doing in HPE in the eyes of staff in other departments, and this contributed toward their acceptance of it and their enthusiasm for taking it up. They also felt that it highlighted the intellectual learning possible in HPE, thus further raising its status in the school. Tayla felt that the TfU initiative was very helpful in validating TGfU and highlighting the educational value of HPE in the school: 'I think the whole concept signifies what we want our students to gain ... that is true understanding of what they are learning' (Tayla, interview 3, August

2009). The teachers also felt that the in-service training in TfU was beneficial for their understanding of TGfU: '[T]he extra in-servicing has been valuable to really bring the concept home for me' (Cathryn, interview 3, August 2009).

Gender

The issue of gender is yet to receive adequate attention in the TGfU literature but those studies that have been conducted suggest significant differences between the nature of experiences, motivation and learning when GBAs are adopted (see, Gutierrez and García-López 2012; Harvey 2009; Mandigo, Holt, Anderson and Sheppard 2008). It has also been suggested that Game Sense pedagogy is consistent with feminist pedagogy (Light and Kentel 2010). Responses to the implementation of TGfU at Vastground differed along gender lines and particularly in the early stages of the implementation. During these early stages the resistance from staff came from the male teachers within what could be seen as a dominant, masculinist approach to coaching sport and teaching physical education. This resistance was, in turn, strongest among the older males who promoted a top-down, authoritarian approach that they suggested the headmaster follow. The participants' views on this is clearly identified in the following quote from Cathryn:

> I think that one of the massive issues is that people who really believed in this approach were female. We have had sort of a really big battle on that because we were fighting against a male tradition of co-curricular sports and weren't necessarily accepted in our views. Most of the fight came from female staff and support from our HOD.
>
> (interview 1, August 2008)

Mark (HOD) was male but he had been educated in a state system that, he suggested, placed less emphasis on the traditional, 'old school' direct instruction, sports-skills mastery approach. This gender division saw general support from female teachers, who were more accommodating and willing to try new things, and opposition from the males during the early stages implementation. Indeed, during the shaky beginning of implementation, one female teacher, Rosie, was instrumental in supporting Mark and the TGfU approach and preventing its early failure. The gender division dissipated over the duration of the study as the male teachers began to develop a more positive attitude toward TGfU but it never completely disappeared. Throughout the study the female teachers placed more importance on providing inclusive, social and affectively positive learning experiences for their students than the male teachers did.

The pressures of teaching

As is the case in most schools the pressure on teachers' time and energy created by teaching loads and commitments to coaching sport teams made it difficult for the teachers in this study to experiment with innovation (Guskey 1988). In the beginning they were concerned about the extra workload they knew it would entail, which included reading books and journal articles on top of teaching: 'I would like to read more first but I just haven't had a chance' (Cam, August 2008). All the teachers suggested that one of the biggest challenges in the beginning was finding this time to get acquainted with TGfU and this contributed toward slowing the uptake. There had been a couple of workshops in the beginning but Mark had relied heavily upon the teachers reading to become familiar with TGfU. The lack of preparation provided by the HOD contributed to this slow initial development of understanding. Change requires extra work, especially at first, adding to the teachers' already heavy workload as Rosie outlines:

> It is the culture of the school, the dual roles and some people have many other commitments in their life so they're tutors, or they're heads of houses or they're MICs (master in charge) of sport, directors of sport or coaches of first teams, so our other commitments outside our face-to-face teaching are time consuming and energy sapping, therefore that influences our willingness and energy to devote taking on a new concept or new idea.
> (Rosie, interview 3, August 2010)

There was also a concern about the quality and availability of resources to help take up TGfU that exacerbated Mark's misinterpretation of TGfU. A lack of resources meant the teachers had to come up with ideas themselves and this proved challenging. The attention paid to the intellectual domain in TGfU (Pearson, Webb and McKeen 2008) was foreign to them and developing appropriate questioning arose as the major problem: 'I find the questioning hard, I feel like the kids just look at me trying to work out what I'm doing' (John, interview 1, August 2008). This is a common problem identified in the literature (Roberts 2011; Wright and Forrest 2007; Light 2013 and Forrest in Chapter 11). However, this improved over time as the implementation progressed as Tayla suggests late in the study: 'The students are used to being questioned now and I am much more comfortable with it than I was at the beginning' (interview 3, August 2010).

Discussion

This study conceptualised teachers' experiences of the implementation as a process of learning in which previous experience, knowledge, beliefs and dispositions shaped their interpretation of the implementation process adopted by the head teacher of HPE. This confirmed findings in the literature, suggesting how teachers' beliefs about teaching and learning can conflict with the theories of learning underpinning TGfU (see, for example, Butler 1996; Light 2008). It also highlighted the significance of the specific socio-cultural and institutional context for the learning process as suggested by some previous studies (see, for example, Light and Tan 2006) and by Quay and Stolz in Chapter 1. The contextual factors influencing the implementation were dynamic and changed significantly over the period of the study. This study also suggests that despite the powerful influence of structures such as the historical dominance of sport in the school and the culture of excellence and performance, individual agency played a significant part in shaping the eventual outcome of the implementation.

For example, the influence of the headmaster was significant but fluctuated over the period of the study of the school between support and opposition. Mark's influence was clearly the key to implementation, driven by his belief in TGfU as a tool for making a cultural change in the HPE department, but his initial misunderstanding of the approach and his poor managerial strategies hindered progress. The initial support of Rosie and the departure of a few very resistant coaches were also pivotal influences on the outcome. On the other hand, structures such as the dominance of sport in the school remained a constant influence on the implementation of TGfU and on the teachers' practice of it. While recognising the dynamic nature of the context, how it interacted with teacher beliefs and the management process, and the ways in which different factors interacted within it, we discuss them separately as those that facilitated the process and those that impeded it.

Impeding factors

The importance of competitive sport in the school emerged as the most significant factor limiting the implementation of TGfU. It was, however, exacerbated by Mark's misunderstanding of TGfU and his lack of early con- sultation with staff. In his enthusiasm to use TGfU as a way of distancing HPE from sport he threatened the roles of coaching staff and set up TGfU in opposition to sport. He promoted a view of it as being anti-competition, therefore challenging competitive sports such as rugby. This, and his lack of consultation with HPE teachers and coaches, created unnecessary conflict early in the process with staff in his department who were also head coaches of major team sports in the school. The central role that social interaction and dialogue plays in learning was limited for the eight key informants by Mark's initial approach and their lack of understanding about TGfU, and his misinterpretation created problems with coaching staff. For example, a group of irate coaches approached the headmaster to complain about the threat to success in school sport that they felt TGfU represented at the end of a com- paratively poor season for most school sports. In the first months of the intervention a researcher working on Game Sense in an elite-level rugby union presented on its benefits for sport at the school, but there was no follow up and this one lecture had little effect upon the coaches who were so quickly opposed to the implementation of TGfU.

This misinterpretation and poor management of the implementation formed such a major problem because of the emphasis on excellence and competition across the school, and particularly with sport. These problems were manifested in the relationship between sport and HPE and its positioning as an area of the curriculum that served sport. Indeed, Mark had recognised this problem from his appointment at the school and had set correcting this inappropriate relationship between sport and HPE as his major goal, choosing to use TGfU to achieve it. It also exerted a significant influence upon the teachers' interpretation and use of TGfU as was very evident in the intense opposition to TGfU from some staff involved with sport.

The headmaster's attitude toward TGfU, which changed over the period of the study, had a significant influence on the progress of the implementation. He was a traditionalist who emphasised the value of sport in the school. His original support for TGfU was due to its alignment with the TfU programme, but this was tested when he was encouraged to think that TGfU was reducing the performance of the school's sports teams. He questioned Mark after the first year to suggest that what the HPE department were doing had contributed toward a decline in sport results. This upset many of the HPE teachers as it reinforced their feelings that HPE was undervalued within the school: '[U]nfortunately the value of our subject is low, there is so much emphasis on what are considered the more academic subjects' (David, August, 2009). The original misconception of TGfU by Mark did not allow him to highlight what it could offer intellectually and to emphasise its links with TfU.

From the very first day of the implementation some of the coaches were resistant to protect the continued opportunity for extra sports training in PE classes. As Rosie suggested: 'There's always going to be conflict with staff members that are employed to be directors of sport wanting to teach them the basic skills rather than doing a games for understanding approach' (Rosie, interview 2, August 2009). Such pressure on staff to meet the demands of both areas makes it difficult for them to develop innovation in schools (Connell and Payne 1985). There were also other factors that presented challenges for the implementation of TGfU, such as the demands of the workload placed on teachers and competing demands of other commitments such as coaching. This and the lack of available TGfU resources and initial misinterpretation created significant problems for the implementation in the early stages.

Facilitating factors

The TfU initiative was the most significant contextual factor facilitating the implementation of TGfU. It encouraged all staff in the school and the executive body to be positively disposed toward TGfU and provided greater knowledge and understanding of the concepts used in it. This was further assisted by the school being open to educational change and up to date with educational innovation. While the alignment with TfU was clearly a great help in the implementation of TGfU this was disrupted at times by the tensions that were perceived to exist between TGfU and performance in school sport by some staff and the headmaster.

The original support from the headmaster was significant, and although this faltered at the end of the first year, he was again supportive after realising that TGfU had not hindered the performances of the sports teams. The early problems caused by extreme resistance from a few staff working as coaches and their commitment to derailing the implementation disappeared when these staff left the school and this helped considerably. This allowed for a happier and more positive environment for teachers to embrace TGfU:

> We've had a few staff retire, we've had a couple of staff leave that probably were very negative towards any change, or anything a little different, and having those people leave, it's really opened up, it's put some fresh air in the department, and we've had some new people come in who are very open to different ways of teaching.
>
> (Mark, interview 3, August 2010)

During the early stages gender also influenced the progress of the implementation and teacher experiences of it, with the female teachers being more supportive of the challenge to sport's dominance and more inclined to be positive about TGfU. During the first year of the implementation most of the male teachers did not see the need for the change as they felt their approach to teaching HPE was working well, as John suggests in an early interview: 'I think we are ensuring our students leave here with good skills and that is important' (John, interview 1, August 2008). All the early 'trouble makers' were male coaches and their departure led to improved acceptance of TGfU. The female teachers tended to accept this change sooner and became prominent in leading the uptake of TGfU with strong support from female staff providing much needed support for Mark.

In the second year the male teachers began to see the benefits, particularly for their students, and were able to slowly move away from the directive approach. As time progressed and all the teachers became more comfortable with TGfU they found it easier to embed the approach in their practice, and taking the opportunity to discuss TGfU and share ideas helped the process: 'I love hearing what others are doing and getting new ideas to try' (Rosie, interview 3, August 2010). By this stage TGfU and the dispositions it can encourage toward discussion, reflection and collaboration among teachers were very evident. This could also be seen as re-establishing cognitive equilibrium after a 'perturbation' for the teachers as learners from a Piagetian constructivist perspective (see, for example, Fosnot 1996).

Conclusion

This chapter identifies the significant influence that socio-cultural and institutional contexts can have on the implementation of a significant pedagogical innovation. In doing so it focuses on an area that has received significant attention in the GBA literature over the past half decade, as illustrated by

Jarrett and Harvey in this volume, and is the focus of a philosophical discussion in Chapter 1 by Quay and Stolz. It identifies a dynamic, changing context shaped by both traditions and culture of the school, contemporary develop-ments in pedagogy, broader educational developments and the influence of individual agency such as that of the teachers, the head teacher and the headmaster. Our division of contextual factors into those impeding and facilitating the implementation of TGfU is helpful in understanding how the progress of the implementation was influenced by context but should not detract from, or be seen as an attempt to reduce, the complex interplay of these factors in this particular setting.

There is an important methodological implication here in regard to the duration and nature of the study. Other studies that have explored the imple-mentation of TGfU have been of far shorter duration from a few weeks to a few months (see, for example, Light and Tan 2006; Harvey and Jarrett in press and Chapter 6 by Jarrett and Harvey in this volume). While Light and Tan looked at the development of TGfU teaching across the last two years in PETE programmes and the first two years of teaching, they took a cross-sectional snapshot, this study examined teacher experience over a two-and-a-half-year period in one school. The positive outcomes identified in the study are pro-mising for expanding the uptake of game-based approaches and would not have been identified in a shorter study.

In Chapter 6 Jarrett and Harvey suggest that there is a need for long-itudinal research designs, and the breadth of research methodologies used to generate information about subjective experiences of learning in and through GBA. The study reported on in this chapter supports this contention by illustrating how studies of longer duration can provide a deeper under-standing of the issues involved in implementing GBA, and of how to develop strategies to address them and how important the subjective dimensions of teaching are. Following on from the approach adopted in this study might usefully involve longitudinal and/or ethnographic approaches to research. Such approaches can provide more nuanced understandings of the dynamics of schools and HPE departments, and assist in developing successful strate-gies for innovation in physical education, such as Game Sense, TGfU and other GBAs. They can also account for the important differences between the contexts within which they are undertaken.

Discussion questions

1. One factor impeding the implementation of TGfU was opposition from coaches who saw it as a threat to the success of competitive inter-school sport due to misunderstanding it. Write a short expla-nation to the coaches explaining how TGfU would not threaten the performance of the schools sports teams and how it could be used to improve performance.

2. This chapter highlights the complexity of the contextual factors shaping the implementation of TGfU and changes in it over time. What does this suggest about implementing TGfU or any other innovation in schools?

3. Explain the significance of the design and length of the study drawn on in this chapter for the results that it reports on in regard to how context shaped the implementation of TGfU, and discuss the advantages offered by longitudinal studies in this area.

References

Butler, J. (1996) 'Teacher responses to Teaching Games for Understanding', *Journal of Physical Education, Recreation and Dance*, 67: 28–33.

Butler, J. and Griffin, L. L. (2010) *More Teaching Games for Understanding: Move Globally*, Champaign, IL: Human Kinetics.

Cohen, D. K., McLaughlin, M. W. and Talbert, J. E. (eds) (1993) *Teaching for Understanding: Challenges for Policy and Practice*, San Francisco: Jossey-Bass.

Connell, R. (1996) 'Teaching the boys: New research on masculinity, and gender strategies for schools', *The Teachers College Record*, 98(2), 206–235.

Connell, R. W. and Payne, R. (1985) *Teachers' Work*, Sydney: Allen & Unwin.

Fosnot, C. T. (ed.) (1996) *Constructivism: Theory, Perspectives and Practice*, New York: Teachers' College Press.

Glaser, B. G. (1978) *Theoretical Sensitivity: Advances in the Methodology of Grounded Theory*, Mill Valley, CA: Sociology Press.

Guskey, T. R. (1988) 'Teacher efficacy, self-concept, and attitudes toward the implementation of instructional innovation', *Teaching and Teacher Education*, 4(1), 63–69.

Gutierrez, D. and García-López, L. M. (2012) 'Gender differences in game behaviour in invasion games', *Physical Education and Sport Pedagogy*, 17(3), 289–302.

Harvey, S. (2009) 'A study of interscholastic soccer players' perceptions of learning with Game Sense', *Asian Journal of Sport and Exercise Science*, 6(1), 29–38.

Harvey, S. and Jarrett, K. (in press) 'A review of the game-centred approaches to teaching and coaching literature since 2006', *Physical Education and Sport Pedagogy*.

Holt, J. E., Ward, T. and Wallhead, T. (2007) 'The transfer of learning from play practices to game play in young adult soccer players', *Physical Education and Sport Pedagogy*, 11(2), 101–118.

Kirk, D. (2010) 'Towards a socio-pedagogy of sports coaching', in J. Lyle and C. Cushion (eds) *Sport Coaching: Professionalisation and Practice*, Edinburgh: Elsevier.

Light, R. (2002) 'The social nature of games: Pre-service teachers' first experiences of TGfU', *European Physical Education Review*, 8(3), 291–310.

——(2005) 'Introduction: An international perspective on Teaching Games for Understanding', in R. Light (ed.) An international perspective on Teaching Games for Understanding, special issue of *Physical Education and Sport Pedagogy*, 10(3), 211–212.

——(2008) *Sport in the Lives of Young Australians*, Sydney: University of Sydney Press.

——(2013) *Game Sense: Pedagogy for Performance, Participation and Enjoyment*, London and New York: Routledge.

132 *Christina Curry and Richard L. Light*

Light, R. and Butler, J. (2005) 'A personal journey: TGfU teacher development in Australia and the USA', in R. Light (ed.) An international perspective on Teaching Games for Understanding, special issue of *Physical Education and Sport Pedagogy*, 10(3), 241–254.

Light, R. and Kentel, J. A. (2010) 'Soft pedagogy for a hard sport: Disrupting hegemonic masculinity in high school rugby through feminist-informed pedagogy', in M. Kehler and M. Atkinson (eds) *Boys' Bodies*, New York: Peter Lang Publishers.

Light, R. and Kirk, D. (2001) 'Australian cultural capital – Rugby's social meaning: physical assets, social advantage and independent schools', *Sport, Culture, Society*, 4(3), 81–98.

Light, R. and Tan, S. (2006) 'Culture, embodied understandings and primary school teachers' development of TGfU in Singapore and Australia', *European Physical Education Review*, 12(1), 100–117.

Mandigo, J., Holt, N., Anderson, A. and Sheppard, J. (2008) 'Children's motivational experience following autonomy-supportive games lessons', *European Physical Education Review*, 14(3), 407–425.

Pearson, P., Webb, P. and McKeen, J. (2008) 'Developing cognitive ability through games: a conundra?' *Australian Journal of Gifted Education*, 17(1), 30–37.

Roberts, J. (2011) 'Teaching Games for Understanding: the difficulties and challenges experienced by participation cricket coaches', *Physical Education and Sport Pedagogy*, 16(1), 33–48.

Sherrington, G. (1983) 'Athleticism in the antipodes: The AAGPS of New South Wales', *History of Education Review*, 12, 16–28.

Wright, J. and Forrest, G. (2007) 'A social semiotic analysis of knowledge construction and games centred approaches to teaching', *Physical Education and Sport Pedagogy*, 12(3), 273–287.

9 The nature and importance of coach–player relationships in the uptake of Game Sense by elite rugby coaches in Australia and New Zealand

John Robert Evans

Introduction

Despite the fact that it was first introduced in 1997 (den Duyn), Game Sense can still be seen as an innovation due to the ways in which it proposes such a different approach to traditional skill-focused coaching approaches and because it is still not widely adopted. The ways in which it challenges well-established coaching methods as well as beliefs and conceptions of those involved in sport about what constitutes good coaching have contributed to a limited uptake in elite-level sport (Light 2004, 2006). The Game Sense approach involves far more than merely using games or modified practice games, as is reasonably common practice in many sports (see, for example, Light and Evans 2010). The use of small-sided modified games characteristic of teaching games for understanding (TGfU) approaches (Bunker and Thorpe 1982) is only one aspect of a Game Sense pedagogy, which promotes player-centred, inquiry-based learning, indirect coaching and player empowerment through the typical presentation of a problem for its uptake (Kidman 2005; Light 2013). Its implementation thus presents a range of challenges for coaches including the use of questioning to generate thinking and dialogue. Communication is also very different. Where 'traditional' approaches emphasise a monologue from coach to player(s) and direct instruction by the coach, Game Sense emphasises productive dialogue between players and between players and the coach. This is thus a very different approach to coaching that also requires, and builds, very different relationships between the coach and the players, and between the players.

In both physical education and coaching literature there has been some attention paid to specific aspects of Game Sense, TGfU and other game-based approaches (GBA) that present challenges for coaches and teachers such as meeting the challenges of effective questioning (see, for example, Roberts 2011; Wright and Forrest 2007) and the issue of game design (addressed by Adrian Turner in this book in Chapter 13). There has, however, been little attention paid to the change in relationships involved in implementing Game Sense and other GBA. This chapter attempts to redress this issue by drawing on a study that investigated the interpretation and use of Game Sense by elite-level rugby coaches in Australia and New Zealand (see Evans 2010, 2012; Light and Evans, 2010). It explores the nature of relationships developed by the coaches with their players and how they related to both the coaching approaches used and their perspectives on good coaching.

Game Sense

Game Sense is a variation of Teaching Games for Understanding (TGfU) developed in Australia during the 1990s (see den Duyn 1997) through collaboration between the Australian Sports Commission (ASC), Rod Thorpe and local coaches (Light 2004). Although very similar to TGfU there are some notable differences in that Game Sense was developed specifically for sport coaching while TGfU was developed for physical education (Light 2013). Many coaches in Australia at the time were already using Thorpe's ideas, such as games-based coaching to contextualise learning, but he provided a structure for this work and, most importantly, introduced an emphasis on questioning in place of direct instruction (Light 2013). This use of questioning, as opposed to directing players in what they should do, shifted the focus of coaching away from traditional coach-directed methods towards more player-centred approaches. The key features of a Game Sense coaching pedagogy are that (1) most learning is shaped and contextualised within games or game-like activities that involve competition and decision making and (2) that the coach asks players about technique and strategy to stimulate thinking and players' intellectual engagement.

In coaching contexts Game Sense is typically used with players who know how to play the game in a basic way and who have chosen to play it. This applies to six-year-old children in a soccer club as much as it does to elite-level professional rugby union or cricket players. The focus then is not on developing an overall ability to play the game as it typically would be in physical education lessons but is, instead, more on developing particular aspects of play typically focused on the next competition match. This could arise from analysis of the previous week's match aimed at correcting mistakes or addressing weaknesses in play, or could arise from strategies developed to exploit the next opponents' perceived weaknesses or counter their strengths, considered within an overall season-long plan. Further, this could involve working on particular skills, such as passing under pressure, by constructing a context that replicates or even exaggerates the pressure under which passes must be made in competition matches, or setting up particular match scenarios where particular players must make instant decisions.

The core idea of both TGfU and Games Sense is the use of a game as a context for learning along the lines of the pedagogy suggested by Dewey (1916/97), in which learning occurs through interaction with the environment rather than by direct instruction (see Bunker and Thorpe 1986; Light 2013). Further, problematising the separation of 'technique' from 'tactical knowledge' that so often characterises traditional 'skill drills', a Game Sense approach rejects the notion that skills have to be learnt *before* a game is played (Light

2008). Attention is shifted from the teacher/coach to the student/player through the adoption of inquiry-based, student/player-centred pedagogies. In particular, this is achieved by taking a problem-solving approach that sees aspects of the game as being problems, and which challenges students/players to solve them while being guided by teacher/coach questioning. This encourages students/players to think about what they are or should be doing and places them at the centre of the learning process. This emphasis on questioning is the most distinctive feature of Game Sense when compared with traditional, directive instruction (Light 2006).

The pedagogy used in Game Sense and TGfU places an emphasis on the coach/teacher designing the learning environment (the modified games), setting problems for the students/players to solve, using questioning to stimulate thinking and reflection, facilitating group discussion and collaboration and allowing players to test and reflect upon strategies, tactics and/or skills formulated to solve the problem(s). Inherent in this approach is the contribution of both the coach and players towards generating new knowledge as, what Davis and Sumara (1997) refer to as, 'co-participants' in learning. The relationship embraces discussion and interaction and the dialogue that emerges (Kidman 2005, 2007; Kidman and Davis 2007; Light and Fawns 2003). It also requires a significant shift in power relations, which is often difficult in situations where knowledge is used to exert power and confirm unequal power relations (Foucault and Gordon 1980; Gore 1997).

Methodology

The sites and participants

The study focused on eight rugby union coaches working at the most elite levels in Australia and New Zealand over 2007–8 (four in Australia and four in New Zealand). The participants all worked with teams at national or provincial levels competing in the Super 14 (at the time) and Tri Nations competitions between Australia, New Zealand and South Africa. In addition, one participant at the Australian site and one in New Zealand coached their national teams (the All Blacks and the Wallabies). Purposive sampling was used in this study as accessing such elite-level coaches is difficult and I had strong connections and networks in rugby that I was able to draw on. The participants were chosen because they coached at elite level, or had particular features or characteristics, which enable detailed exploration and understanding of the central themes that, as the researcher, I wished to study (Baumgartner and Hensley 2006; Neuman 2006).

Data generation and analysis

Data were generated through a series of three extensive, semi-structured interviews and field notes taken during my visits to their places of practice. Interviews were mostly conducted before or after training but occasionally at other settings to fit in with the busy schedules of the coaches. The interviews were structured around a number of themes and/or questions and conducted on a one-to-one basis with each participant to gain an understanding of the real world experiences of coaches working in a professional environment. The study was conducted over a two-year period in New Zealand and Australia. Interviews were generally of 45–60 minutes in duration and were digitally recorded, transcribed verbatim and returned to the participants for member checking.

Content analysis was used to analyse the data inductively as an approach that produces a systematic summary or overview of the data set through the reduction of information that is categorised into themes by finding relationships and grouping similar topics (Krippendorff 2004). As the transcriptions were the unit of analysis the process began with reading and re-reading the interview transcripts to identify recurrent themes. These themes were then systematically identified across the data set and re-grouped together into significant categories. Pseudonyms have been used to protect the identity of participants with the Australian coaches referred to as Ellery, Lincoln, Elvis and Joseph and the New Zealand coaches as Arnold, Paul, Walter and Rodney.

Results

The Australian site

Two strong, interrelated themes emerged from the data. They were that (1) coaches sought to establish and maintain a business relationship with players and that (2) they sought to foster respect and honesty from players, which will be discussed here.

Coaches sought to establish and maintain a business relationship with players

Ellery, Lincoln and Elvis felt that it was important to establish a working relationship that focused on the business of rugby. They also felt that it was difficult to maintain close social relationships with players and be able to do their jobs properly. Ellery felt that having a professional relationship that involved mutual respect between him and the players meant he was in a much better position to improve them as players. He made this comment in response to a question about his relationship with players:

> One of the things that I probably learned early was that it's very important to have a professional relationship with the players. They're never your friends and you can't treat them like your friends. You must treat them like players. So you need to have a professional relationship. That doesn't mean you can't like the players but at the end of the day I think yeah the

coach is there to improve the players. So I think the most important aspect of that relationship is respect.

(Ellery, interview 2, 19 April 2007)

Lincoln, like Ellery, was conscious of establishing relationships with players that were focused on the business of coaching rugby. Lincoln maintained a relationship with players that distanced him from them and ensured that they were not part of his social group. He felt he needed to have this type of relationship in order to be honest with players. Lincoln felt strongly that players should see him as approachable and that he cared about them and their development. Lincoln was measured in his response to his relationship with the players when he said:

> Well I try and maintain it as a business relationship, so certainly friendly with them, but not matey with them. So they're certainly not part of my social group. But the key thing is to be approachable and for them to genuinely believe that you care and that you want them to be the best they can be without having to be matey-matey, that it is a business so you can tell them, you can be absolutely honest with them which is the key for it.

(Lincoln, interview 2, 20 April 2007)

Elvis had made the transition into coaching immediately after finishing his playing career and was coaching players who he had played with. Therefore, he felt it was important to establish a new relationship that distanced him from the players so that his role as a coach was clear. Elvis made this comment in response to a question about his relationship with players:

> I actually drew a line in the sand and said okay I'm the coach now, so I went from the back of the bus to the front of the bus, didn't drink with the blokes. I made it very clear that now I'm coaching so I didn't socialise with the players hardly at all, so I made a very clear line in the sand.

(Elvis, interview 2, 18 July 2007)

Coaches sought to foster respect and honesty from players

All the Australian coaches highly valued being respected by their players for demonstrating the same values that the coaches expected to see in their players. Ellery, Lincoln and Elvis felt that respect and honesty were central to their relationships with players. Ellery thought that his role was to improve players and that this meant that players should respect his knowledge and this knowledge formed the basis of improving player performance:

> The coach is there to improve the players. So I think the most important aspect of that relationship is respect. Yeah, well I think that there

is mutual respect, I respect the player, respect his individuality. That I respect their individuality and they respect my knowledge and hopefully what I bring to the table in terms of helping to improve them as players because a coach's main job is to improve players.

(Ellery, interview 3, 12 July 2007)

Lincoln, however, appeared to view his relationships with players as integral to the organisation's ability to reach its fullest potential. Lincoln wanted people to see him as honest, approachable and with genuine intentions. He felt that in order for everybody to improve he needed to be honest. In response to a question about his relationship with the players he said:

So hopefully they all find me approachable, hopefully they all find me honest, and hopefully they understand if I say something, I mean it. And that I want them and the organisation to be as good as it can be. If we all believe that, then that's fine.

(Lincoln, interview 3, 9 August 2007)

Elvis, like Ellery, viewed respect as an important part of his relationship with players. He felt that it was much easier to be liked by players but harder and more important to be respected. He believed that earning player respect required the coach to be consistent with his decisions, being honest and being fair on a regular basis:

Yeah respect. I think it's easier to generate an environment where everyone likes you can easily go and you know shout everyone drinks and do things like that and everyone likes you, but I think it's respect. Respect comes from consistency of decision making, fairness, honesty. So that's how I see the difference.

(Elvis, interview 2, 18 July 2007)

Joseph saw his relationship with the players slightly differently to the others. He felt that it was important to work closely with the players but made it clear that coaching staff were in control and that players expected the coaching staff to be in control: 'My relationship, as I said, is working with the players to get a result. But there's no doubt that we're running the show and I think players want that direction' (Joseph, interview 2, 18 December 2007).

The New Zealand site

Two interrelated themes emerged from the data generated at the New Zealand site, suggesting that (1) the four coaches favour a humanistic and player-centred approach in their interactions with players, they value being respected and trusted by players and that, (2) they believed that coaches learn from players through appropriate interaction and relationships. The two themes are discussed below in order of importance in the analysis.

Relationships are humanistic and player centred

Paul, Walter and Rodney expressed strong player-centred views. From the data it appears they wanted to establish positive relationships with players and considered players as being particularly influential and integral to team decision making. Each supported the idea that players should be responsible for making the final decision about activities associated with team culture, leadership and team building. On the other hand, Arnold felt that the coaching staff should lead and then the players should take responsibility: 'So the players have got to have buy-in but the whole thing in the first place I think if it's not driven by your coach then you're in trouble' (Arnold, interview 2, 16 October 2007). Paul was uncomfortable with the traditional view of the coach being detached from, and disengaged with, players. He said he had a humanistic relationship with his players: 'Had a sort of a maybe social's the wrong term but humanistic relationship prior to the actual work relationship' (Paul, interview 2, 7 September 2007). He felt that the closer he got to players the better they would perform. Paul favoured a relationship that was more interactive where he could take a personal interest in the players:

> You read material that says you can't be too close to your players. But I think the pendulum's swinging for the generation Y. I think the more individual and the more interactive you can be at a personal level, the more you can get out of them in the field.
>
> (Paul, interview 3, 12 February 2008)

His relationship was centred on maintaining the self-esteem of players without diminishing his own credibility and integrity. Walter had learned from his recent coaching experiences that the most important principle in his relationships with players was that they come first: 'It's something I've had to learn over the last probably five years, got to learn that the player comes first in all engagements' (Walter, interview 2, 11 February 2008). He believed that if a player made the effort to come and talk to him he had to ensure he was committed to resolving their issues or problems in a sensitive, but fair, manner. Walter felt that there needed to be some social distance between him and the players but in reality this often became 'blurred' resulting in strong bonds with players, which led to long-lasting friendships. Walter also felt that his relationship with the players involved helping the players to become 'better people' in order to become better players.

Rodney made the connection between caring and respect for his players. Indeed, the notion of care was emphasised by all four coaches. He felt that caring meant helping players identify their own needs and providing them with an enjoyable training environment in which they could thrive, and that by taking this approach it may lead to him gaining the players' respect. In response to a question about his relationship with players he said:

> I guess, the respect from their end is their choice, but from my perspective I simply try to be motivated by trying to cater for their needs so that they hopefully not only have a good experience but thrive in their environment and if they identify with the way I go about my work, first and foremost I care, probably I might be lucky enough to earn some respect as well back.
>
> (Rodney, interview 3, 6 January 2008)

The optimum relationship for Rodney involved him assisting the players in identifying their own needs through asking questions and getting them to think for themselves:

> Well, the optimum would be for me to assist them to find the solutions that they need as fast as is possible. I mean that's two-way effort obviously. It's not a matter of me telling, and to do that it's probably as much about asking as it is about telling.
>
> (Rodney, interview 3, 6 January 2008)

Valued respect and trust from the players

All the coaches valued being respected and trusted by the players they coached. Paul saw his role as attending to the business of coaching, which meant doing everything in his capacity to prepare a winning team. However, when asked to describe his relationship with the players he coached he reflected on the fact that he knew most of his players growing up and felt he was a 'father figure'. He recognised that coaching often meant making difficult decisions but he was confident because he had the trust and respect of the players:

> You want to be a sort of a father really. You want to be able to have their respect first and foremost. They're not necessarily going to like everything that you tell them but they're going to respect you for telling them and that they're really willing to do everything they can to be part of the group that you're trying to work with together.
>
> (Paul, interview 3, 12 February 2008)

Walter needed to continually ensure that his actions gained the trust and respect of the players. When asked about his relationship with his players he said: 'I'd come back to respect. I think it's really important, I think trust is a huge thing you know, the sort of thing that you've got to earn and you can lose it bloody quickly' (Walter, interview 3, 26 March 2008). Walter asserted that leading by example was critical to maintaining the trust and respect of players. He used this quote by Ralph Waldo Emerson as an analogy for the importance of his actions with players: 'what you do shouts so loudly in my ears that I can't hear what you say' (Walter, interview 3, 26 March 2008). Rodney also felt that the relationship he had with players was built on trust and respect. He was also keen to point out that the relationship needed to be a working one where the respect was mutual by saying that, 'I mean, I aim for a working relationship and by a working relationship I mean one of mutual respect probably sums it up' (Rodney, interview, 6 January 2008). Arnold felt that the players should respect the coach and that without respect coaches would not survive as a long-term professional coach. Arnold indicated that the nature of coaching involved making decisions about selection and this made it difficult to maintain friendships with players, which meant coaches had to engender an environment of respect: 'Unless there's a reasonable amount of respect you don't really have longevity with a team. I don't think you last very long if you strive to have buddy-buddy relationships with all your players, it's too tough' (Arnold, interview 3, 26 March 2008). Arnold felt team selection was the main reason for players not being happy: '[T]hey won't all respect you because players get affected by non-selection' and it can often affect players' self esteem. He felt that it was not possible to make all the players in a squad happy: 'You can't make them [players] all happy all the time' (Arnold, interview 3, 26 March 2008).

Coaches learn from players

All the coaches said that they learn from the players they coach and that this learning occurs on a daily basis. In particular, this type of learning was considered imperative for keeping information current, for the coach's individual development and, in the case of Rodney, for providing insights about how to create environments that foster player empowerment. Learning from the players, or with them, involved having appropriate relationships that enabled productive dialogue. Paul valued the currency of the knowledge he got from players and felt that this helped him to be a better coach:

> I think symbiotic is the term, unless you're able to feed off each other and learn from each other, then you're not getting the full benefit of being a coach, because the players do have a wealth of understanding and knowledge. And as a coach, the ability to tap into that and draw that out so that the next generation of players are getting that information via the horse's mouth as opposed to third party, as the coach generally is, the stronger you'll be.
> (Paul, interview 2, 7 September 2007)

Walter felt that coaches who think they 'know everything' are doing a disservice to the players they coach. Players had knowledge and coaches could benefit from the players' understanding. He felt one of the best characteristics of a good coach was to be open to learning and this meant being open to the players' interpretations as the individuals experiencing training and competition:

Yeah I think the coaches don't know it all and if they think they do then they're doing their players a disservice. You know, I think the ability to think and the openness to learning are two of the biggest, best characteristics of the coach. And that the players who are out in the heat of the battle and doing it, often have a lot to teach you.

(Walter, interview 2, 11 February 2008)

Rodney saw the ability to learn from players as being based on the belief that questioning was the way to gather information from players. He viewed questioning as a part of his relationship with players and a desire to maintain a player-centred approach to coaching. Questioning was a strategy that created motivation and enthusiasm in players, which can potentially lead to creativity and innovation on their part. Rodney made this point when asked if he learned from the players he coached:

Huge, yeah, 'cause they've got the greatest motivation to actually do well, so they're going to have the greatest, hopefully, the greatest enthusiasm to actually get better at what they do, and to find the solutions before the crisis, so they'll drive a lot of innovative and creative and constructive thinking.

(Rodney, interview 2, 7 September 2007)

Arnold, like the others, recognised the importance of learning from players. At a practical level he was able to cite recent examples of adjusting his training and implementing strategies for games based on the feedback from players: 'You got to learn, like just even in the tactical sense, for instance this week, two of the changes we have made to our tactics have come from one of our players' (Arnold, interview 3, 26 March 2008).

Discussion

Game Sense and TGfU require different relationships between coaches/teachers and players/students than traditional, teacher/coach centred approaches (Griffin and Butler 2005; Kidman 2005, 2007; Kidman and Davis 2007; Light and Fawns 2003). Much learning in Game Sense arises from dialogue as emphasised in social constructivism (see, for example, Bruner 1966) instead of the monologue of directive coaching used to convey information. This requires more equal relationships between coach and players and there was a distinct difference between the Australian and New Zealand coaches that seemed to be related to the extent to which they adopted positions congruent with the pedagogic assumptions of Game Sense.

The Australian coaches said that they wanted to establish distance between themselves and their players. They wanted to 'draw the line between' coach and players. This suggests a managerial approach and the desire to sustain a hierarchy where there is a distinct difference in the distribution of power between coaches and players. This reflects a coach-centred approach in which the coach is positioned as most knowledgeable with wisdom to impart to the players. The Game Sense approach embraces a more equitable distribution of power than this in that players are seen as making a contribution to the development of new knowledge that can even extend to coaches being co-learners with the players. The Australian coaches also wanted to earn respect from their players by displaying qualities and characteristics that they felt were valued by all involved in elite-level rugby. They wanted to be respected for making the hard decisions, being strong and fair and taking responsibility for their actions and decisions. They wanted respect for displaying the qualities that they felt were necessary for players to succeed in elite-level rugby.

The relationships valued by the New Zealand coaches appeared to be quite different to the Australian coaches, as was the importance they placed on developing a holistic approach to coaching. They valued respect and trust from players but emphasised developing humanistic relations with them as being necessary for coaching. This is more than just preferring an athlete-centred approach to coaching. Two coaches clearly said that humanistic relationships needed to be built before any professional ones. They also stressed how coaches needed to be open to learning from players on a daily basis through positioning both parties as co-learners and, in doing so, confirming the importance they placed upon relationships that produced dialogue. Such relationships are difficult to establish without a reasonably equitable power relationship between coach and players and are necessary for the implementation of Game Sense coaching (Light 2006, 2013). They all spoke about empowering players to make decisions in training and matches and as part of the personal growth of players. They felt players should have a significant input in all the decisions made about the team, often placing their own views secondary to those of their players. Placing athletes and their learning at the centre of activities is an essential attribute when implementing a Game Sense approach.

The difference between the two sites regarding relationships highlights the humanistic values taken up by the coaches at the New Zealand site compared with the directive coach-centred approach of those at the Australian site. Indeed, during the fieldwork component I felt very welcomed by the coaches I observed at the New Zealand site but, even though I was well known to a number of the Australian participants, I did not feel the same welcome at the Australian site. It felt more like a clinical business environment. The participants in New Zealand provided opportunities for discussion among players and between the players and the coach. They also used questioning during training whereas in Australia the emphasis was on highly organised sessions that followed a schedule with little or no time for discussion, either between players or between the players and the coach. The Australian coaches in the study gave detailed feedback and direction to players on the run throughout the sessions but asked far fewer questions. This results in limited opportunities for the type of learning that emerges from discussion between players and with coaches when viewed from a constructivist perspective (Andriessen 2006) and which Game Sense emphasises.

Conclusion

This study provides some valuable insights into the issue of coach–player relationships and particularly in relation to adopting GBA such as Game Sense as an area that has received limited attention. The larger study strongly suggests that, at the time it was conducted, the New Zealand coaches had all been guided by a Game Sense approach and had accepted it as being more common sense than an innovation, while the approach had far less influence on the beliefs and practices of the Australian coaches. Other research and writing on rugby in New Zealand has long suggested that it drives the 2011 Rugby World Cup-winning All Blacks' training approach and has a significant influence on rugby coaching at other levels in New Zealand (Kidman 2005). This chapter suggests that reconfigurations of traditional coach–player relationships from a directive, coach-centred approach to a more participatory Game Sense approach, together with the establishment and maintenance of conditions that allow these relationships to develop, are integral to the implementation of more productive and holistic coaching pedagogies.

Discussion questions

1. Explain why different relationships are required for a Game Sense approach to coaching when compared to a direct instruction approach.
2. Outline the differences between the two sites and what the author suggests is the reason for these differences.
3. Humanistic relationships and valuing caring for each other could seem at odds with a heavy contact sport like rugby and particularly played at the most elite levels. Discuss this apparent contradiction.

References

Andriessen, J. (2006) 'Arguing to Learn', in R. K. Sawyer (ed.) *The Cambridge Handbook of the Learning Sciences*, New York: Cambridge University Press, pp. 443–459.
Baumgartner, T. A. and Hensley, L. D. (2006) *Conducting and Reading Research in Health and Human Performance*, Boston, MA: McGraw Hill.
Bruner, J. S. (1966) *Toward a Theory of Instruction*, Cambridge, MA: Belknap Press of Harvard University.
Bunker, D. and Thorpe, R. (1982) 'A model for the teaching of games in secondary school', *Bulletin of Physical Education*, 18: 5–8.
——(1986) *The Curriculum Model: Rethinking Games Teaching*, Loughborough: Department of Physical Education and Sports Science, University of Technology.

Davis, B. and Sumara, D. J. (1997) 'Cognition, complexity, and teacher education', *Harvard Educational Review*, 67: 105–125.

den Duyn, N. (1997) *Game Sense. Developing Thinking Players*, Canberra: Australian Sports Commission.

Dewey, J. (1916/97) *Democracy in Education*, New York: Free Press.

Evans, J. R. (2010) 'Elite rugby union coaches' interpretation and use of Game Sense in Australia and New Zealand: An examination of coaches' habitus, learning and development', unpublished thesis, University of Sydney.

——(2012) 'Elite rugby union coaches' interpretation and use of Game Sense in New Zealand', *The Asian Journal of Exercise and Sports Science*, 9: 85–97.

Foucault, M and Gordon, C. (1980) *Power/Knowledge: Selected Interviews and Other Writings, 1972–1977*, New York: Harvester Wheatsheaf.

Gore, J. M. (1997) 'Power relations in pedagogy: An empirical study based on Foucauldian thought', in C. O'Farrell (ed.) *Foucault: The Legacy*, Kelvin Grove, QLD: Queensland University of Technology, pp. 651–663.

Griffin, L. L. and Butler, J. (2005) *Teaching Games for Understanding: Theory, Research, and Practice*, Champaign, IL: Human Kinetics.

Kidman, L. (2005) *Athlete-centred Coaching: Developing Inspired and Inspiring People*, Christchurch: Innovative Print Communications Ltd.

——(2007) 'Humanistic coaching – Teaching Games for Understanding', in R. Light (ed.) *Conference Proceedings of the Asia Pacific Conference on Teaching Sport and Physical Education for Understanding*, Sydney: University of Sydney, pp. 59–71.

Kidman, L. and Davis, W. E. (2007) 'Empowerment in coaching', in W. E. Davis and G. D. Broadhead (eds) *Ecological Task Analysis and Movement*, Champaign, IL: Human Kinetics.

Krippendorff, K. (2004) *Content Analysis: An Introduction to its Methodology*, Thousand Oaks, CA: Sage.

Light, R. (2004) 'Coaches' experience of Game Sense: opportunities and challenges', *Physical Education & Sport Pedagogy*, 9: 115–132.

——(2006) 'Game Sense: Innovation or just good coaching?', *Journal of Physical Education New Zealand*, 39: 10–21.

——(2008) 'Complex learning theory – its epistemology and its assumptions about learning: Implications for physical education', *Journal of Teaching in Physical Education*, 21: 21–37.

——(2013) *Game Sense: Pedagogy for Performance, Participation and Enjoyment*, London: Routledge.

Light, R. and Evans, J. R. (2010) 'The impact of Game Sense on Australian rugby coaches' practice: A question of pedagogy', *Physical Education & Sport Pedagogy*, 15: 103–115.

Light, R. and Fawns, R. (2003) 'Knowing the game: integrating speech and action in games teaching through TGfU', *Quest*, 55: 161–177.

Neuman, W. L. (2006) *Social Research Methods: Qualitative and Quantitative Approaches*, Boston, MA: Pearson/Allyn and Bacon.

Roberts, S. J. (2011) 'Teaching Games for Understanding: the difficulties and challenges experienced by participation cricket coaches', *Physical Education & Sport Pedagogy*, 16: 33–48.

Wright, J. and Forrest, G. (2007) 'A social semiotic analysis of knowledge construction and games centred approaches to teaching', *Physical Education & Sport Pedagogy*, 12: 273–287.

Part III

Issues in adopting game-based approaches

10 Subjectivity as a resource for improving players' decision making in team sport

Alain Mouchet (translated by Rémy Hassanin)

The complexity and subjectivity of in-match decision making in elite players

In team sports, outstanding players seem to possess an uncanny sense of the game that allows them to be in the right place at the right time, have more time to respond and make effective decisions under pressure (Light, Harvey and Mouchet 2012). Such players are typically described as possessing a remarkable 'practical sense', characterized as a seemingly innate mastery of what is practical, even in dynamic circumstances (Bourdieu 1980). The speed and efficiency with which decisions are made under pressure suggest that this sense of the game, which involves an adaptation to a very dynamic environment with little separation between perception, decision making, mind and body, or the player and the situation, demonstrates tactical intelligence, as does the ability to adapt with precision, speed and efficiency to evolving game situations. There is, however, typically a distinct paradox between the coaches' discourse and player training, with a general tendency to prioritize a rationalistic, reductionist approach to decision making, which is often accompanied by criticism of the players for their inability to adapt in action. There is also a significant problem in research conducted on decision making and the activity of coaches in verbalizing what constitutes this expertise in action, often depicted as instinct, intuition or experience (Nash and Collins 2006) with the implication that it cannot be coached (Light and Evans 2010; Willliams and Hodges 2005). Such attempts in coaching and conducting research to reduce an inherently complex phenomenon severely limit our understanding of what is going on and our ability to improve in-match decision making.

Research that has considered the subjective dimensions of decision making provides some insight into these two problems (Mouchet 2005a, 2008). It suggests that elite rugby union players' decision making in matches is both complex and subjective and is shaped by a subjective personal logic. Thus, decisions occur in situ, following the actions of the ball carrier in a 'local context', meaning that the circumstances are shaped by these actions whilst also being influenced by a general context labelled 'the decisional background' (see, for example, Light *et al.* 2012). This latter decisional background is constituted by the relative socio-cultural context of the club, the game plan, strategies, team and individual experiences, such as the many elements displayed in the outer extremities of the model (see Figure 10.1 below). These influences act as a system, which embeds the decision making in action. Each player is constructing his/her world (i.e. his/her own situation) by integrating each level (environment, ball carrier and his team mates) in accordance with his/her subjective logic. Such a model highlights the dynamics between collective and individual action and portrays the subtle articulation between strategies and tactics (Mouchet 2005b).[1]

Studies conducted on subjectivity in match play in France have typically employed a psycho-phenomenological approach, with the aim of describing and exposing the subjective lived experience of players. This approach is beneficial for understanding the subjective dimensions of play and decision making and can expose the internal decisional logic from the constructed view of the player in action (Mouchet 2008). This allows for the investigation of significant indications of the player's lived experience by accessing the micro-operating modus as stemming from a level of pre-reflective consciousness (Vermersch 2001).[2] Such characterization of player activity in a match permits emphasizing the importance of this subjective facet of players' experiences of play and its influence on awareness and/or decision making (Mouchet 2008; Light *et al.* 2012). The data obtained through this work have revealed the capacity of elite-level players to make a 'deliberate decision' in a 'light pressure' situation (e.g. far counter attack) and 'decisions at action' when required to make an instant decision. However, the results suggest that one's own personal logic may not always conform to the rational logic (strategies) of the game. It seems then to be important to consider this player subjectivity in developing an approach that attempts to optimize all these decision-making factors of performance.

To understand and document this complexity and subjectivity within a match, research in France has employed several methods (Mouchet 2005b, 2008; Mouchet, Vermersch and Bouthier 2011) that also have use in sports coaching. The objective of this chapter is to present a framework for coaching in decision making through the use and the articulation of the lived experience of players as a way of developing expertise. This framework has been implemented in high-performance rugby institutes in France and can be used in other team sports if consideration is given to the inter-subjectivity between player(s) and coach(es) to optimize team effectiveness. This framework is organized with the following idea: the co-construction of a common reference in which the key is the capacity to articulate a reflection in action, an analysis of the lived experience and an intervention that promotes adaptation and game intelligence. Consequently, our propositions for sports coaching aim to contribute to player development.

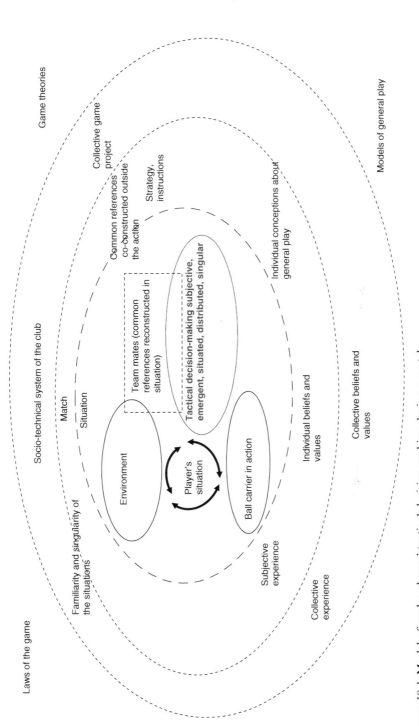

Figure 10.1 Model of rugby players' tactical decision making during a match
Source: Translated from Mouchet 2005a, 2010b

The co-construction of common references: towards an inter-subjectivity between coaches and players

Game plan and common references

A game plan is defined as a set of articulated strategic and tactical principles that represent an ideal game defined by its creator(s). It contains, most of the time, set plays from which to launch an attack after a phase play (Mouchet 2010b). Phase play is play that arises from rucks and mauls between the set plays of scrums and line-outs. The game plan is usually constructed by the coaches and is presented explicitly to the players with different media such as written documents, PowerPoint presentations or DVDs. However, such shared knowledge is moulded in pre-match strategies adapted to the opposition – and enriches the collective, lived experiences of previous matches. This shared knowledge, explicit and previously defined, is a resource for action as it defines the priorities of the game, the collective organization, the player's role and so on. This promotes the creation of a 'common reference' (Deleplace 1979).

This common reference is inscribed in the game plan and defines it. It possesses two characteristics: it is declarative and functional. Declarative in the sense that it mobilizes the shared knowledge such as the game plan, and functional as it orients and coordinates players' decisions in action, according to a rational (or theoretical) logic of the game. However, it is permanently reconstructed in situ, and, as such, possesses an ephemeral character (Bencheckroun and Weill-Fassina 2000).

Within a team-sport framework, and in rugby union in particular, one of the emblematic theoreticians of French rugby, Deleplace (1979), defined the common reference as 'a common representative system of the opposition's effects'. He defines the logic of the game as shifting between attack and defence at three operational levels: (1) the 'total plan' (teams), (2) a 'partial plan' (for example, the two backlines) and (3) 'inter-individual plan' (man-on-man, for example, two against one). This common reference then constitutes a common base of tactical awareness. It could also be formulated with particular decisions such as 'if the defence is tight, we must attack wide'. Bouthier (2000) puts forth, in a cognitivist view, the need to make subjective a common analytical reference and tactical decision making. For example, this would allow the support play to anticipate individual initiatives of the ball carrier, which would enhance coherent action and decision making. Thus, there is a necessity to elaborate on a common reference that has been set but which is adaptable and constantly evolving. Therefore, we are more reserved when ideas prioritize the environment as being static, controllable and predefined, wherein an adaptation occurs according to rationalistic processes. The individual initiative (Deleplace 1979) can be considered using another framework for analysis, which integrates the subjective and personal experience of the players' adaptation to the dynamic nature of the situation.

Locating and evaluating the theoretical appropriation of a collective reference

The theoretical options discussed in the previous section are to be connected with practical constraints. Coaches, most notably in professional teams, are required to manage a constant player turnover with each new season. This problem is exacerbated by the nature of rugby as a global game and the increasing movement of players between countries, with significant numbers of foreign players typically found in teams competing at elite professional levels. For example, in France in the 2011/2012 season 42 per cent of the players in professional competitions were foreign players. Thus, it is necessary, on the one hand, to create a game plan that takes into account the diversity of the players and, on the other hand, to be assured the players have a good understanding of the 'set' game plan. This has led to research interest in considering inter-subjectivity in decision making, by developing a preliminary, co-constructed game plan and some common references with the aim of optimizing collective effectiveness (Mouchet and Bouthier 2006; Mouchet 2010b). Indeed, in the dynamic construction of shared knowledge, it is necessary to highlight the active roles played by the individuals when appropriating such knowledge and their transformation (Barbier 1998). Consequently, ignoring this aspect brings forth a possibility and risk of misunderstanding and a lack of player cohesion. I would also suggest that such a cooperative learning environment is best accompanied with the training cycles set for the rugby season. This learning rests upon a co-constructed organization between coaches, senior players and a researcher or outside consultant.

Such a development necessitates evaluating the theoretical appropriation of the game plan and its common references that could occur at the beginning of the season whilst the game plan is being put in place, or with respect to particular training cycles focused on different themes such as defence, attacking plays, player circulation and so on. In studies conducted on subjectivity and the complexity of decision making (Mouchet 2005a, 2008) short (approximately 15-minute) individual semi-structured interviews (Weill-Barais 1997) were performed to identify the players' conceptions. The results were synthesized and presented visually with the use of a diagram (see Figure 10.2) that clusters, in the centre, the words or groups of words most often cited (e.g. in Figure 10.2, by six or seven people), and thus represents the shared beliefs amongst the group. The more we diverge towards the peripheries, the fewer the number of people who had made mention of the words. Each player was attributed a letter of the alphabet for identification: each item is thus personalized. In Figure 10.2 I make mention of only a few of the examples.

This allows the coaches a quick and clear descriptive response to the elements used by the players, the shared aspects but also the ambiguities and misunderstandings which it is necessary to come back to. Additionally, the diagram allows for the identification of leading representations of the game

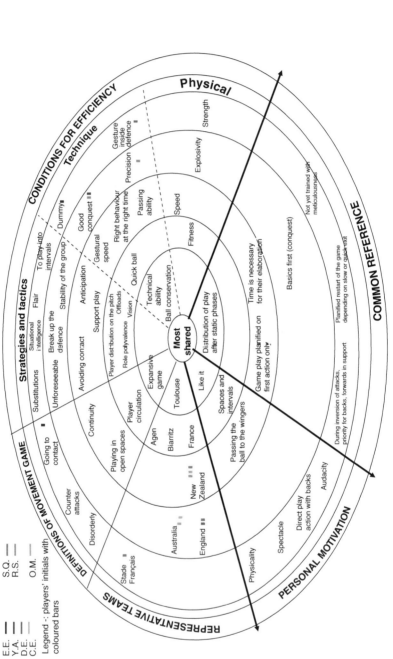

Figure 10.2 Players conceptions of match play: words most commonly used

plan, and players who seem more congruent with the ideas of the coaches. Finally, such reporting allows for personalized work that may help in understanding the common references. It is there that such work, not only with respect to the diversity inherent in the players, but with each passing season affected by a high degree of player roll-over, is important. It then requires a means of understanding and considering player subjectivity to regulate the coach's interventions (Mouchet and Bouthier 2006).

Performance analysis and transforming practice

I now turn to the concept of reflective learning for professional practice in respect to Schön's (1983) propositions. The main idea is that reflection on one's practice is a means of enhancing practice because it allows constant access to knowledge-in-action. The importance of this form of learning was highlighted in various other works relating to coach education (see, for example, Werthner and Trudel 2006; Abraham and Collins 2011). I also draw on various propositions in the professional didactics[3] field in France, through which a retrospective reflexive analysis can become a resource for transforming practice (Pastré 1999). Consequently, the role of verbalization in the analysis of practice and to develop expertise is enhanced by structuring 'education that combines learning through practice and learning through analysing practice' (Pastré 1999: 26). Different interview methods could be used, but that chosen corresponded with the aim of characterizing the subjective experience of the players. My proposition in this respect is an educative scheme based on the use of individual explicitation interviews (Vermersch 2009) to bring forth and make accessible the 'lived experiences' of practice. My references to lived experience derive from the idea of the 'lived body' (Husserl 1962) as a subjective, social entity that is lived and involves forms of action, intention and intimate interaction.

Describing the lived experience in a game through the explicitation interview

Work on the reflective practitioner is concerned with reflection in action and reflection on the act of action but it underestimates the non-conscious dimensions of action, or a 'pre-reflexive phenomenological' consciousness. Moreover, we break away from such work by focusing on the explicitation interviews carried out individually, not on a reflection on action but 'thinking' on it (Vermersch 2009; Maurel 2009). Such thinking emerges and makes real a reflective consciousness within the subject (Vermersch 2001). The explicitation interview thus aims to create a reflective consciousness; a verbalized and conceptual form of experiential knowledge. The objective of the explicitation interview is to characterize the subjective experience, which was momentarily non-conscious at the moment of the lived experience. It allows the interviewee to take consciousness of his/her acts and his/her cognitive processes in a past act/situation.

Research on lived experiences of play has led to the development of a systematic approach that utilizes an explicitation interview used in conjunction with video (Mouchet 2005b; Mouchet *et al.* 2011) to capture the subject's (first-person) viewpoint with an exterior viewpoint on the action.[4] This involves a brief stimulated recall in which video of the sequence of play concerned is presented to the player with the task being to highlight the most important moment(s) that structured his/her actions and decisions made at the time. After this the explicitation interview is used in search for deeper and more descriptive details on the mentioned moments as a reliving of the situation/experience. The interview guide for the explicitation interview is structured by excerpts from the match in which the player can be seen to have made successful and unsuccessful decisions and responses. Two aspects are thus elicited and explored.

We compare the 'situation resource' (e.g. where the player was successful) and the 'situation problem' (e.g. where the player is challenged or fails) (Faingold 2002) to study the intrinsic logic of the subject in the two cases and figure out the differences to identify factors contributing to success or the source of an error. The analysis of such failures is pertinent as it represents a natural means of uncovering facets of expertise. This comparison can help a subject to better understand why situations were challenging by shifting the centre of attention from describing tacit knowledge in an effective performance towards a critical analysis of the strategies, assumptions and formalizations of the problem that are often the source of poor performance/failure.

Alternatively, we can compare the situations of a similar format where the player has been successful to promote consistency in the subject's decision making. With this approach we align with Schön's (1983) propositions relating to learning as a reflective transfer, noting that it is important to interview players who are willing to participate in order to optimize authentic data, and we present below extracts from an interview. The extract below is from a successful task, and highlights the precision and the amount of information taken into consideration by the player.

An illustration of reliving player experience of decision making in rugby

The following reliving of player experience focuses on a moment in play for the player referred to as J. C. It describes the sequence of play and then focuses on the experience of finding the gap in the defensive line. The text relates to the video stills (Figures 10.3, 10.4 and 10.5) taken from the video footage played by J. C.

Play-sequence description

The sequence of play that was focused on began with the set play of a lineout followed by a maul for the offensive team (dark jerseys) 25 metres from the opposition's try line. After the maul the ball carrier (dark number 13) follows

Figure 10.3

Figure 10.4

Figure 10.5

a pre-determined strategy to receive a lateral pass and breaks the first defensive line. He runs towards the last defender (white number 15) and passes the ball to his team-mate on his right side (dark number 14) who should have scored a try but the ball was knocked on (he dropped it forward). I present

Figure 10.6

Figure 10.7

Figure 10.8

the following extracts of data concerning the continuity of the game play after the defensive line break as the part of the game we agreed to focus on. Extracts of the player verbalization of experience are presented in parenthesis and quotation marks.

Finding the gap in the defensive line

As soon as the defensive line is crossed, J. C. (the ball carrier) aims to exploit the overlap created ('what is important for me was to score, my goal is to accelerate quickly and look for solutions') (Figure 10.4). He recounts the following actions: 'I raised my head, I accelerated'. Here he is providing information on the new break in play created by reliving the moment. He recounts how his peripheral vision enables him to identify the positions and movements of the opponents around him. The first and principal cue for him is an opponent located opposite him ('it appears there is a defender in front of me [Figure 10.4], I see a person opposite, a silhouette that I see more distinctly than the others'). He recounts other cues but with less descriptive detail ('there are other opponents who are moving towards me', 'on my left I see a white patch. In fact it is the jersey colour of the opponent that I notice'). Here it seems that the decisional background intervenes to shape a 'visual feeling' ('I have this general impression'). Thus, the subject refers to similar, previous situations he has experienced ('several times I have been in this situation, and sometimes I didn't pay attention precisely enough to information at the side of or behind me, it is by experience or intuition'). This background also includes knowledge relative to defenders moving back into position in this kind of game situation ('it is known that they are there') while he also remembers the noise, which accompanies the action ('there are shouts from the spectators') as part of the moment he relives.

Apart from recognizing the distance that separates J. C. from the defensive line ('I must be within seven–eight metres'), he provides additional information about the experience that influenced his decision making. We can speak about focusing details extended to the body of the opponent ('I see a more or less definite silhouette; I do not see precise details; I do not see what he does with his body, I do not see precisely if he is looking to the right or the left'). The most significant aspect of this moment is his perception of a silhouette he considers to be an obstacle, and which appears to constitute a sufficient cue for action and thinking at this moment ('I see just that there is a body, that there is somebody opposite me').

Fragmenting the action during the explicitation interview makes it possible to obtain new data that can facilitate the reconstruction of J.C's awareness. He hears a shout close to him, without being able to clearly identify it ('and then I hear, I hear somebody who shouts from beside me; as soon as I break the line, I look, I see him shouting, I know that he is there, I do not need to worry about him being there any more').

The video stills above clearly confirm the fact that J. C. accelerates and raises his head to look forward; he is approximately 17 metres from the try line. Moreover, such awareness is confirmed by the presence of the defenders (Figures 10.3 and 10.4). The white fullback (15) is the last defender in front of him, there are also two close opponents pursuing J. C. on the left about two metres away (they have run back to cover from the first defensive line). There is also confirmation of focusing on the fullback located approximately seven or eight metres in front as the subject affirms it (Figures 10.4 and 10.5). Although the video still (Figure 10.5) cannot confirm this because I don't have audio data of the player, the content data suggests that he heard shouts next to him and saw his teammate at this moment. His supporting teammate is unmarked and runs into the same gap that J. C. did. We can see from Figure 10.5 and his open mouth that his supporting player called for the ball. The two sources of data (i.e. visual and audio) of the partner are simultaneous and very brief and I suggest that here we have a good example of the co-construction of a common reference between these two players who have analyzed the situation in the same way.

Structure and intervention for on-field player development

Let us recall that the approach I have outlined is designed to accommodate player development. To do this it needs to be integrated into the season plans at integral moments and assimilated into organized periods of training structured in the team's training cycles and micro-cycles and combine different factors influencing performance (e.g. tactical, technical, physical and mental). Consequently, my proposition is situated in this organization, in accordance with coaches' conceptions and the importance placed upon general play in the game plan, time of the season, needs and expectations of the players as well as performance and wins.

Such a pedagogical approach requires developing tactical intelligence and player adaptation in situ, resulting in less focus on the technical components of play. Through this approach tactics are prioritized, but while the focus on technical development is reduced it is not overlooked. This is not incompatible with an organized collective strategy, as I have shown earlier in the chapter. Thus, within the context of French rugby, Villepreux, Jeandroz and Brochard (2007) recommend autonomous player development prioritizing a high degree of freedom.

The Game Sense approach for coaching also emphasizes player autonomy and responsibility successfully employed by the 2011 Rugby World Cup-winning All Blacks (Evans 2012; Light 2013). However, this requires, first, developing 'game play' (under game conditions), as it is in these collective phases that a player's adaptability due to the dynamic nature of game play is best expressed. It must focus on the 'reality of the game' in proposing situations that require players to adjust according to the 'three oppositional plans' defined by Deleplace (1979). Such a pedagogical approach is characterized by a teaching/coaching approach developed in France named 'pedagogical models for tactical decision-making' (PMDT) (Bouthier 1993; Gréhaigne, Godbout and Bouthier 2001). The proponents of this approach argue that the cognitive process is decisive in guiding the choice and motor control of actions. It assumes that key moments (e.g. cues), and the rational principles of what is tactical (e.g. theory), organize effective action in terms of quality and execution. It is, thus, similar to the Anglo-Saxon TGfU (Light and Fawns 2003; Gray and Sproule 2011), which prioritizes understanding in learning to become better decision makers, and in which the focus is on modified games within which technique develops. However, PMDT relates better in certain respects to Game Sense (den Duyn 1997; Light 2013). These approaches recognize that good decision making is inseparable from effective technical execution but PMDT and TGfU are based on a paradigm that is essentially cognitivist whereas Game Sense is based on socio-constructivist learning theory (Light 2013). Typically, from a Game Sense perspective, the coach would stop the game for brief questioning that would stimulate critical reflection and collaborative problem solving. This would then lead to the formulation of ideas that would be tested in the game that may refine successful tactical decisions and eliminate those that did not work (see, for example, Light *et al.* 2012).

This process in PMDT, TGfU and Game Sense highlights the central role of language in learning that requires conscious, rational processing. Furthermore, without suggesting this to be a new theory, I would support the use of a rational logic of action that is objective and common across players. Knowledge of these intrinsic logics is an essential skill for the coach to be able to adapt his interventions. Indeed, whilst referring to the cognitivist approach apparent in PMDT, Bouthier (2000) highlights how the common reference is not simply reduced to decisional aspects, but also important in motor, sensational and social aspects of play as well. Consequently, we should consider the importance of integrating the subjective dimension of play within player activity as I have demonstrated. In order to convey such a perspective, I refer to the possibility of exploiting differently one of the means of action in PMDT 'the laws of exercise',[5] defined by Deleplace (1979) and developed by Bouthier (2000).

Thus, one of the laws consists of preserving, in proposed situations, alternative choices. This, according to Bouthier (2000), allows a person to: (a) categorize various possible states of physical activity and a structured class of problems; (b) identify the class of problems; (c) understand the logical notions corresponding to typical states of physical activity; (d) have reliable (pertinent) criteria of choice adequate to the situation.

Indeed, I would estimate the capacity to provide understanding, and propose pathways with which to further integrate player/subject subjectivity:

(a) Over and above the generic classification of a class of problems, we should consider the player's personal characteristics in regards to their abilities.
(b) It is difficult to direct all players to the same cues, particularly as they are defined in the third person. This can affect player development, as one must manage and adapt to situations (e.g. adapting the material, environment or the activity). Thus one can stimulate the preferred sensorial channels and solicit a sensorial mode in action, and develop in crucial zones and key moments a greater awareness and thus dispositions towards more effective decision making.

(c) If a logical sequence of actions is defined as per an analysis of a situation from an objective view, which is useful in optimizing decision making, then we can positively adhere to such use as mentioned above. Indeed, such models are varied and these appropriations are in themselves diverse, be it for the coaches or the players. It is necessary to identify players' subjective logic in order to operationalize differentiated and adapted interventions.

(d) I do not suggest that decision making is only specifically based upon a model that is preordained. But that it is important to construct situations that have varied temporal and physical pressures in order to activate such rational decision making (deliberate) and those decisions that are more instinctive (e.g. 'at action').

Some leads have been proposed in this regard, for example, organizing team discussions is useful for collaboration and a helpful tool for finding solutions to test in the real game (Wallian and Chang 2007), or again a functional link between action and a reflective analysis of action (Light *et al.* 2012). We can envisage exploiting verbalization to on-the-field interactions. This aims to manipulate coach and player interactions by explicitation means. It is not only possible to solicit a reflective consciousness with commentary, opinions or declarative knowledge of the lived action, but also promote in situ consciousness or pre-reflexive aspects, as these elements relate to a description of the action that has been lived at the decision organization – 'at action'. These explicitation cues of the lived action are based upon a different manner through which to promote player verbalization, based upon techniques used in the explicitation interview. Thus, we envisage questions of this format:

And when you receive the ball, what do you deem important?
What did you start with?
And just when you want to draw the defender, what do you do?
When you straighten your running line, what are you aware of?
Are there other things of which you are aware?
How do you know that you've drawn the defender?

These questions evoke the lived situation with a reflective description of the objective motor acts and awareness or internalized cues that act as a form of appreciation to guide the subsequent actions.

Conclusion

Tactical coaching constitutes a fundamental part of coaching for player development with a co-constructed common reference as an important facet of it. It provides an interface between the pre-determined team game plan and individual decision making, or more generally between the team's shared experience, and player subjectivity. From this perspective, I have presented a valid and rigorous method of documenting this subjective player experience to optimize decision making in practical contexts. As I have argued, it is important to understand these subjective experiences to be able to transform them into practical resources that can be drawn upon to improve performance. In this chapter I have outlined a method developed through research and through which it is possible to access these subjective player experiences in order to understand, interpret and operationalize them for player development. Rogalski and Leplat (2009) suggested that it is possible to learn from episodic experiences that play a role in developing expertise. Furthermore, the proposed methodology presented in this chapter can be mobilized in other parts of the game such as in scrums and line-outs, or to analyze other composite activities such as a specific skill or stress management (e.g. the goal kicker in a penalty or the lineout thrower), or in other team sports.

A similar methodology has been operationalized in research on coaching during a match to study coaches' observations and analyses of a game (Mouchet 2010a), and coach/player communication (Mouchet and Le Guellec 2012; Mouchet, Harvey and Light in press). Furthermore, work on coaches' half-time speeches in an elite-level rugby club is currently in progress, within which the explicitation interview is at the heart of a systematic approach that articulates a relationship between research and the development of game play (Mouchet 2012). Understanding the intrinsic logic of players, or more generally accounting for such subjectivity, is a coaching skill required to manage peculiarities and to adapt his/her interventions. It is also a skill for players in the sense that a better understanding of the organizational modes of his colleagues promotes efficient team play.

Discussion questions

1. What does the author mean by the subjective aspects of game play and decision making and how is this different to an objective view of play and decision making?
2. What are the aims of research on decision making in matches outlined in this chapter that employs a psycho-phenomenological approach and how does it strive to achieve these aims?
3. Explain how the author suggests that understanding the subjective aspects of decision making can be used to improve it in sport coaching and suggest what implications this might have for teaching games in physical education.

Notes

1 A strategy is a decision made of an activity that is preordained to guide and structure the sporting action, whereas tactics correspond to the decision-making process in situ. However, the articulation between these two decisional modalities

was highlighted in previous works (Bouthier, Barthes, David and Gréghaine 1994; Gréghaine, Bouthier and David, 1997; Mouchet 2005b; Eloi, 2009).

2 In his consciousness theory, Vermersch (2001) distinguishes between 'consciousness in action' (i.e., pre-reflective experience, implicit mode of reflection) and 'reflective consciousness' (i.e., conceptualized knowledge, judgements or explanations about a process). A part of the subjective experience unfolds below the threshold of reflective consciousness; for example, day-to-day activities are embodied in consciousness. It is possible, however, to become aware of pre-reflective experience.

3 The professional didactics approach aims to analyze work duties to identify the competencies required and thus include them in learning and development programmes: www.didactiqueprofessionnelle.org (last accessed 7 May 2013).

4 The first-person viewpoint corresponds to what appears to the subject who lived the experience, thus the third-person viewpoint develops, for example, through observations from a coach/researcher.

5 The laws of exercise that allow the interviewer to organize situations are as follows: (a) designation/delimitation of space and clear objectives of the game; (b) adequate personnel; (c) two-part action: with players starting off and then introducing the ball; (d) alternative choices of motor solutions; (e) starting positions are either calibrated or de-calibrated according to the opposition (spatial or numerical); (f) reversing roles and positions.

References

Abraham, A. and Collins, D. (2011) 'Taking the next step: Ways forward for coaching science', *Quest*, 63(4), 366–384.

Barbier, J. M. (1998) *Savoirs Théoriques et Savoirs d'action* [Theoretical Knowledge and Knowledge-in-action], Paris: PUF.

Bencheckroun, T. H. and Weill-Fassina, A. (2000) *Le Travail Collectif. Perspectives Actuelles en Ergonomie* [Group Work. Ergonomic Perspectives], Toulouse: Octarès.

Bourdieu, P. (1980) *Le Sens Pratique* [The Practical Sense], Paris: Minuit.

Bouthier, D. (1993) *L'approche Technologique en S.T.A.P.S.: Représentations et Actions en Didactique des APS* [The Technological Approach in Exercise and Sport Science: The Didactic Representations and Actions in Physical Activity], Diplôme d'habilitation à diriger des recherches. Orsay: Université Paris-Sud.

——(2000) 'La coordination des décisions individuelles; contribution de l'intelligence tactique' [The Organization of Individual Decisions: Contributions of Tactical Intelligence], paper presented at the Symposium for Olympic Preparation [Colloque Préparation Olympique] *L'évolution de la pensée tactique* [Developments in tactical thinking], Noisy le Grand, 14–15 November.

Bouthier, D., Barthes, D., David, B. and Gréhaigne, J.-F. (1994) *Tactical analysis of play combinations in rugby with video computer: rationalizing French Flair*, paper presented at 2nd World Congress of Notational Analysis of Sport, Cardiff, 25–30 November.

Deleplace, R. (1979) *Rugby de Mouvement, Rugby Total* [Movement Rugby, Total Rugby], Paris: Edition EPS.

den Duyn, N. (1997) *Game Sense: Developing Thinking Players*, Canberra: Australian Sports Commission.

Eloi, S. (2009) 'Style d'un passeur de haut niveau en volley-ball' [Passing style of a high-level volleyball player], *eJRIEPS*, 17, 76–105.

Evans, J. R. (2012) 'Elite rugby union coaches' interpretation and use of Game Sense in New Zealand', *Asian Journal of Exercise and Sport Science*, 9(1), 85–97.

Faingold, N. (2002) 'Situation problème, situation ressource en analyse de pratique' [Problem situation, resource situation in analysing action], *Expliciter*, 45, 38–41.

Gray, S. and Sproule, J. (2011) Developing pupils' performance in team invasion games, *Physical Education and Sport Pedagogy*, 16(1), 15–32.

Gréhaigne, J.-F., Bouthier, D. and David, B. (1997) 'Dynamic-system analysis of opponent relationships in collective actions in soccer', *Journal of Sports Sciences*, 15, 137–149.

Gréhaigne, J.-F., Godbout, P. and Bouthier, D. (2001) 'The teaching and learning of decision-making in team sports', *Quest*, 53, 59–76.

Husserl, E. (1962) *Ideas: General Introduction to Pure Phenomenology*, translated by W. R. Boyce Gibson, London and New York: Collier, Macmillan.

Light, R. (2013) *Game Sense: Pedagogy for Performance: Participation and Enjoyment*, London and New York: Routledge.

Light, R. L. and Evans, J. R. (2010) 'The impact of Game Sense pedagogy on elite level Australian rugby coaches' practice: A question of pedagogy', *Physical Education and Sport Pedagogy*, 15(2), 103–115.

Light, R. and Fawns, R. (2003) 'Knowing the game: Integrating speech and action in games teaching through TGfU', *Quest*, 55, 161–175.

Light, R. L., Harvey, S. and Mouchet, A. (2012) 'Improving "at-action" decision-making in team sports through a holistic coaching approach', *Sport, Education & Society*, DOI:10.1080/13573322.2012.665803.

Maurel, M. (2009) 'The explicitation interview: Examples and applications', *Journal of Consciousness Studies*, 16(10-12), 58–89.

Mouchet, A. (2005a) 'Modélisation de la complexité des décisions tactiques en rugby' [Modelling the complexity of tactical decisions in rugby], *eJRIEPS*, 7, 3–19.

——(2005b) 'Subjectivity in the articulation between strategy and tactics in team sports: example in rugby', *Italian Journal of Sport Sciences*, 12, 24–33.

——(2008) 'La subjectivité dans les décisions tactiques des joueurs experts en rugby' [Subjective tactical decision-making in elite rugby players], *eJRIEPS*, 14, 96–116.

——(2010a) 'Le coaching des sélections nationales en rugby: observation et analyse du jeu en début de match' [National selection in rugby: game observation and analysis], in C. Amans-Passaga, N. Gal-Petitfaux, P. Terral, M. Cizeron and M. F. Carnus (eds) *L'intervention en Sport et ses Contextes Institutionnels: Cultures et Singularité de l'action* [Sport interventions and their institutional contexts: Cultures and specificity of action], Rodez: Presses du Centre Universitaire de Champollion.

——(2010b) 'Co-construire un référentiel commun en rugby. Approche coopérative de l'entrainement en sport de haut niveau' [Co-constructing a common reference in rugby. Cooperative approaches to training in high level sport], in F. Darnis (ed.), *L'apprentissage Cooperatif* [Cooperative learning], Paris: EPS.

——(2012) 'Compétences des entraîneurs de rugby en match: les discours à la mi-temps' [In-match rugby coaching skills: the discourse at halftime], proceedings of the 2nd International Symposium on Professional Didactics, 'Learning and Professional Development', Nantes, 7–8 June.

Mouchet, A. and Bouthier, D. (2006) 'Prendre en compte la subjectivité des joueurs de rugby pour optimiser l'intervention' [Considering rugby players' subjectivity to optimise interventions], *STAPS*, 72, 93–106.

Mouchet, A. and Le Guellec, L. (2012) 'Les communications entraineurs/joueurs en match de rugby international' [Coach/player communication in an international rugby match], in C. Spallanzani, R. Goyette, M. Roy, S. Turcotte, J. F. Desbiens and

S. Baudoin (eds) *Mieux Former et Intervenir dans les Activités Physiques, Sportives et Artistiques: Vivre Actif et en Santé* [Better Development and Interventions in Sport, Physical Activity and Art: Live Active and Healthy], Sherbrooke, QC: PUQ.

Mouchet, A., Harvey, S. and Light, R. (in press) 'Match coaching: communications with players during the game', *Physical Education and Sport Pedagogy*.

Mouchet, A., Vermersch, P. and Bouthier, D. (2011) 'Méthodologie d'accès à l'expérience subjective: entretien composite et vidéo' [Approaches to subjective experience: composite interview and video], *Savoirs* 27, 87–105.

Nash, C. and Collins, D. (2006) 'Tacit knowledge in expert coaching: science or art?', *Quest*, 58, 465–477.

Pastré, P. (1999) 'La conceptualisation dans l'action: bilan et nouvelles perspectives' [Conceptualisation in action: overview and new perspectives], *Education Permanente*, 139, 2, 13–35.

Rogalski, J. and Leplat, J. (2009) '*Des expériences dans l'Expérience*' [Experiences in experience], paper presented at round table on 'Experience' at the International Symposium of the Association Francophone Research and Professional Practices in Teaching, Agrosup, Dijon, 2–4 December.

Schön, D. A. (1983) *The Reflective Practitioner: How Professionals Think in Action*, New York: Basic Books.

Vermersch, P. (2001) 'Conscience directe et conscience réfléchie' [Direct consciousness and reflective consciousness], *Expliciter*, 39, 10–31.

——(2009) 'Describing the practice of introspection', *Journal of Consciousness Studies*, 16(10-12), 20–57.

Villepreux, P., Jeandroz, M. and Brochard, F. (2007) *Rugby. le Jeu, les Joueurs, les Entraîneurs* [Rugby: the Game, the Players, the Coaches], Paris: Vigot.

Wallian, N. and Chang, C. W. (2007) 'Language, thinking and action: Towards a semio-constructivist approach in physical education', *Physical Education and Sport Pedagogy*, 12(3), 289–311.

Weill-Barais, A. (1997) *Les Méthodes en Psychologie* [Approaches in Psychology], Rosny: Bréal.

Werthner, P. and Trudel, P. (2006) 'A new theoretical perspective for understanding how coaches learn to coach', *The Sport Psychologist*, 20, 198–212.

Williams, A. M. and Hodges, N. J. (2005) 'Practice, instruction and skill acquisition in soccer: challenging tradition', *Journal of Sport Sciences*, 23(6), 637–650.

11 Questions and answers

Understanding the connection between questioning and knowledge in game-centred approaches

Greg Forrest

Introduction

Over the last 20 years, there has been considerable enthusiasm for approaches to teaching games and sports that use a game-centred approach (GCA). GCA is an umbrella term for pedagogical approaches and models that have game play and reflection on game play as central elements of the learning process. However, they should not be confused with the games concept approach used in Singapore and reported on in Chapter 3. The underlying philosophy of the GCA approaches described here is that students need to develop an understanding of *how* to play rather than an overriding focus on *what* to do when they do play and that this understanding is developed through their active participation in, exploration of, and reflection on, their play. The *how* element can be developed because GCAs have the capacity to examine a broad range of game-play elements, such as strategy and tactics and decision making, as well as movement skills, and to explore the relationships these elements have with performance. As a result of this learning through games via progressions from simple to more complex practice games and the use of questioning, students in classes characterized by GCAs can recognize that there is more to play than movement alone. This, in turn, provides them with the opportunity for greater learning, engagement and participation.

The study presented in this chapter investigates how physical and health education (PHE) pre-service teachers may gain an understanding of how to effectively use GCAs (see Forrest 2009; Forrest, Wright and Pearson 2012). Conducted over a five-year period, it examined the development of GCA understanding in second- and third-year PHE pre-service teachers arising from their engagement in a formal course of study focused on GCAs. The study revealed a range of issues associated with pre-service teachers developing an understanding of GCAs. Prominent amongst these was the management of more open questions and discussions in a GCA lesson. This is an important area as it has direct links to the quality of student learning experiences in GCA lessons (Light 2013). However, data from this study strongly suggests that while the participants (pre-service PHE teachers) valued the role of appropriate questions and question structures, and understood the role these played in improved learning, they could not sustain this type of questioning. This chapter will use participant self-reflections as well as comments and exchanges from GCA lessons to demonstrate this and other issues relevant to the investigation.

Method

The data presented in this chapter were collected as part of a larger study that inquired into the development of understandings of GCAs by pre-service PHE teachers studying at a university in New South Wales, Australia. The course undertaken by participants (n = 119) involved them in four consecutive practical studies subjects over four semesters (two years) that covered the three *categories* of invasion, net/court and striking/fielding sports and games.

The common *elements* in sport and games that GCAs examine are strategy and tactics, decision making, concepts of movement skill and game performance. These four elements, as well as the additional areas of communication and concentration, became the foundation of the knowledge in games and sports to be learnt by the participants through their course. These were applied in game play in tutorials. This approach builds on that suggested by Light (2013) who argues that teachers of Game Sense (a GCA) should develop a basic theoretical knowledge of learning and pedagogy to empower them to make their own decisions about their teaching. For example, if one understands an underlying principle of strategy and tactics such as deception – defined by Gréhaigne, Richard and Griffin (2005) as the deliberate intent to deceive the opposition – then it does not matter whether or not one 'fakes' an overhead smash and plays a drop shot in a net /wall court game, dummies a pass in an invasion sport or plays a bunt in a striking fielding context. It is still the application of the principle of deception. The elements can then be used as templates for game play observation to further develop analysis skills to allow greater understanding of the elements of GCAs and, from this, to teach using a GCA more effectively.

Participants were not required to develop knowledge of these elements in specific sports but focused on comprehending the underlying *principles* of play for each game category. This idea is evident in the work of Hopper (1998) and Hopper and Bell (2001) in net/wall court games, Memmert and Harvey (2010) in invasion/field territory games and Howarth (2005) in viewing games as problems to be solved. Each principle has a range of tactical underpinnings (understood by the participants as *action rules*) that help students deepen their understanding of the principles. For example, in striking/fielding sports, the underlying principles of play for the team in the field is to minimize the scores made 'from the bat' and minimize the scores made not 'off the bat'. This principle can then be achieved through understanding the action rule of 'all throws must be backed up by other fielders', to minimize runs not off the bat and can be applied to all striking/fielding sports. The principles are then combined with the common elements of games and sports, for example, strategy and tactics. The principle of deception can be explored by developing plans to take advantage of teams not following the action rule, such as pretending to sneak a base in softball-style games to force an overthrow, and can also be observed in the sports of cricket and softball as specific contexts. This expanded application deepens knowledge of both the elements of game play and the category of game.

The sport and game categories, elements, principles and action rules were the key areas of knowledge to be acquired in the four practical studies subjects undertaken by participants in the course. This knowledge was applied in the practical tutorial sessions. Assessment across each of the four subjects addressed the ability of the pre-service teachers to work with this knowledge in a teaching situation. This assessment consisted of two parts. Part one required the participants to teach a GCA lesson to their peers. This was aimed at developing their pedagogical skills in an environment less hampered by behavioural and management problems (because the 'students' were their accommodating peers). Each lesson was recorded on an iPod and the participants used these recordings to support the second part of the assessment, which involved reflection on their GCA lesson and development of a presentation made to staff and peers. This reflective analysis was structured by the interrelated aspects of lesson purpose or focus, games and progressions used, and the use of questions in the lesson. Over the four semesters, this produced four self-reflections and presentations on their GCA lessons in three different games and sports categories. These self-reflections were analyzed using a constant comparative qualitative analysis as outlined by Strauss and Corbin (1998). This was further clarified through ongoing discussions with colleagues and comparisons with field notes recorded by the researchers.

Results

Participant responses to knowledge

The participants felt more comfortable with their knowledge in the game and sports areas studied and in their ability to observe and analyze games and sports. They noted improved understanding of games and sports, even in their own specialist sports. Renee noted that:

> I never realized why my coach developed different strategies for different teams. On the weekend, I could see he recognized the resources of our team and the opposition and came up with a great plan. While he used the terms we do, I could see how he used the underlying principles and it actually made more sense. I could actually see what was happening and I felt a little like I was a coach!

Others, however, now armed with a well-developed understanding of the elements and principles of games and sports as well as a better understanding of how to teach using GCAs, were questioning their coach or teacher's expertise. For example, James noted:

> It is really hard because we have not been performing well and people in the different positions are not working together. I can see it is a strategical [sic] issue at a sub-team level but he (the coach) just blames everyone and yells at the players.

Luke also noted that:

> It is really annoying that I can no longer be the 'biased observer' when I watch a sport. I am always analyzing the play, even when it is in sports I don't really know. I can see the reasons why the players do things due to the links with, for example, decision making or concentration, and realize why this occurs.

This also translated to improved confidence when approaching their GCA lessons. For example, Nikki wrote that: 'I felt really well prepared to use a GCA before we began and prepared a range of questions to use that would really allow the class to explore the content knowledge I want them to know'. These comments indicate that the pre-service PHE teachers felt they were developing in their understanding of games and sports and felt they could apply this knowledge and the attendant observational skills to their own sports within categories and, to an extent, across categories. However, in each of these comments, the participant was able to concentrate on observation and analysis without interference from other factors. The question became whether this enhanced knowledge of game elements, principles and action rules would assist them when they had to analyze the responses of those in their class, then use these responses to create more meaningful learning experiences through a key element of all GCAs: the use of questions.

Questioning, question structures and GCAs

Questioning can be seen as representing the practical application of a teacher's content knowledge in their everyday work as a teacher (Ball, Thames and Phelps 2008). Thus they are very important in GCAs. Questions and question structures are a common element of all GCAs. They allow a teacher to contextualize the learning by encouraging students to identify and explore solutions to the problems that game play presents (Pill 2009). For example, using a 'Game Sense' approach, the teacher sets the game form and, after an initial bout of game play, questions students on technique, rules and tactics (Webb and Thompson 1998). In the tactical games approach, the teacher manages a questioning session on an initial game and the answers received allow the teacher to progress the lesson to a contextually appropriate stage (Mitchell, Oslin and Griffin 2006). Questions in GCA should be thought provoking and stimulate further discussion but also develop further questions from both the teachers and the players, allowing a genuine interaction between those in the lesson (Light 2013). As a result of the prominent role that questioning plays in GCAs, authors such as Metzler (2000), Bailey (2001) and Light (2013) suggest that the structure of questions and the ability to ask higher order and probing questions are key elements for achieving success in creating GCA environments that promote quality educational outcomes.

The skill of asking questions and managing discussions has been an area of major interest for those researching games and sports environments, especially in GCAs (see, for example, Wright and Forrest 2007; McNeill *et al.* 2008; Forrest, Wright and Pearson 2012). One of the most common problems involves the use of the three-way exchange, often referred to as an IRE or IRF exchange (initiate – response – evaluation / follow-up or feedback). Lemke (1990) describes this as a 'triadic dialogue', a three-way move between the teacher (as questioner) and the students (as responders). While a number of resources related to GCAs outline a range of questions to ask to assist GCA users, they use an IRE/F structure (see, for example, Turner 2005 and Mitchell, Oslin and Griffin 2006). However, this may be problematic in a GCA environment because the demonstrated structures often reduce student responses to simple confirmations of what the teacher wanted to know, while presenting knowledge as fixed rather than allowing the exploration of a range of possibilities that game play scenarios present (Wright and Forrest 2007). This issue is evident in the following exchange drawn from this study. After initial game play, the pre-service teacher conducting the session called the 'students' (their peers) in to begin the questioning process:

PRE-SERVICE TEACHER: So after that game, did you find that putting the bird to a space was the best way to win a point?
MEGAN (PARTICIPANT): Yes.
PRE-SERVICE TEACHER: Excellent!

Due to the closed structure of the question, the possibilities here for the participants are quite limited as they are reduced to 'responders' to the student teacher's query, which in turn reduces the value of the learning experience. There is little exploration allowed and little examination of the range of possibilities. The student teacher has placed a statement within the 'initiate' question, received a yes/no response and evaluated it as appropriate, to allow the progression of the lesson. The questioning sequence is therefore of limited value in relation to student involvement in the learning process due to its structure.

For lessons to more actively involve the students and to be of greater educational value, van Zee and Mistrell (1997) recommend an expanded IRE/F exchange. When the teacher initiates the discussion, the opening question should be much broader and divergent to provide for a wider conceptualization of the topic, allowing for responses from more students. To continue this process, evaluation/feedback must be more than just an evaluation of the answer. It should allow further exploration of the ideas developed from these responses. Van Zee and Mistrell (1997) refer to this as a 'reflective toss'. Such a move throws the responsibility of the thinking back to the students and creates an environment to then examine the range of issues associated with and related to the opening question and responses. This process, applicable in GCAs, allows the teacher to facilitate, encourage and guide students to articulate their own thoughts and ideas and incorporate these into the progress of the lesson. It also places greater demands on the user's knowledge as they have to make judgements on the relevance and appropriateness of the responses generated (both verbally and in play) and then use them 'on the spot' to further learning in class.

Participant responses to questioning in practice

When examining the use of questions in the GCA presentations, the majority of undergraduate presenters attempted to use a range of questioning structures but by far the most dominant was the problematic IRE/F structure. What was of interest was that most evolved from the question structures suggested by GCA literature. Most undergraduates attempted to use more divergent questions such as the reflexive toss but this became problematic for the participants in the study. In the example above, the student teacher was ready to move on, having evaluated the answer as 'correct' with her 'excellent' evaluation. However, the peers, as 'students in the class', were quite involved in the lesson, and unwittingly forced her into a situation where she had to use the 'reflexive toss' when 'Ash' used the polite 'hand up'. As the pre-service teacher responded, the following occurred:

PRE-SERVICE TEACHER: Excellent. Ok, next we will … Yes Ash?
ASH: Well it depends.
PRE-SERVICE TEACHER: Sorry, depends?
ASH: 'The best way'. It depends where you are on the court.
NIC: Yes, and where the other player is and what they are thinking.
ASH: You could actually hit it at them and force an upwards shot!
TIM: Or they could give you the space and then be already moving there when you hit it. Then you would be hitting it to a space where they wanted it, which would be a poor option.
PRE-SERVICE TEACHER: Yes? (uncertain)
ASH: Yes. (agreement from others)
PRE-SERVICE TEACHER: But if you hit it to space, wouldn't it be good?
ASH: (pause) I suppose it could be?
PRE-SERVICE TEACHER: Excellent!

For the participants in the study, this second half of the exchange represented a common scenario if the range of responses moved beyond what they believed was 'correct' or required more analysis of the play action that had occurred. In this example, the discussion explored a very valid range of possibilities with excellent 'class' involvement. However, the pre-service teacher's uncertain response indicated that these possibilities had not been considered and were beyond her present capacity to apply this knowledge in a GCA context. Her response was to shift back to an IRE/F, gain a positive affirmation from a closed question, evaluate this affirmation as an indication of understanding and progress the lesson. Here, it seemed it was not a structural issue related to the question but the student teacher's application of knowledge in practice that hindered the learning. It seemed that the student teacher used a closed IRE/F structure, both initially and in response to the discussion, to avoid or control what was becoming a difficult situation for her. This was confirmed in the student teacher's self-reflection, when she wrote:

> During that presentation, I felt terrible. The students came up with a range of answers that were all beyond what I knew. They went off on their own discussions, which seemed to be all on topic but I was excluded. I really had no idea; I had not seen or considered any of the answers they were talking about. I just ended up closing the discussion to end it. I really felt pretty useless.

This feeling of 'uselessness' created by the use of more open question structures was repeated regularly in participant self-reflections on their GCA presentations. Steve, another student teacher, found himself in a similar situation to the one above. He wrote:

> I felt really confident at the beginning of the presentation. I asked a number of different types of questions in relation to strategies but as time went on it would not have mattered what structure I used or what type of question I asked. I did not really understand the answers I received and did not really see them or connect the answers given to their play.

Even Jenna, who loved the flexibility questions gave her and enjoyed using GCAs, wrote:

> The use of more open and intuitive questions meant I had to think on my feet, but I really liked the flexibility it gave to the lesson due to the range of responses I received. However, it was scary and just because I liked it, it didn't mean it always worked. For example, after the second game, I asked an open question and the students came up with a range of answers. At that point, I just went blank. I did not know whether they were answering appropriately or not. I did not come up with anything definitive at the end. The discussion seemed to fade away because I was unsure whether what they said was appropriate in relation to the topic. In the end, I just closed the discussion and we moved on.

These reflections clearly indicate that the issue for these pre-service teachers was not related to questions and question structures. It was related to their ability to manage the outcomes of the more open, divergent questioning *process*. The pre-service teachers felt comfortable with the elements of questioning noted as important in GCA literature: the purpose of questioning, the type of questions to ask, the value of good questioning, the need to generate a wide range of responses, both verbally and in game play. They were also willing to try these more open structures. The issue for these pre-service teachers was the application of their knowledge in practice, to adequately respond to the answers emerging from the questions and develop the emerging discussions into meaningful learning experiences. While they demonstrated confidence in their content knowledge in the area prior to presentations, the demands created by the questioning practices – such as determining whether the range of responses represented appropriate solutions and whether they would lead to improved learning – meant they were overwhelmed and struggled to use it in relation to the answers. Without this, even those most supportive of GCAs felt forced into using a closed IRE structure, though they knew it stopped the discussion and went against the principles of GCAs.

It became evident that pre-service PHE teachers need to develop another form of knowledge to allow them to address the issues that emerged for them in GCA presentations, one that relates to the work of teachers in using GCAs in everyday practice. This knowledge was identified by the work of Ball, Thames and Phelps (2008) who describe it as specialized content knowledge, the knowledge that builds on common content knowledge of the subject area but is specific to the teaching of the content. Developing this knowledge allows the teacher to 'do' games and sports but also to talk the language of games and sports, to understand the different interpretations of the games and sports content in ways that their students do not, to unpack the elements of this content to make the features apparent to students and finally develop extended expertise in a range of practices to effectively teach the content. Developing this specialized content knowledge in undergraduates can help them make sense of not only the content but of the different interpretations students make in relation to games and sports.

The development of this knowledge in pre-service teachers is a challenging task considering the misunderstandings and challenges already presented when implementing GCAs such as teaching games for understanding (as noted by Curry and Light in Chapter 8) and the addition of extra complexity to GCAs may seem unwarranted. However, this area must be addressed if questions are to be used more appropriately in GCAs and the approach is to develop more long-term sustainability.

At present, adjustments to courses are a work in progress and there is as yet no definitive answer on how to develop this knowledge (as is the case in subjects such as math and science). However, the better understanding of the common elements of all games and sports has demonstrated great promise in this area. A number of participants from this study used these elements in their teaching when on their final, fourth-year practicum. Self-reflections from a number of these students suggested increased confidence in their ability to manage questions and discussions with their classes, even in sports they were not familiar with, through a focus on these common elements. For example, Scott wrote:

> I decided to focus on the elements of strategy and tactics in my Frisbee unit, as I was more comfortable with this content knowledge. I used questioning both before, during and after each activity around the different aspects of strategies and tactics and the students really started taking the concepts on board and explored them in the games, which was great to see. One student used a specific example from soccer and suggested how it could be used. Another brought an example up from cricket. This helped me to further develop the discussion and explain how the components of strategies and tactics relate to all sports, invasion and net court and striking. I was really comfortable with what I was asking and they all were really involved in the discussion.

Another student, Jess, noted that:

> I wanted to use a GCA on practicum but I panicked a little when I had a number of units based on different sports that I knew very little about. However, when I focused on the elements and principles, I felt much more in control. I found it did not matter what sport I taught: I could focus on an element such as their decision making, generate questions around this and set meaningful tasks. I felt I could manage discussion better as I was the one with expertise in the classes and could really help the students understand the different elements of decision making in play.

These responses demonstrate encouraging initial development in the areas relating to that of specialized content knowledge such as the ability to unpack the elements of strategy and tactics or decision making and the ability to explain them in ways students can understand them. Importantly, this focus has also allowed better questioning and represents a much more positive view in relation to the use of questioning. While these are small steps in an ongoing process, they are encouraging signs in relation to future possibilities in the area of GCAs.

Conclusion

This chapter has examined PHE pre-service teachers' experiences of a course of study aimed at developing their understanding of GCAs. From their use of GCAs in practice it also identifies the issues that typically emerge for undergraduate GCA users when utilizing the questions and question structures in a GCA context (see, for example, Wright and Forrest 2007). By doing so it draws attention to an area that features in much of the GCA literature: the knowledge needed by those using GCAs to manage the questioning process effectively. It demonstrates that in practice, despite the willingness of the pre-service teachers to use more open question structures, their inability to manage the outcomes forced them to revert to more traditional question structures. This then points to the need to develop further forms of content knowledge in relation to games and sports, such as specialized content knowledge to assist future GCA users in the area of questioning and GCAs in general.

The chapter also illustrated the value of long-duration research studies into how teachers (present and future) understand GCAs and implement them in practice, whether in schools, coaching environments or as in the case of this chapter, tertiary education environments. The ongoing, needs-based development of courses to improve outcomes related to pre-service teacher understanding of GCAs demonstrated in this chapter has been assisted by the collection and analysis of qualitative data over a five-year period. The data provides insight into the experiences of users of GCAs in practice, throwing some light upon what occurs for them when trying to implement GCAs in classes and tutorials and how these experiences impact upon on their understanding of GCA. I suggest that this can make a valuable contribution towards enhancing quality GCA implementation by pre-service PHE teachers in a range of contexts and improve teaching and learning outcomes in games and sports for their students.

Discussion questions

1. The use of closed IRE/F structures can impede quality learning. Explain why the undergraduates in this study used a closed IRE/F in the management of their questions and question structures?
2. Undergraduates in the study struggled to translate the confidence and understanding of content knowledge into GCA practice. Outline why this was the case and demonstrate possible solutions for this problem.
3. The chapter suggests that the management of the answers in a GCA context needs the development of specialized content knowledge in games and sports. Demonstrate how the specialized content knowledge of a teacher would differ from that of a student.

References

Bailey, R. (2001) *Teaching Physical Education: A Handbook for Primary and Secondary Teachers*, London: Kogan Page.

Ball, D. I., Thames, M.H. and Phelps, G. (2008) 'Content knowledge for teaching: What makes it special?', *Journal of Teacher Education*, 59(5): 389–407.

Forrest, G. (2009) 'Using iPods to enhance the teaching of games in physical education', in J. Herrington, A. Herrington, J. Mantei, I. Olney and B. Ferry (eds) *New*

Technologies, New Pedagogies: Mobile Learning in Higher Education, Wollongong, NSW: Faculty of Education, University of Wollongong, 87–99.

Forrest, G., Wright, J. and Pearson, P. (2012) 'How do you do what you do – examining the development of quality teaching using a GCA in PETE undergraduates', *Physical Education and Sport Pedagogy*, 17(2): 145–156.

Gréhaigne, J.-F., Richard, J.-F. and Griffin, L. L. (2005) *Teaching and Learning Team Sports and Games*, London and New York: RoutledgeFalmer.

Hopper, T. (1998) 'Teaching games centered approach using progressive principles of play', *Californian Association of Health, Physical Education and Dance*, 64(3): 3–7.

Hopper, T. and Bell, R. (2001) 'Can we play that game again?' *Strategies*, 14(6): 23–27.

Howarth, K. (2005) 'Introducing the teaching games for understanding model in teacher education programs', in L. L. Griffin and J. Butler (eds) *Teaching Games for Understanding: Theory, Research and Practice*, Champaign, IL: Human Kinetics.

Lemke, J. L. (1990) *Talking Science; Language, Learning and Values*, New Jersey: Ablex Publishing Corporation.

Light, R. (2013) *Game Sense: Pedagogy for Performance, Participation and Enjoyment*, London and New York: Routledge.

McNeill, M., Fry, J. M., Wright, S. C., Tan, W. K. C. and Rossi, T. (2008) 'Structuring time and questioning to achieve tactical awareness in games lessons', *Physical Education & Sports Pedagogy*, 9(1): 3–32.

Memmert, D. and Harvey, S. (2010) 'Identification of non specific tactical tasks in invasion games', *Physical Education and Sport Pedagogy*, 15(3): 287–305.

Metzler, M. W. (2000) *Instructional Models for Physical Education*, Boston, MA: Allyn & Bacon.

Mitchell, S. A., Oslin, J. L. and Griffin, L. L. (2006) *Teaching Sports Concepts and Skills. A Tactical Games Approach*, Champaign, IL: Human Kinetics.

Pill, S. (2009) 'Preparing middle and secondary school pre-service teachers to teach physical education', *Curriculum Perspectives*, 29(3): 24–32.

Shulman, L. S. (1987) 'Those who understand: Knowledge growth in teaching', *Educational Researcher*, 57: 1–22.

Strauss, A. and Corbin, J. (1998) *Basics of Qualitative Research: Techniques and Procedures for Developing Grounded Theory* (second edition), Thousand Oaks, CA: Sage.

Turner, A. P. (2005) 'Teaching games for understanding at the secondary level', in L. L. Griffin and J. Butler (eds) *Teaching Games for Understanding: Theory, Research and Practice*, Champaign, IL: Human Kinetics.

Webb, P. and Thompson, C. (1998) 'Developing thinking players. Games sense in coaching and teaching', National Coaching and Officiating Conference, 25–28 November, Melbourne Convention Centre, Victoria.

Wright, J. and Forrest, G. (2007) 'A social semiotic analysis of knowledge construction and games centred approaches to teaching', *Physical Education and Sport Pedagogy*, 12(3): 273–287.

van Zee, E. H. and Mistrell, J. (1997) 'Using questioning to guide student thinking', *The Journal of the Learning Sciences*, 6: 229–271.

12 The body thinking

Assessment in game-centred approaches to teaching and coaching

Stephen Harvey, Edward Cope and Ruan Jones

> Knowing is not enough; we must apply. Willing is not enough; we must do.
> (Johann Wolfgang von Goethe)

Introduction

The importance of authentic assessment in teaching and coaching settings cannot be understated as it provides a way to assess *knowledge-in-action* (Schön 1983), referred to by Light and Fawns (2003) as the 'body thinking'. Light and Fawns (2001, 2003) provide a couple of thought-provoking treatises on the issue of embodied cognition or *enacted knowledge* (Bruner 1966), describing this development of knowledge in game-centred approaches to teaching and coaching games (specifically teaching games for understanding: TGfU) as an embodied endeavour comprising cognition, affect, motor development and social learning: 'If we envisage games play as a form of language this then suggests that the TGfU lesson can be seen as a holistic learning process in which the movements of the body are the grammar of the game' (Light and Fawns 2003: 162).

While their proposition for movement as a form of speech is worthy of note within the field of physical education and coaching – and specifically the teaching and coaching of games – these ideas can be traced to the existential phenomenological philosophy of Merleau-Ponty (1962/2008) and the work of the influential and enlightened educationalist John Dewey (1936/1986), also drawn on by Quay and Stolz in Chapter 1. The work of Merleau-Ponty and Dewey, among others, disavows the long-prescribed Cartesian view of the person as a *res cogitans* or 'thinking thing' separate and superior to the body (Cottingham 1978). Furthermore, there is a growing body of literature that speaks of the embodied and situated nature of cognition (Anderson 2003; Varela, Thompson and Rosch 1991). The axiom, borrowed from Brown, Collins and Duguid (1989), evokes, fundamentally, the premise of embodied cognition: knowing is inseparable from doing.

Light and Fawns' (2003) work was indicative of the fresh perspective adopted in relation to TGfU and other game-centred approaches at the dawn of the new millennium (for example, Gréhaigne and Godbout 1995; Kirk and Macdonald 1998; Kirk and MacPhail 2002). While proponents of a situated and embodied epistemological perspective may have espoused views informed by different theoretical branches (situated learning, socio-semiotics), we suspect they would agree with Lave's (1988) sentiment that cognition is distributed or 'stretched over … mind, body, activity and culturally organised settings' (p. 1). This, therefore, goes to the heart of assessment within game-centred practice. It prompts us to state that if, as practitioners, irrespective of the teaching or coaching setting, we believe fundamentally that our athletes and students are embodied and situated irrevocably within a social and cultural world, it is then logical to assume that assessment practice *must* also reflect this.

Although there are numerous practitioner-orientated journal articles and books showcasing different modes of assessment in games, the use of these by both researchers and practitioners is limited (Harvey and Jarrett in press). It is with this sentiment in mind that this chapter has been written. First, we offer a brief overview of assessment: its historical roots and gradual evolution over time. Second, we examine the extent to which assessment tools – specifically those reported in the game-centred approaches to teaching and coaching literature – match the four key criteria for authentic assessment outlined by Wiggins (1989). Following this, we discuss the substantive nature of the review we have conducted for the purposes of this chapter in order to present strategies to overcome the challenges of authentic assessment in game-centred pedagogies, which we suggest could more widely include the infusion of elements taken from the Francophone research and perspectives on games teaching and assessment (see Gréhaigne, Richard and Griffin 2005).

History of assessment

While physical education in developed and developing nations continues to suffer from the historical focus on the recording of effort, punctuality, dress, etc., assessment conducted in sporting contexts has tended towards the natural scientific disciplines (physiology and biomechanics) and technical markers of performance through the use of laboratory or field-based tests. Arguably, these assessment procedures have been easier to conduct, due mainly to their objective nature, than those assessments associated with the learning and development of tactical decision-making skills and socio-affective elements (see Williams and Hodges 2005). This focus on biophysical and technical skills has resulted in programmes of learning that have placed a heavier emphasis on fitness and emulation of the *right* technique, rather than the development of, for example, game understanding skills and the affective experiences of the participants, as noted by Light in Chapter 2. Consequently, those with *talent* in areas outside the biological and technical aspects of performance may be ignored (Brown and Hopper 2006), with resources being focused on a select few who perform well on a limited number of performance-based summative assessments that perhaps do not truly reflect the nature of performance required in that field (Wiggins 1989).

Siedentop and Tannehill (2000) have defined assessment in physical education as involving 'a variety of tasks and settings where students [or athletes/players in the context of coaching] are given opportunities to demonstrate their knowledge, skill, understanding and application of content in a context that allows continued learning and growth' (p. 179). This definition highlights the notion that assessment should be more than just an evaluation or a measurement of the expected *product* of a course of learning at one point in time. Assessment *should* be used to help participants understand the *process* of learning as well as help teachers and coaches evaluate how well participants have met the learning outcomes set at the beginning of the programme. Finally, assessment can help identify those with, for example, 'the motivation to succeed or commitment to practice', which can 'be more important than their initial skill level or talent' (Ward *et al.*, cited in Williams and Hodges 2005: 639–640).

Hay (2006) recently argued that assessment has two central purposes – accountability *and* learning – suggesting a shift from assessment *of* learning to assessment *for* learning. Assessment *of* learning is generally associated with end-of-unit summative assessments, while assessment *for* learning attempts to inform and provide feedback to students on their progress so as to modify their learning *within* the tasks they are engaged in during a unit of work. The main purpose of assessment *for* learning is to, therefore, inform students about their progress in learning the subject matter, and can be either formative or summative (i.e. contribute to an end of unit summative grade) in nature. A key difference, however, between assessment *of* learning and assessment for learning is that assessment *for* learning is *ongoing* assessment, which recognizes the need for day-to-day practitioner, peer and self-assessment in order to inform progress within tasks, lessons and units and thereby develop learning (Casbon and Spackman 2005).

Much like Siedentop and Tannehill (2000), Hay (2006) also noted that an assessment *for* learning perspective calls for using authentic assessment tasks that allow students to demonstrate the skills and knowledge that would apply in real-world contexts. For example, participants in a youth sports coaching domain may peer assess each others' invasion game performance in a modified four against four *over the line* soccer game using the team sport assessment procedure (TSAP; see Gréhaigne *et al.* 2005). Participants may also rate their game performance on a profiling chart supplemented by descriptions of their own and/or peers' performance (see MacPhail and Halbert 2010). And while the teacher/coach could be assessing psychomotor, cognitive and/or social/ emotional skills within this game, the important point of note here is that the participants are assessed within the context in which the skills are being developed (i.e., *in* the game), as this is what makes the assessment authentic.

An important development in assessment practices over the past two decades is the recognition that teachers' assessment function must go hand in hand with their instructional function in order to be relevant and useful (e.g.,

Greenwood and Maheady 1997). This view recognizes assessment as a central teaching function that occurs on a session-by-session basis. Assessment *for* learning has allowed a shift in attention towards how to support student learning rather than merely how to judge it (Carless 2005). This shift has come about as a result of an attempt to align curriculum, instruction and assessment in such a way that these are interdependent (Biggs 2003).

MacPhail and Halbert (2010) outlined four key principles of this *practice-referenced* framework to ensure this alignment: (a) sharing learning intentions with students, (b) sharing the success criteria, (c) involving students in assessing their own learning and (d) providing feedback, which helps students to recognize where they are making progress and what they must do to close any gaps in their performance and understanding. Gréhaigne *et al.* (2005) earlier noted that 'teachers need to understand that planning what to teach is the same as planning what to assess and that there should be a strong link between the two facets of the teaching-learning process' (p. 98). In games, these authors suggested a three-phase cycle so that the teaching-learning process is more congruent:

1. Students are confronted with a situation or problems to solve – this may be how they prevent opponents scoring from lay-up shots in basketball.
2. Students are in action and play the game – albeit this may be a small-sided game or game-focused practice scenario.
3. Students are given the opportunity to reflect on their action so as to engage in critical thinking and problem solving, facilitated by the teacher/ coach, if needed.

In this regard, the key function of the teacher/coach is one of facilitator, who sets up the environment for learning to enable the participants to construct knowledge and skills via reflective and reflexive thinking (Gréhaigne *et al.* 2005). Gréhaigne *et al.* also noted that using questioning – both by the students and the teacher – was an important part of the social process involved in assessment.

A framework for authentic assessment

In the previous section we provided some suggestions for how we feel authentic assessment may work in physical education and youth sport settings and outlined how a social constructivist perspective underpins authentic assessment (Shepard 2000). In this section we provide an overview of Wiggins' (1989) framework, which outlines four characteristics of authentic assessment.

Criterion 1 – designing assessment to be truly representative of performance in the field

The task to be assessed must resemble the context within which the learning is occurring. If we think of techniques, skills and tactics in games, therefore, an authentic context will be one where the participant has to apply their learning in a real world situation (i.e. in a match as a player, or as an official or coach). A good example of this in the relatively recent game-centred approaches literature is the game test situations (GTS) of Memmert (2006). For example, to examine the non-specific tactical task, *identification of gaps*, one team of three attacking players situated on one side of the playing area has the task of playing the ball beyond a team of two defending players and below an upper limit (height) into the opposite side of the playing area, to another team of three attacking players.

Criterion 2 – greater attention to be paid to teaching and learning the criteria to be used in the assessment

It is important that the assessment task resembles both the physical and social context so as to be authentic. The game situation described above is socially situated, in that it mimics the situation a player may face in a game when confronted by opponents and also requires that the players use pertinent physical skills to solve the problem. Performers should also agree assessment criteria within this GTS before the teaching of the sessions/lessons begin.

Criterion 3 – self-assessment to play a greater role than traditional testing

As we have seen in the previous examples from MacPhail and Halbert (2010) and Gréhaigne *et al.* (2005), peer and self-assessed performances offer positive possibilities. For example, the TSAP assessment may be conducted using video-taped records of performance as well as the players' own perceptions of their performance, so there is not an over-reliance on subjective data, but the use of a combination of subjective and objective data in the self-analysis process.

Criterion 4 – learners expected to present and defend their work publicly and orally to ensure mastery has been achieved

The examples we have provided in the opening section of the chapter require that the players debate and discuss their own performances with peers, defending publicly their decisions as to why they used certain skills and tactics in particular situations. The *debate of ideas* set up described by Gréhaigne *et al.* (2005) is helpful in this regard for two reasons. First, so players can bring aspects of their performance to the conscious level via expressing the subjective experiences of their performance. And, secondl, speaking publically about performances would allow for a more holistic assessment of the social/ emotional and affective dimensions of learning. Another method that could either substitute or formalize the *debate of ideas* is the think aloud protocol (TAP) (Ericsson and Simon 1980). TAP is a procedure through which cognitive processes can be explored by the retrospective description of lived events, commonly stimulated by video sequences (Lyle 2003). The TAP, under the alias of the *point interview*, has been used within game-centred research in PE settings (for example, French, Werner, Taylor, Hussey and Jones 1996), nevertheless, its use in physical education and youth sport coaching environments *per se* has been particularly infrequent (Lyle 2003; Nilges 2004). Notwithstanding the infrequency of use, TAP has been shown to successfully allow performers to recall their lived and subjective experiences within the public domain.

Next, we would like to examine the extent to which the current game-centred teaching and coaching literature exemplifies the use of authentic assessment practices within current physical education and youth sport coaching environments.

Findings on game-centred practice and authentic assessment

In order to determine the extent to which authentic assessment has been incorporated in game-centred approaches, we used the two literature reviews of Harvey and Jarrett (2012) and Oslin and Mitchell (2006). These two reviews focused on the game-centred literature post-2006 and pre-2006, respectively, helping us to identify potential contributions. We examined the studies highlighted in these reviews for evidence of authentic assessment using the framework previously highlighted by Wiggins (1989). While this does not provide an overview of *all* the studies encompassed in the reviews undertaken by Harvey and Jarrett (in press) and Oslin and Mitchell (2006), we focus on examples that we believe demonstrate Wiggins' criteria.

The need to be designed to be truly representative of performance in the field

Perhaps the two most publicized game performance assessment instruments are the TSAP (see Gréhaigne, Godbout and Bouthier 1997) and the Game Performance Assessment Instrument (GPAI) designed by Oslin, Griffin and Mitchell (1998). The main objective of the TSAP is to provide reliable data on student and/or player performance in different invasion and net games in ecologically valid learning situations (Gréhaigne *et al.* 2005). The TSAP focuses on assessing the offensive components of game play, notably how the learner gains possession, and the decisions they make once in possession. For example, in Nadeau, Godbout and Richard's (2008) study, ice hockey players 'volume of play per minute' and their efficiency index were measured. These were combined to represent players' TSAP performance scores. An important point to make is that the authors of the TSAP had the notion of peer assessment in mind when it was constructed, and thus it was based on a constructivist learning theory. In contrast, the GPAI attempts to measure both on- and off-the-ball aspects of play in both offence and defence via the assessment of game components such as on-the-ball decision making and skill execution and off-the-ball movement such as support, cover, adjust and guarding/marking. For example, in Harvey *et al.*'s (2010) study soccer player's ability to defend as a unit was assessed. Findings revealed that the GPAI was a robust method for measuring defensive off-the-ball game performance.

As well as these game assessment instruments, others have been used for more specific purposes. For example, Memmert (2006) and colleagues' (Memmert and Harvey 2008) GTS procedure recorded the learner's ability to solve tactical solutions in different learning situations. Additional assessment instruments employed include the game-performance evaluation tool (G-PET) designed by Gutierrez and García-López (2012), the tactical awareness test (Van de Broek, Boen, Claessens, Feys and Ceux 2011), game test understanding (Blomqvist, Vanttinen and Luhtannen 2005) and tactical skills inventory (Gray and Sproule 2011). G-PET assesses defensive skills as well as two levels of decision-making skills separately, concerned with technical–tactical skills selection and tactical context adaptation. The tactical awareness test employs computerized technology to animate two teams playing small-sided games. Participants are then required to observe and make judgement as to whether the correct tactical decision was being made. In a similar fashion, the tactical skills inventory measures the learner's perceptions of his/her own ability to perform the right action at the right time within a unit of a game, whilst the game test understanding procedure used by Blomqvist *et al.* (2005) is a video-based test used to evaluate learners' game understanding, as is the tactical awareness test of Van de Broek *et al.* (2011).

The main aim of most of these instruments is to assess enacted knowledge *in vivo* during game play performance (Gréhaigne *et al.* 2005). Additional instruments have assessed declarative and procedural knowledge *in vitro* – outside of the natural environment – via video-based and/or cognitive tests. Thus an obvious limitation of some instruments identified in the game-centred literature has been that they are not conducted *in vivo* or *in situ*. However, they are useful in that they provide an underlying understanding of what players think and say they do, which provides a basis for further exploration of what occurs during actual game play performance. Indeed, an essential component of any assessment instrument is that it measures on- and off-the-ball movement (Blomqvist *et al.* 2005). It has also been suggested that these methods of assessment are more authentic than standardized testing procedures as they capture the cognitive and psychomotor components of performance. Therefore, by appreciating the complex demands of authentic game play through formative assessment, students and/or players have the potential to be subjected to *richer* and more meaningful learning experiences (MacPhail and Halbert 2010). Having said that, this is dependent upon the extent to which students and/or players are included in the assessment process. From this examination of relevant studies, it has been identified that a number of them do not include students and/or players as assessors of their peer's performance, as the main concern has been on hypothesis testing rather than examining learning using the aforementioned practice referenced approach (MacPhail and Halbert 2010).

Greater attention to be paid to teaching and learning the criteria to be used in the assessment

Whilst findings of the current review suggest that game performance instruments validly assess game performance, thus giving results that provide an accurate picture of a learner's skills more so than standardized and isolated skills testing (Light and Fawns 2003), there is little research that provides an understanding of how easily practitioners are able to adopt these assessment procedures in their practices. Moreover, practitioners are not the only individuals who need to be considered as active participants in assessment practices. The role of the learner is also critical if they are to be considered active participants in assessment. Having said that, their ability to be able to reliably assess their peer's game performance is something that requires considerably more attention from researchers and practitioners alike. If peer feedback is to be integrated into the assessment process then learners need to be taught how to use such protocols, as the assessment data will be of little use if it fails to accurately reflect performance.

When using the TSAP, Nadeau *et al.* (2008) suggested that in less than an hour of observation training, learners were able to assess performance with a moderate level of reliability. However, to improve accuracy when observing decision-making skills learners needed more time. Consideration of the time needed to do this is required in the planning stage of assessment. Unfortunately, there appear to be few instances in the literature that illustrate both the utilization of peer assessment and the processes undertaken to adequately prepare learners for peer assessment. We propose that more studies are required to explore and evaluate learners' abilities to reliably peer assess and the processes they go through in learning about such processes.

Self-assessment to play a greater role than traditional testing

Memmert and Harvey (2008) suggest that through formative assessment, learners have the opportunity to reflect on their own performance and thus identify areas for self-improvement, whilst assessing the performance of their peers. So instead of learners receiving purely objective information related to their ability to execute a particular skill, formative assessment situates them as central components in the assessment process. Yet despite this, a dearth of evidence exists that has a focal point on self-assessment. An exception to this is a study conducted by Casey and Dyson (2009). The authors interviewed students allowing them to reflect on the games unit they had been taught. The interview specifically focused on students' understanding of the game in relation to their use of offensive and defensive tactics. Group reflection sheets were also incorporated into each session where students discussed results from conducting the GPAI. MacPhail, Kirk and Griffin (2008) also adopted an interview technique with students to gain awareness into their thinking and reflections of a game unit. On the whole though, studies have not reported learners' involvement in self-assessment practices.

Learners expected to present and defend their work publicly and orally to ensure mastery has been achieved

Of the empirical assessment studies reviewed only a small number have expected learners to present and defend their work publicly and orally. For example, Hastie and Curtner-Smith (2006) asked the learners in their study to explain the games that they had invented to find out if they really understood the central components of these games. In a similar way, Gray and Sproule (2011) posed a series of questions to learners to enable them to discuss their knowledge about the game of basketball.

Requiring learners to present and defend their work can help facilitate the mapping of procedural knowledge (Thomas and Thomas 1994), the knowledge domain most accessible to manipulation. However, very few studies have explored the relationship between declarative, procedural and enacted knowledge: 'if-then-do' (Thomas and Thomas 1994). Exceptions to this can be found, for example, in the work of Wallian and Chang (2007) and Mahut *et al.* (2003). Without explanation from learners there is no certainty that the decisions learners make are purposeful, or in fact intended.

Assessment of the body thinking

What the review of empirically based assessment papers has demonstrated is that there is currently a dominant focus on assessing performance within game-related contexts. This has resulted in the design and implementation of various game assessment instruments in order to accurately assess successful performance. The data that is produced as a result of using these instruments reflect learners' *doing* skills, and subsequently their procedural knowledge. For example, the amount of correct skill executions or offensive decisions made show what the learner can do. Only through asking learners to present and defend their actions via some form of explanation can it be confirmed that the decisions made are as intended. By doing so, learners are displaying their declarative and procedural knowledge of why and how their actions are appropriate in game contexts.

A shift toward assessment within games has emerged as new theoretical perspectives have been suggested and implemented in the game-centred approaches literature. For example, we noted that the early research in game-centred approaches was focused on comparative research designs, which were underpinned by the information processing theoretical perspective. This theoretical perspective limited the type and form of assessments that could be used within these studies. Thus, studies were restricted to paper and pencil or video-based knowledge tests and/or relatively straightforward game play protocols and even skill tests. The introduction of different theoretical perspectives in game-centred research, such as constructivism and socially situated perspectives on learning, has enabled researchers and practitioners alike to more adequately meet the needs of the four criteria required for authentic assessment highlighted in this chapter.

Certainly, studies such as the ones undertaken by Nevett, Rovegno, Babiarz and McCaughtry (2001) and Rovegno, Nevett and Babiarz (2001) – which have conceptualized learning in games as active, relational and co-constructed – have more adequately enabled researchers, and the practitioners in their study, to lay claim to the fact that they are assessing the pupils authentically. The fact that these researchers used a *practice-referenced* (MacPhail and Halbert 2010) approach to the teaching and learning of games, and considered the ongoing development of the pupils' learning against these learning outcomes, made for a more ecologically valid environment in which learning could be assessed (Criterion 2). Similarly, the situated nature of the learning tasks and their design also meant that the assessment met Criterion 1. However, an important point to note is that no study has met all four criteria as outlined by Wiggins. A possible reason for this is that studies have lacked an alignment between teaching, assessment and learning processes. In other words, there is more of a concern as to what is being taught and how, rather than evidencing the impact these practices have on learning.

Nonetheless, this does not mean that meeting all four criteria is not practicable. While students may not have actually been given the opportunity to defend their work publicly and orally or self-assess in its truest sense (due to this process being conducted within interviews), some amendments to the research methodologies – such as using drawings or the photo-elicitation interview (PEI), and/or having students reflect on video-taped records of game play (TAP, for example) – could have allowed the researchers to meet Criteria 3 and 4, which have received the least attention. Chiefly an anthropological and sociological method (Curry 1986), PEI has been effectively employed to capture 'student voice' and provide insight into meaning in physical education and sport (Chen and Light 2006; Enright and O'Sullivan 2012; Light and Quay 2003). It has been described as the use of photographs and/or other visual methods in natural settings to facilitate reflection and, discussion. Extending this point further, we suggest that incorporating relatively *new* research methodologies enables the possibilities for the affective domain of learning to be better understood from the viewpoint of the learner. Methods such as drawings and PEI (Curry 1986) present learners with the opportunity to discuss their experiences of playing games from their own perspectives, thus sharing their thoughts and opinions as to what games mean for them (Georgakis and Light 2009). From an assessment perspective it is important to comprehend how learners experience and understand games from their own world view in order to complement other methods such as game assessment instruments.

Equally, we suggest that the Francophone literature has much to offer in meeting the demands of the four elements of authentic assessment. We have intimated, via the studies of Mahut *et al.* (2003) and Wallian and Chang (2007), that a theoretical perspective underpinned by semiotics can be a fruitful way of integrating reflection *on* action via verbalization to formulate a set of *action rules* (i.e. exploiting space in attack, challenging opponents progression in defence; see Gréhaigne *et al.* 2005) needed when playing games. The constant iterations between game play and reflection (which may not be supported by statistics generated by observers using the TSAP analyses) therefore enable performers to bring aspects of the game to a conscious level and examine their own and each other's interpretations of game play. This reflection also enables the performers to link the ongoing events in the game to tactical solutions in order to validate the most appropriate game-play solutions. In this methodology, we can see clearly the effect of the four aspects of authentic assessment. There is an appropriate context for discovery as these four aspects set the opening problem for the performers. Second, there are some agreed learning outcomes due to the focused nature of the problem set to the performers. Third, there is ongoing self-assessment throughout the iterations of game play and reflection. And, finally, performers are both orally and publically defending the use of the various *action rules* in order to solve the problem set by the teacher/coach. In order to add more in-depth reflection on action the teacher/coach could also use video-taped records of performance to add an extra level of quality to the ensuing debates of ideas. This method provides a suitable framework in which to consider authentic assessment, and in doing so promotes assessment to the forefront of teaching and learning practices and further encourages more specific alignment between assessment, teaching and learning (Biggs 2003).

Finally, not only does the Francophone literature have much to offer in meeting the demands of the four elements of authentic assessment, but also in terms of theoretical position, as it is arguably more *constructionist*[1] than constructivist. This is because, in the examples provided above from the Francophone literature, language and dialogue are key aspects in the ongoing *conversation* the players have with the game (Light and Fawns 2003) and, thus, their developments in game-play knowledge and performance.

Conclusion

Given the position that an increasing volume of game-centred teaching and coaching literature has taken in recent years, which encompass a number of (social) constructivist epistemological positions, it would seem an opportune moment to make a case for the infusion of methods with a particular Francophone or *constructionist* focus to game-centred teaching programmes and continuing lines of research that are Anglophone in their nature and outlook. The Francophone literature blends assessment seamlessly into the planning and delivery process through its constant iterations between game play and reflection, meeting the demands of a Game Sense pedagogical framework. It is our contention that a consideration of the arguments forwarded in this chapter will prompt researchers and practitioners alike to contemplate how greater alignment between assessment, teaching and learning could be achieved in their future daily practice.

Discussion questions

1. How might you assess learning in the psychomotor, cognitive and affective domains within game-based approaches?
2. Design a way of assessing learning when utilizing a game-based approach, which would meet the four criteria outlined by Wiggins in this chapter.
3. What might some of the benefits be of aligning learning outcomes, your pedagogical approach and assessment in your current coaching/ teaching practice?

Note

1 See, for example, Kenneth Gergen's (1985) paper in which he articulates the features of social constructionism. Burr (1995) also provides an excellent introductory text to social constructionism in which the characteristics are outlined and explained.

References

Anderson, M. L. (2003) 'Embodied cognition: A field guide', *Artificial Intelligence*, 149: 91–130.

Biggs, J. (2003) *Teaching for Quality Learning at University: What the Student Does* (second edition), Maidenhead: Society for Research into Higher Education and Open University Press.

Blomqvist, M., Vanttinen, T. and Luhtannen, P. (2005) 'Assessment of secondary school students' decision-making and game-play ability in soccer', *Physical Education and Sport Pedagogy*, 10(2): 107–119.

Brown, J. S., Collins, A. and Duguid, P. (1989) 'Situated cognition and the culture of learning', *Educational Researcher*, 18(1): 32–42.

Brown, S. and Hopper, T. (2006) 'Can all students in physical education get an "A"? Game performance assessment by peers as a critical component of student learning', *Physical and Health Education*, Spring: 14–21.

Bruner, J. (1966) *Toward a Theory of Instruction*, Cambridge, MA: Belkapp Press.

Burr, V. (1995) *An Introduction to Social Constructionism*, London: Routledge.

Carless, D. (2005) 'Prospects for the implementation of assessment for learning', *Assessment in Education: Principles, Policy and Practice*, 12(1): 39–54

Casbon, C. and Spackman, L. (2005) *Assessment for Learning in Physical Education*, Leeds: BAALPE.

Casey, A. and Dyson, B. (2009) 'The implementation of models-based practice in physical education through action research', *European Physical Education Review*, 15(2): 175–199.

Chen, Q. and Light, R. (2006) '"I thought I'd hate cricket but I love it!": Year six students' responses to Game Sense pedagogy', *Change: Transformations in Education*, 9(1): 49–58.

Cottingham, J. (1978) 'Descartes on "thought"', *The Philosophical Quarterly*, 28(112): 208–214.

Curry, T. J. (1986) 'A visual method of studying sports: The photo-elicitation interview', *Sociology of Sport Journal*, 3(3): 204–216.

Dewey, J. (1936/1986) 'How we think: A restatement of the relation of reflective thinking to the educative process', in J. Boydson (ed.) *John Dewey: The Later Works, 1925–1953*, vol. 8, Carbondale: Southern Illinois University Press, pp. 105–352.

Enright, E. and O'Sullivan, M. (2012) 'Producing different knowledge and producing knowledge differently: rethinking physical education research and practice through participatory visual methods', *Sport, Education and Society*, 17(1): 35–55.

Ericsson, K. and Simon, H. (1980) 'Verbal reports as data', *Psychological Review*, 87 (3): 215–221.

French, K. E, Werner, P. H., Taylor, K., Hussey, K. and Jones, J. (1996) 'The effects of a 6-week unit of tactical and skill instruction on badminton performance in ninth grade students', *Journal of Teaching in Physical Education*, 15(4): 439–463.

Georgakis, S. and Light, R. (2009) 'Visual data collection methods for research on the affective dimensions of children's personal experiences of PE', *Healthy Lifestyles Journal*, 56(3/4): 23–27.

Gergen, K. J. (1985) 'The social constructionist movement in modern psychology', *American Psychologist*, 40(3): 266–275.

Gray, S. and Sproule, J. (2011) 'Developing pupils' performance in team invasion games', *Physical Education and Sport Pedagogy*, 16(1): 15–32.

Greenwood, C. R. and Maheady, L. (1997) 'Measureable change in student performance: forgotten standards in teacher preparation', *Teacher Education and Special Education*, 20(3): 265–275.

Gréhaigne, J.-F. and Godbout, P. (1995) 'Tactical knowledge in team sports from a constructivist and cognitivist perspective', *Quest*, 47: 490–505.

Gréhaigne, J.-F., Godbout, P. and Bouthier, D. (1997) 'Performance assessment in team sports', *Journal of Teaching in Physical Education*, 16: 500–516.

Gréhaigne, J.-F., Richard, J.-F. and Griffin, L. L. (2005) *Teaching and Learning Team Sports and Games*, New York: RoutledgeFalmer.

Gutierrez, D. and García-López, L. M. (2012) 'Assessment of primary school students' decision-making related to tactical content', *New Approaches in Educational Research*, 1(1): 7–12.

Harvey, S. and Jarrett, K. (in press) 'A review of the game centred approaches to teaching and coaching literature since 2006', *Physical Education and Sport Pedagogy.*

Harvey, S., Cushion, C. J., Wegis, H. M. and Massa-Gonzalez, A. N. (2010) 'Teaching Games for Understanding in American high-school soccer: a quantitative data analysis using the game performance assessment instrument', *Physical Education and Sport Pedagogy*, 15(1): 29–54.

Hastie, P. A. and Curtner-Smith, M. D. (2006) 'Influence of a hybrid Sport Education–Teaching Games for Understanding unit on one teacher and his students', *Physical Education and Sport Pedagogy*, 11(1): 1–27.

Hay, P. J. (2006) 'Assessment for learning in physical education', in D. Kirk, M. O'Sullivan and D. Macdonald (eds) *The Handbook of Physical Education*, London: Sage, pp. 312–325.

Kirk, D. and Macdonald, D. (1998) 'Situated learning in physical education', *Journal of Teaching in Physical Education*, 17: 376–387.

Kirk, D. and MacPhail, A. (2002) 'Teaching games for understanding and situated learning: Rethinking the Bunker–Thorpe model', *Journal of Teaching in Physical Education*, 21(2): 177–192.

Lave, J. (1988) *Cognition in Practice: Mind, Mathematics, and Culture in Everyday Life*, Cambridge: Cambridge University Press.

Light, R. and Fawns, R. (2001) 'The thinking body: Constructivist approaches to games teaching in Physical Education', *Melbourne Studies in Education*, 42(2), 69–87.

——(2003) 'Knowing the game: integrating speech and action in games teaching Through TGfU', *Quest*, 55(2): 161–176.

Light, R. and Quay, J. (2003) 'Identity, physical capital and the disjunction between young men's experiences of soccer in school and community-based clubs', *Melbourne Studies in Education*, 44(2): 89–106.

Lyle, J. (2003) 'Stimulated recall: a report on its use in naturalistic research', *British Educational Research Journal*, 29(6): 861–878.

MacPhail, A. and Halbert, J. (2010) '"We had to do intelligent thinking during recent PE": students and teachers' experiences of assessment for learning in post-primary physical education', *Assessment in Education: Principles, Policy and Practice*, 17(1): 23–39.

MacPhail, A., Kirk, D. and Griffin, L. (2008) 'Throwing and catching as relational skills in game play: situated learning in a modified game unit', *Journal of Teaching in Physical Education*, 21: 100–115.

Mahut, N., Chang, C. W., Nachon, M., Chevalier, G. and Gréhaigne, J.-F. (2003) 'Student action reading and meaning attribution: towards a model of interpretation register in game play', paper presented at the 2nd International Conference: Teaching Sport and Physical Education for Understanding, 11–14 December, Melbourne, Australia.

Memmert, D. (2006) 'Developing creative thinking in a gifted sport enrichment program and the crucial role of attention processes', *High Ability Studies*, 17: 101–115.

Memmert, D. and Harvey, S. (2008) 'The Game Performance Assessment Instrument: Some concerns and solutions for further development', *Journal of Teaching in Physical Education*, 27: 220–240.

Merleau-Ponty, M. (1962 [2008]) *The Phenomenology of Perception*, London: Routledge.

Nadeau, L., Godbout, P. and Richard, J.-F. (2008) 'Assessment of ice hockey performance in real-game conditions', *European Journal of Sports Science*, 8(6): 379–388.

Nevett, M., Rovegno, I., Babiarz, M. and McCaughtry, N. (2001) 'Changes in basic tactics and motor skills in an invasion-type game after a 12-lesson unit of instruction', *Journal of Teaching in Physical Education*, 20(4): 352–369.

Nilges, L. M. (2004) 'Ice can look like glass: a phenomenological investigation of movement meaning in one fifth-grade class during a creative dance unit', *Research Quarterly for Exercise and Sport*, 75(3): 298–314.

Oslin, J. and Mitchell, S. (2006) 'Game-centred approaches to teaching physical education', in D. Kirk., M. O'Sullivan and D. Macdonald (eds) *The Handbook of Physical Education*, London: Sage, pp. 627–651.

Oslin, J. L., Mitchell, S. A. and Griffin, L. L. (1998) 'The Game Performance Assessment Instrument (GPAI): development and preliminary validation', *Journal of Teaching in Physical Education*, 17: 231–243.

Rovegno, I., Nevett, M. and Babiarz, M. (2001) 'Learning and teaching invasion-game tactics in 4th grade: Introduction and theoretical perspective', *Journal of Teaching in Physical Education*, 20: 341–351.

Schön, D. A. (1983) *The Reflective Practitioner: How Professionals Think in Action*, New York: Basic Books.

Siedentop, D. and Tannehill, D. (2000) *Developing Teaching Skills in Physical Education*, Mountainview, CA: Mayfield.

Shepard, L. A. (2000) 'The role of assessment in a learning culture', *Educational Researcher*, 29(7): 4–14.

Thomas, K. T. and Thomas, J. R. (1994) 'Developing expertise in sport: the relation of knowledge and performance', *International Journal of Sport Psychology*, 25: 295–312.

Van de Broek, G., Boen, F., Claessens, M., Feys, J. and Ceux, T. (2011) 'Comparison of three instructional approaches to enhance tactical knowledge in volleyball among university students', *Journal of Teaching in Physical Education*, 30: 375–392.

Varela, F., Thompson, E. and Rosch, E. (1991) *The Embodied Mind: Cognitive Science and Human Experience*, Cambridge, MA: MIT Press.

Wallian, N. and Chang, C.-W. (2007) 'Language, thinking and action: towards a semio-constructivist approach in physical education', *Physical Education and Sport Pedagogy*, 12(3): 289–311.

Ward, P., Hodges, N. J., Williams, A. M. and Starkes, J. L. (2004) 'Deliberate practice and expert performance: Defining the path to excellence', in A. M. Williams and N. J. Hodges (eds) *Skill Acquisition in Sport: Research, Theory and Practice*, London: Routledge.

Wiggins, G. (1989) 'Teaching to the (authentic) test', *Educational Leadership*, 46(7): 41–47.

Williams, M. A. and Hodges, N. J. (2005) 'Practice, instruction and skill acquisition in soccer: challenging tradition', *Journal of Sports Sciences*, 23(6): 637–650.

13 Learning games concepts by design

Adrian P. Turner

Introduction

As the coaching facilitator for a small town youth soccer club in the American Midwest, I had the opportunity to conduct a research project with three inexperienced travel coaches during the 2011–12 youth soccer season. The coaches were each attempting to use a game-based approach in their work with their respective teams. On one occasion I observed Sally Simpson (a pseudonym) coaching her under-11 girls team. In the opening activity of the session she began with a modified three versus three soccer game (no goalkeepers) on a 35-by-25-metre field. A five-metre channel (running the length of the field) was marked with discs along one side and two-metre-wide goals (one for each team to attack) were offset at opposite ends on the other side of the pitch. Conventional soccer rules were applied except that when the offensive team maintained possession only one player was allowed to enter the channel with the ball, and could then pass it out to a teammate, while defensive players were not permitted in that area. Sally's intent was to help coach the offense to use space on the flank (away from the goal) to help invade the other team's territory and subsequently create a scoring opportunity. When asked about the success of the activity Sally commented:

> It was kind of slow, I think there was something I could have done to make it more successful, but I don't know what that would have been. It seemed that what I was trying to get them to do was too challenging, I don't know if they were that developed to kick the ball that far.

While Sally attributed limited success in the game to the players' inability to pass the ball over distance, from a coaching facilitator's perspective, the main problem was that when passing the ball out of the channel to a teammate the offense was simply outnumbered by three players to two. By changing the game to allow the channel player a free pass, or allowing that player to dribble out of the channel, it would likely have afforded the offense more attacking opportunities (Turner 2012). The inclusion of a neutral player on 'all-time offense' may also have facilitated more options in the modified game.

Rationale for modified games

Sally's scenario illustrates precisely what many proponents of a game-based approach have noted, that tactics and skills specific to game forms (invasion, net/wall, fielding/run-scoring and target) must be comprehended initially by the coach and then introduced to players through carefully crafted modified games that pose tactical problems (Turner 2005: 73). In Game Sense, inquiry-based approach players participate in small-sided, modified games designed to develop skill and understanding in the game context (Curry and Light 2007: 9). Small-sided games are especially helpful in developing offensive and defensive principles of play (Pill 2012: 44). In invasion sports, the most strategically complex category of games (Mitchell and Collier 2009: 48), four principles of offense (mobility/support, advancement/penetration, width, and depth/retaining possession) and four principles of defense (engagement/restraint, depth, contraction, and expansion) provide the focus for modified games used to teach children to overcome major tactical problems (Wilson 2002: 23). Four of these principles (two offensive and two defensive) will be illustrated in this chapter and represent a starting point for teachers and coaches employing a tactical focus in designing and modifying small-sided invasion games for learning.

The modified games are simple to construct and designed to allow the game to be the teacher. They simplify players' choices in possession (pass, dribble, shoot), provide students with multiple touches of the ball, and permit players to learn to read the game by thinking and anticipating where and when to move when they are off the ball (Evans 2007: 27). The small-sided games also provide greater player participation, more passing and scoring opportunities, multiple one-versus-one encounters and attempt to develop more complete players who operate both offensively and defensively rather than as position specialists (Cooper 2006: 24).

In general, small-sided modified games are useful to expose selected tactical elements of play, for example, in one-versus-one basketball games there are multiple opportunities for transition between offense and defense; likewise two-versus-two (plus a neutral player) field hockey permits depth in defense and combination play on offense to be explored; and three-versus-three StxBall lacrosse allows for any three of the four offensive principles (mobility, width, depth, and penetration) to be practiced simultaneously. In many invasion sports the four-versus-four modified game is regarded as the initial manifestation of an adult game because it provides the minimum number of participants to potentially incorporate all eight tactical principles of play into a small sided game (van Lingen 1997: 104). The modified game should be representative of the full game and retain much of its strategic complexity but be adapted to match the players' size, ability, skill, strength, and motivation (Curry and Light 2007: 9). Although a four-versus-four modified invasion game (with application to Team Handball) is used as a starting point for the four games examined in this chapter, smaller iterations are sometimes desirable based on the specific tactical problem encountered.

Game design template

So how does a teacher/coach begin to design a modified invasion game to enhance player performance and game sense? The initial step is to select a tactical problem from among the eight principles of attack/defense (Wilson 2002: 23). In the initial offensive modified game *Gridiron* (see Table 13.1) the tactical problem is advancement (player and/or ball penetration to attack the opponents' goal/area). Second, there needs to be a specific aim of the game or method of scoring. In Gridiron the ball must be placed on the ground inside the defensive team's semi-circle to score.

In his text *Student-designed Games* Peter Hastie (2010: 90) suggests that once the method of scoring is established the rules of the modified game that impact team *progression* with the ball/object and subsequent rules for a

Table 13.1 Gridiron

Tactical problem	Advancement (player and/or ball penetration to attack opponents' goal)
Aim (scoring)	Place ball on ground inside opponents' semi circle (one point)
Progression rules	Players hold ball for 3 seconds, take 3 steps, dribble (3 bounces), pass/catch Players cannot enter/step in either semi-circle
Possession rules	No stealing ball from ball handler (non-contact game) Either team can recover dropped pass and pass can be intercepted Out-of-bounds results in throw-in from side
Game start and restart	Game starts (and restarts after score) with ball thrown to opponents (modified American football kick-off) Teams start at edge of defending semi-circle; once ball is in air players move
Violations	Free pass/dribble for opponents from side, defenders 3 metres away
Players and area	Four versus four: third of netball court (16 × 12 metres) marked
Equipment	Two 4-metre semi-circles (marked with plastic domes/strips), large nerf/gator skin ball (shape of size 3 soccer ball)
Game variations aim (scoring)	Reduce/increase size of touchdown semi-circle based on offensive success
Progression	No dribbling (or conversely, allow unlimited dribbling), forward passes only, no steps permitted, increase/decrease number of passes prior to scoring
Win possession	Permit two-handed touch on ball carrier to represent turnover (free pass to opponents), players must mark person to person (no zone defending circle)

Table 13.1 (continued)

Game restart	After score, offensive team starts next to circle, defenders begin in own half
Equipment	High bounce volleyball replaces gator ball, encourages dribble penetration
Game Sense	Offensive
Ball handler	Fake pass and attack the gap around circle, use three steps after dribble to penetrate past defender, at end of dribble (or three steps) pass ball to teammate (option of wrist pass)
Passers	Unmarked players provide safe targets, lead passes to receivers, short passes safer, long passes afford quick penetration but with risk, lateral passes offer safer alternative
Receivers	Post, corner, hook routes (change of speed and direction), angles of passing support, crossing patterns to screen defenders.

team's capability to gain *possession* need to be determined. In Gridiron players may *progress* by holding the ball for three seconds, taking three steps with it, dribbling (maximum of three bounces), and passing and catching the ball with their hands. Players cannot enter either semi-circle on the court. Rules regarding a team gaining *possession* include: recovering a dropped pass, intercepting a pass, and earning possession from the courtside when the ball travels out of bounds. Stealing from the ball handler is not permitted. In invasion games possession is also frequently relinquished following a score and so a method of restarting a modified game, and also beginning the match, needs to be selected. In both instances in Gridiron the game commences with both teams starting at the edge of their respective semi-circles and the ball is thrown to the receiving team. As soon as the ball is in the air both teams can move about the court. Finally, it is necessary to establish procedures for rule violations. In the Gridiron game violations result in a free pass or dribble to the non-offending team on the nearest sideline, level with where the infringement took place. All defensive players must be three metres away from the ball handler.

The next step in game design is to establish the playing area, equipment, and the initial number of players involved in the game. All three of these elements, like the game rules, are subject to manipulation by the teacher/coach. Gridiron can be played outside or indoors, on grass or a hard surface. Playing numbers are initially four versus four on an area comparable to a third of a netball court. This will enable a group of 24 players to participate comfortably in three games on an area the size of a volleyball court. The last component in initial game design entails selecting equipment. In the Gridiron game two four-metre semi-circles (marked with plastic domes/poly spots) represent the scoring area at both ends of the court and a nerf/gator skin ball (equivalent to a size three soccer ball) is used for the game.

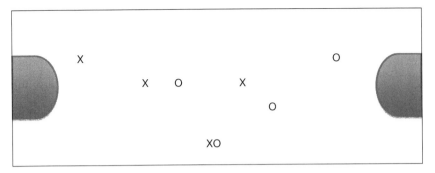

Figure 13.1 In Gridiron a team attempts to penetrate into their opponents' territory and attack the goal area, grounding the ball inside the semi-circle with their hands to score, while remaining outside the actual goal area

Introducing the game

The players want to start playing the modified game (Gridiron) quickly and the teacher should provide only a few instructions concerning scoring, progression, gaining possession, as well as the game boundaries, to enable players to begin to play the game safely. This affords an opportunity for the teacher to observe the game, to see which players understand it during the first few minutes, and allows the participants to develop a feel for the game. They will only learn the game by playing it. Second, the coach may scan the activity to see which players are able to comprehend the major problem in the game. If the modified game is well constructed the tactical problem should begin to emerge and the participants will attempt to solve it if they have the requisite tactics and skills. The coach may try to elicit responses from the players about potential solutions to the game problem. Rather than instructing the players, coaches can question students and encourage them to become part of the learning process through a problem-solving approach (see Turner 2005: 83, for a potential question protocol). In a modified game setting the teacher adopts the role of a facilitator who guides Game Sense acquisition by setting effective learning environments (Evans 2007: 28). Modified games can be varied to enable the players to learn a little more quickly and effective coaches are able to make adjustments to any one of a variety of game elements to make one tactical component of the game more prevalent. For example, in the Gridiron game, if the offense is advancing the ball slowly and that is making offensive players easy to mark then a rule modification in the progression element of the game, removing the 'three steps and three dribble' rule (making it a passing only game), will likely increase the tempo of the game and encourage player and ball penetration via quick passing (see Table 13.1 for additional game variations to Gridiron ball).

In essence the coach is operating like a doctor, observing (reading) the initial modified game, looking for signs in the game, and listening to symptoms from the players, about what is wrong, and then prescribing an adjustment to the game in order to make the players function at a higher level. In many cases the initial solution will not cure the issue in the game and so the teacher/coach needs a repertoire of pedagogical adjustments (game variations) to help the players begin to solve problems involved in a variety of mini-invasion games.

Intra-game variations

In the next section examples of three additional modified invasion games will be provided using a game design template similar to Gridiron (one game is based around a second offensive tactical problem, depth, and the remaining two are based around two defensive tactical problems: engagement/restraint and contraction). Following presentation of a table outlining each game form, two separate categories of potential game modifications will be discussed for each game to illustrate how specific elements might be amended in order to improve the quality of the game and the players' Game Sense in attempting to solve the tactical problem outlined. Several foci for either offensive or defensive Game Sense development are also included in the final section of each modified game table to provide teachers and coaches with ideas about potential teaching content that may emerge from the respective games.

In the modified game 'target to zone' the offensive tactical problem concerns depth and support-players' contributions from behind the ball (see Table 13.2).

Table 13.2 Target to zone

Tactical problem	Depth/retain possession (supporting players' contributions from behind ball)
Aim (scoring)	Receive ball in team's target zone directly from target player (one point)
Progression rules	Players hold ball for 3 seconds, take 3 steps, dribble (3 bounces), pass/catch Team sends ball to target player (T) who plays just in front of target zone Target cannot score but may pass to a teammate who may receive ball in target end-zone (includes three steps after catch to enter target zone, and/or dribble) Target player switches position with scorer on team after score
Possession rules	No stealing ball from ball handler (non-contact game) Either team can recover dropped pass and pass be intercepted Out-of-bounds results in throw-in from side Only one defender may guard the target player
Game start	Game starts with a jump ball
Restart	After score, new offensive team starts next to own end-zone with free pass
Violations	Free pass/dribble for opponents from side, defenders 3 metres away
Players and area	Four versus four: third of netball court (16 × 12 metres) marked

Table 13.2 (continued)

Equipment	Two (2-metre) end zones running width of court (marked with plastic domes/strips), four quarters (marked with plastic domes/strips), large nerf/gator skin ball (shape of size 3 soccer ball)
Game variations aim (scoring)	Extend depth of scoring zone 2 metres into the field of play Two point score for player receiving pass having run from outside final quarter
Progression	Specify number of passes in zones prior to pass to target player Player tagged in possession must pass the ball backwards Tags are unlimited and do not create a turnover but do force a backwards pass At least two backward passes must occur prior to score (one from target player)
Game Sense	Offensive
Ball handler	Look for 'give and go' with target player, use dribble or three steps to buy time
Passers	Look for pass to target player, first option to create scoring opportunity, quick penetration but with risk. Unmarked players provide safe targets Be aware of teammates providing depth for drop pass
Receivers	Move quickly to space, closest receiver prepared to move to support position behind ball for drop pass as defender approaches, or for lateral switch pass

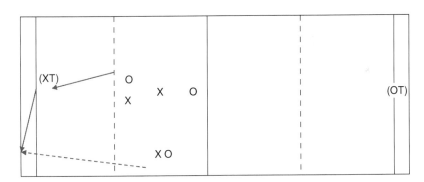

Figure 13.2 In Target to zone a team positions a target player (who cannot score) just in front of the offensive scoring zone and uses supporting players' movements to receive a pass from the target player in order to score

Scoring variation. In the initial version of target to zone, the target player is restricted to an 'assist' capacity and the offensive players must support that player in order to score. As a game variation, by extending the depth of the scoring zone two more metres into the field of play, more opportunities to score are created for offensive players arriving late from deep positions.

Scorers who have made runs from outside the final quarter of the court could also receive two points for a score encouraging depth of support play on offense. Awarding additional points for successful application of a tactical concept is usually quite motivating for players in modified games where they invariably keep score.

Amended progression. While the focus initially in target to zone is on the use of a target player as a catalyst to create offensive depth, the contributions of other players in support play from behind the ball (and in positions much deeper on the court) may also be developed. The progression rule could be added that a player with the ball tagged by an opponent must pass the ball backwards. While tags are unlimited (and do not create a turnover) they do force a backwards pass and a need for support behind the ball quickly (prior to the expiration of the three-second time limit, that would cause a turnover for holding the ball, already in place in the game). Further, depth on offense in invasion games is underpinned by the ability to retain possession. This can be accomplished by specifying a set number of completed passes in each quarter of the court prior to reaching the target player. Another amendment is that two passes must be backwards in any one possession prior to a score. Players will develop an appreciation for the risk–reward structure of different types of passes and appropriate support in various areas of the court. Modifying progression rules to impact game tactics is also common in coaching many adult sports, the two-touch condition in soccer is a similar example.

It is also important to reward defensive endeavors in modified games designed with that tactical focus. In the game 'mini-goal challenge' (see Table 13.3) defensive players receive one point for an interception and one point for blocking a pass through the goal (in effect denying the offense a score). The offense also receives one point for a completed pass, or dribble, through any of the multiple goals.

Table 13.3 Mini-goal challenge

Tactical problem	Engagement/restraint (challenge opponents' progression and win possession)
Aim (scoring)	Defensive interception or blocked pass attempt through goal (one point) Offense dribble, or pass ball to teammate, through any cone goal (one point)
Progression rules	Players hold ball for 3 seconds, take 3 steps, dribble (3 bounces), pass/catch Offense cannot pass for a 'scoring pass' over the defender's upright arm (reach) when he/she is defending a goal No more than one goal can be scored on the same goal consecutively No more than one pass can be made between the same two players in a row
Possession rules	No stealing ball from ball handler but defender can block score attempt at goal Either team can recover dropped pass and pass can be intercepted There is no out-of-bounds

Table 13.3 (continued)

Game start	Game starts with a jump ball
Restart	Offense and defense switch when team scores five points – free pass 5 metres from nearest goal
Violations	Violations result in free pass/dribble for opponent 5 metres from nearest goal
Players and area	Four versus four: third of netball court (16 x 12 metres) marked
Equipment	Four 1-metre goals (marked with plastic domes/cones) spread randomly throughout court area, large nerf/gator skin ball (shape of size 3 soccer ball)
Game variations win possession	Steal from dribbler (no contact), defense score one point and gain possession Tag ball handler, defense score one point Drop ball (defender within 1 metre, offense recover) defense score half point Shot clock equals 10 seconds, if no shot on goal defense win possession
Restarts:	After goal scored, offensive team keeps ball until interception or turnover Ball out of bounds (added 16 x 12 metre court), results in throw-in to opponent
Game Sense	Defensive (individual) Deciding when, where, and for how long to mark is a tactical decision Deciding when to defend a goal or step to pressure a ball handler or receiver Typically, in person-to-person defense players mark opponents by positioning between the attacker and goal Close proximity to the ball handler makes it difficult to shoot, pass or dribble Defenders position on balls of feet (shoulder-width apart), knees bent, leaning forward, arms slightly out to side for balance As attacker dribbles/passes the defender steps closer to block the ball

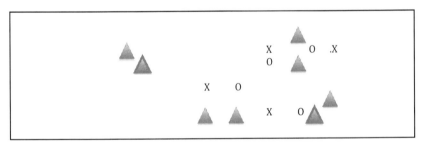

Figure 13.3 Mini Goal Challenge focuses on winning possession in defence with minimal contact but encourages looking for opportunities to appply pressure when they cannot win possession

Winning possession. With the focus on challenging opponents and winning possession in the mini-goal challenge (MGC) the level of defensive intensity may be increased with appropriate game modifications but the level of player contact needs to remain minimal. In addition to blocking goal-scoring attempts and intercepting passes, defenders are now allowed to steal the ball from attackers dribbling with it (without making any contact on the dribbler's hands/arms) in the amended game. Defenders receive one point for a clean (non-contact) steal and also win possession. For tagging a player in possession defenders also receive one point. Further, an offensive player who fumbles, but then recovers a pass, with a defender within one-metre proximity, entitles the defender to a half-point. Teams can be given scoring targets to accomplish on both offense and defense. Finally, the offense has ten seconds to attempt a scoring pass on any goal. If the offense fails to meet this challenge then the defense wins possession in what parallels a basketball shot clock violation.

From a Game Sense perspective it is important for defenders to recognize that while winning the ball is often the optimal scenario, for a defender there are secondary objectives when this cannot be accomplished. Pressure and proximity to offensive players can make it difficult for them to run, pass, catch, shoot or dribble with the ball in order to create a good scoring opportunity. By virtually eliminating body contact, defensive players learn positioning and funneling to create pressure on offensive players and force them away from scoring areas in a safe and non-threatening environment.

Game restart. In the initial version of MGC teams reverse offensive and defensive roles after scoring five points. By adding the modification that after a goal the offense keeps the ball until an interception or turnover occurs in the game, the need for players to be aware of two of the main moments in invasion games, losing possession and regaining possession, is highlighted. The instant transition from offense to defense and vice versa during open play and the need for game players to learn to react to these situations (moments) is critical to players' Game Sense development. In contrast, by modifying MGC to include the out-of-bounds component the deliberate restart point creates a very different scenario. In this situation players have vital seconds to prepare for a clear delineation between their roles on either offense or defense (the other two main moments in invasion sports). By varying restart processes in modified games players can be made aware of four crucial moments in invasion games: their own team in possession, the sudden loss of possession, their opponent in possession, and instantly regaining possession (van Lingen 1997: 27).

In the fourth modified game, guard the goal, the defensive tactical problem pertains to the movement of players to protect the goal (see Table 13.4). In the first version of the game, offensive players are not permitted to shoot until defensive players return to their six-metre semi-circle and no offensive player is permitted inside the defending team's circle.

Playing area. An inner circle with a four-metre radius is added inside the defensive teams circle and the width of the goal can be varied to assist the offense or defense. The defending team must now position one or two players inside the inner circle and two or three players inside the outer circle prior to the attack. By varying the playing area and placing restrictions concerning players' movements the defense will need to make specific adjustments.

Table 13.4 Guard the goal

Tactical problem	Contraction (movement of defensive players to protect the target)
Aim (scoring)	Defensive blocked shot at goal (one point) Offense throw ball into goal (one point), shot must bounce before enters goal
Progression rules	Players hold ball for 3 seconds, take 3 steps, dribble (3 bounces), pass/catch No offensive players are permitted inside the defensive team's semi-circle Offense cannot shoot until at least 3 defenders are inside defensive circle Offense must leave player in own half to prevent shot into goal on turnover
Possession rules	No stealing ball from ball handler but defender can block shot attempt Either team can recover dropped pass Pass can be intercepted at edge of defensive circle only Out of bounds results in throw-in from side Defensive stall (returning to circle) results in a violation (see violation below)
Game start	Game starts with a jump ball
Restart	After score, new offensive team starts with free pass from top of own circle
Violations	Free pass/dribble for opponents from side, defenders 3 metres away If defenders stall returning to defensive circle, offense gets penalty shot from edge of circle against only one defender who can protect goal
Players and area	Four versus four: third of netball court (16 × 12 metres) marked
Equipment	Two 1-metre goals (marked with plastic cones), two 6-metre-semi-circles (marked with poly spots/strips), gator skin ball (shape of size 3 soccer ball)
Game variations playing area	An inner circle is added (4 metres) and the goal width is doubled to 2 metres Size of goals and distance of shooting circle varied to assist offense/defense Add the role of an official goalkeeper to each team (GK save equals one point)
Players	Defending team must have at least one player in inner circle (GK plus one other) and two or three players inside the outer circle to defend any attack
Equipment	Nerf/sponge ball
Game Sense	Defensive (team) Defense must retreat to form a zone to protect its goal and decide whether it is advantageous to position more defenders closer to the shooter or goal Addition of inner circle (on court) and goalkeeper encourages use of a 1:3 zone Primary defender steps toward ball handler and others provide cover Defenders set up a 'help triangle' behind first defender Defensive roles are switched as point of attack is changed by the offense Defenders slide across in their zone and force offense away from central shots, creating lower percentage scoring options and providing more defensive stops

Initial field area   *Game Playing Area Variation*

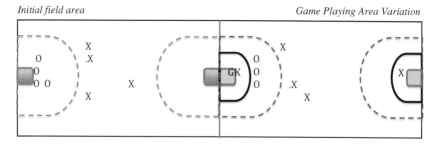

Figure 13.4 Guard the Goal focuses on the defensive tactical problem of moving players to protect the goal

Defenders in effect form a 1:3 zone or 2:2 zone due to the changes that have been made to the playing area. They will likely experiment with one or two deep defenders on the goal line and decide whether it is advantageous to position more defenders closer to the shooter (1:3) or closer to the goal (2:2) zone. The change in the structure of the playing area with the additional circle encourages the defense to make strategic game decisions.

In most invasion sports the larger the space, the less are the demands on game skill and spatial awareness. By subsequently increasing the radius of the outer circle in this modified game the deep defenders would be put under less pressure by the offense enabling them to function well both technically and tactically. As Launder (2001) has indicated, 'space = time = skill (good decisions and good execution)' (p. 59). The playing space (court size) should attempt to provide adequate challenge and flow within the game and should be proportional to the number of players involved.

Equipment. There are also situations in modified games where changing or modifying the equipment would be particularly beneficial. Using a low bounce lightweight nerf/sponge ball will cause defensive players less apprehension about being hit by a fast moving projectile in guard the goal.

Playing role variations (including offense–defense ratio). The position of a goalkeeper is subsequently added to each team from among the game playing personnel in guard the goal. Only the goalkeeper is now allowed inside the smaller semi-circle. In what approximates a 1:3 zone (goalkeeper plus three defenders), one defender will guard the ball handler (stepping toward the ball) and the others provide cover (off-the-ball defenders). A 1:3 zone also permits defenders to set up a 'help triangle' when the offense attack from a central position. Defensive roles are switched as the point of attack is changed by the offense. Defenders slide across in their zone. Forcing the offense away from central shots (and potentially onto players' non-preferred shooting sides) creates lower percentage scoring opportunities, likely providing more defensive stops. The goalkeeper begins to coordinate the defense by covering gaps, as the defenders attempt to block shots, and also narrows the shooter's angle by effective positioning behind shot blockers.

Varying the number of offensive or defensive players as part of an overload scenario in modified games can also be used to achieve a specific tactical objective.

In guard the goal an overload of defensive players (five versus four) will likely enable the defense to operate more effectively by contracting to form a defensive wall in front of the goalkeeper, which provides additional cover. Both offense and defense can suddenly find themselves outnumbered, particularly when there is a change of possession in many invasion games and players learn to react to these situations through coach manipulation of playing numbers. A neutral player who serves as 'all-time' offense or defense will also likely impact the achievement of the games' tactical objective quite effectively. In practice scenarios coaches have used additional players on either offense or defense to facilitate tactical success and this concept is a useful addition to modify game play.

Inter-game development

While at least two separate categories of potential variations have been provided for each of the four small-sided invasion games presented in this chapter it is important to recognize that any modified invasion game could be amended further by adjusting any of the categories of variations presented in the game template (scoring, progression, possession, start and restart procedures, playing area, equipment and players) based on the desired tactical or skill-related objectives. Each of the four modified games also incorporated dribbling, throwing, and catching using the hands. For many students (although not all) using their hands represents a comfortable starting point in their games education (Mitchell, Oslin, and Griffin 2003: 26) and from a skill-learning perspective the application to netball and basketball is quite evident in each of these modified games. By changing the medium employed for object manipulation, for example, switching from the hands to feet, the modified games are immediately applicable to learning soccer where all four games would provide valuable environments for learning new skills, with similar tactical objectives, as they morph into a different modified game. Similarly, by including both hands and feet as methods of object manipulation the games have application to other invasion sports (speedball and Australian rules football), and with additional progression and possession rule variations, they could serve as precursors to rugby and American football. By adding modified implements the games also provide valuable learning experiences in preparation for ultimate frisbee, any form of hockey (field, ice, floor), lacrosse, and even hurling. Finally, a change of venue from the court or field to the pool could also invoke their application to learning to play water polo.

Summary

This chapter has been designed to provide teachers with a potential template for designing modified games for learning in the invasion games category. The four example games were each based on a specific tactical principle designed to improve player performance during game play. Several types of modifications were presented to illustrate how specific elements might be amended in each game in order to improve the quality of play and the participants' Game Sense in attempting to solve the offensive or defensive tactical problem.

Discussion questions

1. What additional tactical problems could you focus on in the invasion category to design games around beyond the eight principles (four offensive and four defensive) referenced in this chapter?
2. What tactical problems would you focus your modified game design around in other games categories (net/wall, striking/fielding and target)?
3. This chapter focused on the design of modified games for learning in the invasion games category. How would you use and/or change the proposed design template to construct modified games in other categories?

References

Cooper, P. (2006) 'Why the 4 v 4 format is the answer for youth football', *Soccer Coaching International*, 17, 22–25.

Curry, C. and Light, R. (2007) 'Addressing the New South Wales quality teaching framework in physical education: Is Game Sense the answer?', in R. Light (ed.) *Proceedings for the Asia Pacific Conference on Teaching Sport and Physical Education for Understanding*, pp. 7–19, www.proflearn.edsw.usyd.edu.au/proceedings_resources/index.shtml (last accessed 16 May 2011).

Evans, J. (2007) 'Developing a sense of the game: Skill, specificity and game sense in rugby coaching', in R. Light (ed.) *Proceedings for the Asia Pacific Conference on Teaching Sport and Physical Education for Understanding*, pp. 20–31, www.proflearn.edsw.usyd.edu.au/proceedings_resources/index.shtml (last accessed 16 May 2011).

Hastie, P. (2010) *Student-designed Games: Strategies for Promoting Creativity, Cooperation and Skill Development*, Champaign, IL: Human Kinetics.

Launder, A. G. (2001) *Play Practice: The Games Approach to Teaching and Coaching Sports*, Champaign, IL: Human Kinetics.

Mitchell, S. and Collier, C. (2009) 'Observing and diagnosing student performance problems in games teaching', *Journal of Physical Education, Recreation & Dance*, 80 (6), 46–50.

Mitchell, S., Oslin, J. L., and Griffin, L. L. (2003) *Sport Foundations for Elementary Physical Education: A Tactical Games Approach*, Champaign, IL: Human Kinetics.

Pill, S. (2012) 'Teaching game sense in soccer', *Journal of Physical Education, Recreation and Dance*, 83 (3), 42–46.

Turner, A. P. (2005) 'Teaching and learning games at the secondary level', in J. Butler and L. Griffin (eds) *Teaching Games for Understanding: Theory, Research, and Practice*, Champaign, IL: Human Kinetics, pp. 71–90.

——(2012) *Coaching soccer at its grass roots: Tackling a games for understanding approach*. Paper presented at the Fifth International Teaching Games for Understanding Conference, 14–16 July, Loughborough University, Loughborough, UK.

van Lingen, B. (1997) *Coaching Soccer: The Official Coaching Book of the Dutch Soccer Association*, Spring City, PA: Reedswain.

Wilson, G. E. (2002) 'A framework for teaching tactical game knowledge', *Journal of Physical Education, Recreation and Dance*, 73 (4), 23–26, 56.

Conclusions

Stephen Harvey, John Quay and Richard L. Light

Introduction

Mitchell (2005) suggests that although the range of variations of GBA may be different in detail, they should be seen as taking 'different paths up the same mountain'. This collection provides support for Mitchell's contention by demonstrating the commonalities among some of these different GBAs while confirming their efficacy.

Bunker and Thorpe's innovative approach to teaching games, first published in 1982, was directly influenced by new thinking about teaching and coaching games in the UK, evident in the work of Wade (1967) and Maulden and Redfern (1969), that prioritized the game. It has also been suggested that all GBA have their roots in France in the work of Mahlo and Deleplace (Gréhaigne, Richard and Griffin 2005) around the same period. Underpinned by a cognitivist theory of learning, this work suggests that cognitive processes were necessary for the correct execution of motor skills within game situations. Drawing on more sophisticated theories of learning that can account for the complexity of learning as a whole-person process, the collection of chapters in this volume move beyond the limits of a cognitivist perspective to suggest that learning in and through games is a holistic processes. This perspective highlights how these approaches are underpinned by epistemological positions grounded in social theories of learning. These manifest in GBAs via the use of a certain *brand* of pedagogy that foregrounds the body and experience to emphasize reflection on action, dialogue, teacher/coach questioning, and a form of debate that challenges the division of mind from body by promoting the development of knowledge-in-action – *enacted* knowledge.

The book showcases various examples of how game-based approaches can facilitate positive learning experiences, but – as Light reminds us in his chapter on positive pedagogy – contributions to the cognitive (tactical), physical (technical), social, moral, and personal development of participants engaged in GBAs are not automatic. Such development, however, is enhanced through the coach or teacher having a well-refined conceptual model of teaching/ coaching aimed at achieving these aims.

In this conclusion we frame our examination of the content of the book with Côté and Gilbert's (2009) conceptual model of coaching. Although based on coaching it has been constructed using a combination of conceptual models adapted from education and teaching, thus offering a suitably comprehensive framework for interrogating the content of this current collection with its focus on teaching physical education. The conceptual model is based around the three components of: (a) knowledge, (b) learner outcomes, and (c) context, each of which we deal with.

Knowledge

Côté and Gilbert (2009) divide knowledge into three areas: (a) professional, (b) interpersonal, and (c) intrapersonal. Professional knowledge is based on declarative, sport-specific, and pedagogical knowledge with accompanying procedural knowledge. Interpersonal knowledge is based on individual and group interactions and intrapersonal knowledge refers to understanding oneself and the ability for introspection and reflection.

Professional knowledge

The review of literature in Chapter 6 by Jarrett and Harvey reveals how many teachers and coaches lack the declarative (articulated) and procedural (enacted) knowledge to effectively deliver GBAs (see also Díaz-Cueto, Hernández-Álvarez and Castejón 2010; Harvey, Cushion and Massa-Gonzalez 2010; Roberts 2011; Wright, McNeill and Fry 2009). This point is supported by recent research reported on in other chapters in this volume, such as those by Mooney and Casey (Chapter 7), Curry and Light (Chapter 8), and Forrest (Chapter 11), where the effectiveness of the utilization of the GBA was very dependent upon the conceptual understandings of the teachers and coaches. A fragmented understanding of GBAs results in an 'epistemological gap' (Davis and Sumara 2003) between a superficial understanding and actual practice, where a deep knowledge of the ideas about learning underpinning them and the subsequent pedagogical approach is needed. This weak understanding leads to the employment of a 'cafeteria' or 'watered down' version of GBAs (Curtner-Smith, Hastie and Kinchin 2008) and is typically doomed to failure, which encourages the view that GBAs don't work. These cafeteria versions of GBAs are often driven by misunderstandings that assume: (a) questioning is the *only* coaching [teaching] behaviour to be used; (b) there is no place for technical or skill-based practice; (c) GBAs are nothing new and no more than simply discovery learning; and (d) participants must *always* be physically or socially active to learn.

Beyond inadequate understanding there are further conceptual and pedagogical challenges for teachers and coaches utilizing GBAs. Harvey, Cope and Jones (Chapter 12) show how the alignment between learning outcomes, pedagogical approach and assessment requires an epistemological belief that all learning is embodied with knowing inseparable from doing to enact authentic GBA teaching. As several chapters in this volume confirm, this can be quite challenging for teachers and coaches. Moreover, aligning assessment practice so that it reflects the same social world that the pedagogical approach to be used does and the learning outcomes to be met may also present significant challenges. The challenge of developing effective questioning technique is typically a major challenge for teachers and coaches taking up a GBA approach. As various authors have done before him (see, for example, Roberts 2011; McNeill, Fry, Wright, Tan and Rossi 2008), Forrest highlights the difficulty teachers and coaches have in designing questions to befit the environment the teacher/coach wishes to create. While questioning is not the *only* pedagogical approach it is critical for the authentic implementation of GBA because of its central role in provoking thinking and dialogue between teachers/coaches and their participants (Light 2013). Such questioning also needs to support the ongoing development of higher-order thinking skills in the development of enacted knowledge. If this does not occur, then many lessons can become 'roll out the ball' (Graham 2008; Light 2004) where participants end up 'just playing games' (Metzler 2011).

In Chapter 1 Quay and Stolz support the need for the coach/teacher to conceptually comprehend the need to shift away from learning techniques first. Employing a Deweyan experiential framework they note how GBAs more clearly concern themselves with the context within which learning is occurring. However, they also highlight how the game itself is not the broadest level of context to be considered experientially, revealing a series of ever-broadening layers: the technique or skill, the strategies and tactics, the game, the sport, and the social context (or team). In making this argument they point out the importance of recognizing the integration of curriculum (what is experienced) and pedagogy (how this is experienced), which engenders an occupation (who you are when having this experience). This is reflective of the 'holistic' conceptualization of games that underpins GBAs and supports Harvey, Cope and Jones' argument for the alignment between the learning outcomes to be met (subject matter or curriculum), assessment practice and the pedagogy (or mode of experiencing).

Interpersonal knowledge

Another constructive aspect of this volume is the argument presented in Chapter 2 by Light that GBAs can provide positive experiences for all learners. He draws on the 'concepts of *flow* and *mindfulness* that have been used to inform positive psychology (Seligman and Csikszentmihalyi 2000) as positive states that generate positive affective and learning experiences. The positive state of experiencing flow arising from the right degree of challenge provided in practice games is also referred to by Piltz in Chapter 5. This is presented by Light in contrast to the negative conditions that emphasize what participants *cannot* do, so evident in more *traditional* directive, technical methods of coaching and teaching. For example, by placing participants in the context of an initial game form at the beginning of a practice session, they learn to appreciate *why* and *how* skills learned later on in the practice session may be important to their ongoing learning and development. This is particularly prominent in the mantra of Play Practice (see Chapter 5) where 'what is tactically desirable must be technically possible' and 'what is technically desirable must be physically possible'.

Intrapersonal knowledge

Mouchet's chapter demonstrates how a focus on the subjective experiences of the players 'at action' could help them to develop decision-making capabilities by understanding the various physical, cognitive and social effects of their decisions, a point we return to later. His chapter suggests that coaches could use a similarly introspective and reflective approach to interrogate their own subjective experiences of critical coaching incidents to improve levels of self-awareness in order to become better coaches. This is certainly an avenue that could be of interest to researchers concerned with issues of educating teachers and coaches on how to develop their use of GBAs, especially in relation to how these mediate the experiences of the learner (see Wright *et al.* 2009; Díaz-Cueto *et al.* 2010). Indeed, Mooney and Casey suggest that greater levels of introspection and reflection on the part of the practitioners in their study enabled them to reassess their positioning and so consider the 'limitations of dominant and pervasive practices, and second, the potential for other approaches' (Chapter 7). This introspection seems to have afforded the practitioners in their study more opportunities to offer 'contextually relevant learning opportunities for adolescent girls'. Vygotsky's (1978: 86) notion of a proximal zone of learning where the learner's 'more capable peers' can support them in scaffolding their knowledge suggests the benefits of such reflection and introspection for teaching and learning using GBAs.

Jarrett and Harvey's review of the literature published since 2006 suggests a need for ongoing support in the development of teachers' and coaches' utilization of GBAs; a position that is empirically supported by Curry and Light's study (Chapter 8) and Forrest (Chapter 11). Instruction of and support for pre-service and in-service teachers tends to be limited to short induction and training periods, which then lack further support (see Chapter 6). A study by Nash (2009) where she used communities of practice to support teacher development of GBA teaching suggests other possibilities. In her innovative approach Nash successfully engaged pre-service teachers in communities of practice to exchange and draw on peers' experiences of TGfU implementation in local schools. This warrants further research, not only with pre-service teachers, but in-service teachers and coaches. The use of communities of practice and social-networking opportunities to enhance professional development through active online communities of practice could further foster the development of GBAs through dialogue, discussion, debate, reflection and action (see also Occhino, Mallett and Rynne 2013) as well as support from more capable peers, as Vygotsky's (1978) work suggests.

Athlete outcomes

Côté *et al.* (2010) have applied the four-Cs framework to athlete outcomes, which incorporates: (a) competence, (b) confidence, (c) connection, and (d) caring/character. In terms of developing competence Côté and Gilbert (2009) highlight a major research focus in physical education and sport coaching: examining how teacher/coach behaviours affect learner competence that has guided much of the developmental sport psychology research. They argue that this is consistent with a view on 'holistic' coaching as a way of nurturing positive youth development (see Light, Chapter 2). Certainly, in this volume we have seen the ways in which games-based pedagogies change the dynamics of the power relationships between the teacher/coach and their learners through the use of pertinent game design (see Turner, Chapter 13) and via a questioning protocol that stimulates dialogue (as opposed to monologue) in various contexts, including those associated with elite sport as mentioned by Evans (Chapter 9), Light (Chapter 2), Jarrett and Harvey (Chapter 6), and Forrest (Chapter 11). From this non-linear pedagogy perspective the autonomy, competence, and relatedness that characterizes the supportive environment (practice type and coaching behaviour) associated with GBAs has been shown to improve intrinsic motivation in sports coaching (Renshaw, Oldham, and Bawden 2012) and physical education contexts (Mandigo, Holt, Anderson and Sheppard 2008). However – as we have seen in this volume via Chapters 8 (Curry and Light), 7 (Mooney and Casey), and 9 (Evans) – particular cultures and contexts can impinge upon the integration and utilization of GBAs, which is an issue to which we now turn.

Context

Ultimately, positive pedagogies such as those used in GBAs centre on development and learning rather than treating performance as an outcome in and of itself (see Light, Chapter 2). Thus we have seen how GBAs, via the work of Curry and Light, can confront the traditionally dominant values of the particular cultures of both sport and physical education. These approaches challenge teachers and coaches to overcome their own histories and experiences (Light and Evans 2010) because these are always situated within the wider social and political contexts that impact upon questions concerned with what good teaching/coaching *is* and *should* look like (Light 2004). As games-based pedagogies require coaches to 'step back' and facilitate learning (Light 2004), many parents, head teachers, and club committee members may question the legitimacy of such approaches to teaching and coaching. Moreover, as Jarrett and Harvey illustrate, research on the implementation of GBAs in Eastern cultures provides a stark reminder of some of the challenges teachers face due to the clashes between the philosophy of GBAs and performative cultures (see Chapter 3 by Fry and McNeill).

Evans' cross-cultural comparison of the interpretation and utilization of Game Sense in elite rugby coaching contexts in Chapter 9 also shows how the coaches in New Zealand place a greater emphasis on a 'holistic' approach to coaching than the Australian coaches. This is encapsulated in a primary focus on a humanistic and player-centred coaching style (embracing the four Cs mentioned in the previous section), in contrast to the business-like style of the Australian coaches who tend to emphasize the sport-specific content to be learned (Côté and Gilbert 2009). This 'holistic' approach stems from cultural and historical differences that underpin the 'establishment and maintenance of conditions that allow these relationships to develop', and these conditions have engendered a cultural context that has enabled games-based pedagogical approaches to have an impact at all levels of rugby coaching in New Zealand.

Côté and Gilbert (2009) suggest that 'coaching effectiveness should be defined according to how coaches meet their athletes' needs and help them fulfill their goals, as defined by the specific coaching context'. It is our contention that the positive pedagogy of GBAs enables coaches to meet the needs of athletes in various stages of learning and participation trajectories (i.e. recreation and/ or elite performance) within coaching models such as long-term athlete development (Balyi and Hamilton 2004) and the developmental model of sport participation (Côté and Hay 2002), through an emphasis on creating an environment focused on 'holistic' learning and development.

Summary

This collection of contributions from Europe, Asia, Australia, and North America confirms many of the positive aspects of GBAs that have been increasingly argued for and investigated over the past two decades. The weight of original, cutting-edge research presented in this volume provides support for the claims made in this volume and in other publications on the efficacy of GBA. In doing so it redresses some of the criticisms about a lack of empirical evidence that supports some of the claims made here about GBA. More generally, the writing in this volume suggests that GBA offers an effective way of enhancing learning across all learning domains and providing positive affective experiences for learners. However, practitioners (teachers and coaches) and researchers convinced of the efficacy of GBA face challenges in expanding games-based pedagogies across the teaching and coaching landscape. We would thus encourage readers to draw on the practice-focused content presented in this volume to meet the challenges of taking up these learner-centred, inquiry-based approaches and share them with colleagues.

We would also encourage researchers to consider the suggestions made by the chapters in this volume for future inquiry into GBAs, many of which are innovative and forward thinking. For example, Jarrett and Harvey's suggestion for looking at the possibilities offered by the explication of the affective experiences associated with GBA pedagogy, as illustrated by Mouchet in Chapter 10 on subjectivity and decision making in team sport. There is also opportunity to expand commentary on the potential for GBAs to develop the personal, social, and ethical dimensions of learning critical to the exploration of the holistic learning available within game-based approaches as evident in Light's proposal for positive pedagogy in sport and physical education.

References

Balyi, I. and A. Hamilton. (2004) *Long-term Athlete Development: Trainability in Childhood and Adolescence, Windows of Opportunity, Optimal Trainability*, Victoria, BC: National Coaching Institute British Columbia and Advanced Training and Performance Ltd.

Côté, J. and J. Hay. (2002) 'Children's involvement in sport: A developmental perspective', in J. M. Silver and D. Stevens (eds) *Psychological Foundations of Sport*, Boston, MA: Allyn and Bacon, pp. 484–502.

Côté, J. and W. Gilbert. (2009) 'An integrative definition of coaching effectiveness and expertise', *International Journal of Sports Science and Coaching*, 4 (3): 307–323.

Côté, J., M. Bruner, K. Erickson, L. Strachan and J. Fraser-Thomas (2010) 'Athlete development and coaching', in J. Lyle and C. Cushion (eds) *Sports Coaching, Professionalism and Practice*, Oxford: Elsevier.

Curtner-Smith, M. D., P. A. Hastie and G. D. Kinchin. (2008) 'Influence of occupational socialization on beginning teachers' interpretation and delivery of sport education', *Sport, Education & Society*, 13 (1): 97–117.

Davis, B. and D. Sumara. (2003) 'Why aren't they getting this? Working through the regressive myths of constructivist pedagogy', *Teaching Education*, 14 (2): 123–140.

Díaz-Cueto, M., J. Hernández-Álvarez and F. Castejón. (2010) 'Teaching Games for Understanding to in-service physical education teachers: rewards and barriers regarding the changing model of teaching sport', *Journal of Teaching in Physical Education*, 29: 378–398.

Graham, G. (2008) *Teaching Physical Education: Becoming a Master Teacher* (third edition), Champaign, IL: Human Kinetics.

Gréhaigne, J.-F., J.-F. Richard, and L. L. Griffin. (2005) *Teaching and Learning Team Sports and Games*, New York: RoutledgeFalmer.

Harvey, S., C. J. Cushion and A. N. Massa-Gonzalez. (2010) 'Learning a new method: Teaching Games for Understanding in the coaches' eyes', *Physical Education and Sport Pedagogy*, 15 (4): 361–382.

Light, R. (2004) 'Coaches' experiences of Games Sense: opportunities and challenges', *Physical Education and Sport Pedagogy*, 9 (2): 115–131.

——(2013) *Game Sense: Pedagogy for Performance, Participation and Enjoyment*, London and New York: Routledge.

Light, R. L. and J. R. Evans. (2010) 'The impact of Game Sense pedagogy on Australian rugby coaches' practice: A question of pedagogy', *Physical Education and Sport Pedagogy*, 15 (2): 103–115.

Mandigo, J., H. Holt, A. Anderson and J. Sheppard. (2008) 'Children's motivational experiences following autonomy-supportive games lessons', *European Physical Education Review*, 14 (3): 407–425.

Maulden, E. and H. B. Redfern. (1969) *Games Teaching: A New Approach for the Primary School*, London: McDonald and Evans Ltd.

McNeill, M. C., Fry, J. M., Wright, S. C., Tan, W. K. C. and Rossi, T. (2008) 'Understanding time management and questioning strategies used in a games concept approach to develop "Game Sense"'. *Physical Education and Sport Pedagogy*, 13: 231–239.

Metzler, M. W. (2011) *Instructional Models for Physical Education* (third edition), Scottsdale, AZ: Halcomb Hathaway.

Mitchell, S. (2005) 'Different paths up the same mountain: global perspectives on Teaching Games for Understanding', Keynote presentation at 3rd International Conference: Teaching Games for Understanding, Hong Kong Institute of Education, Hong Kong, 14–17 December.

Nash, M. (2009) 'Using the idea of "communities of practice" and TGfU to develop physical education pedagogy among primary generalist pre-service teachers', *Asian Journal of Exercise and Sports Science*, 6 (1): 15–21.

Occhino, J., C. Mallett and S. Rynne. (2013) 'Dynamic social networks in high performance football coaching', *Physical Education & Sport Pedagogy*, 18 (1): 90–102.

Renshaw, I., A. R. Oldham and M. Bawden. (2012) 'Non-linear pedagogy underpins intrinsic motivation in sports coaching', *The Open Sports Sciences Journal*, 5: 1–12.

Roberts, S. J. (2011) 'Teaching games for understanding: The difficulties and challenges experienced by participation cricket coaches', *Physical Education & Sport Pedagogy*, 16 (1): 33–48.

Seligman, M. E. P. and M. Csikszentmihalyi. (2000) 'Positive Psychology: An introduction', *American Psychologist*, 55 (1): 5–14.

Vygotsky, L. S. (1978) *Mind in Society: The Development of Higher Psychological Processes*, Cambridge, MA: Harvard University Press.

Wade, A. (1967) *The F A. Guide to Training and Coaching*, London: Heinemann.

Wright, S., M. McNeill and J. Fry. (2009) 'The tactical approach to teaching games from teaching, learning and mentoring perspectives', *Sport, Education & Society*, 14 (2): 223–244.

Index

References in **bold** indicate tables and in *italics* indicate figures.

220   *Index*